Volume I


Reminiscences
of
Vice Admiral William R. Smedberg, III
U. S. Navy (Retired)


U. S. Naval Institute
Annapolis, Maryland

July, 1979

## Preface

This is an account of an exceptionable naval career that is highlighted by innovation, initiative, courage and intelligence.

Admiral Smedberg had a series of outstanding assignments in the U. S. Navy. His account of them is most valuable historically. Researchers will find that the narrative is eminently readable in that the Admiral's intrepid nature and natural dynamism give many of the events he describes a quality of high drama.

Admiral Smedberg gave us taped interviews in Annapolis, Maryland, the Naval Historical Center in Washington, D.C. and at his home in Crystal River, Florida. This was over a period extending from May, 1975 to December, 1978. The tapes were transcribed. The Admiral corrected the transcript and it was re-typed. Inasmuch as the memoir is too long for a single volume it appears in two volumes with a separate index for each one.

John T. Mason, Jr.<br>
Director of Oral History<br>
U. S. Naval Institute

VICE ADMIRAL WILLIAM R. SMEDBERG, III, U. S. NAVY, RETIRED

William Renwick Smedberg, III, was born on September 29, 1902, at Fort Grant, Arizona, son of Mrs. W. R. (Louise Chaffin) Smedberg and the late Brigadier General Smedberg, U. S. Army. Before entering the U. S. Naval Academy in 1922, he was graduated from Middlesex School, Concord, Massachusetts, and Shadmann's Preparatory School, Washington, DC. Graduated and commissioned Ensign in the U. S. Navy on June 3, 1926, he subsequently advanced to the rank of Vice Admiral, with date of rank March 21, 1959.

After graduation he remained at the Naval Academy for the summer course in aviation, and reported in October 1926 to the USS NEW MEXICO. In June 1927 he was transferred to the destroyer MULLANY, in which he served until March 1930. He was next assigned to the Bethlehem Shipbuilding Corporation, Quincy, Massachusetts, for duty in connection with fitting out the USS NORTH-HAMPTON, and served on board that cruiser from her commissioning in May 1930 until May 1933. He then reported to the Naval Postgraduate School, Annapolis, for the course in Communications.

From June 1935 to July 1937 he served as Radio Officer on the staff of Commander Cruiser Division Three, Battle Force, U. S. Fleet. During the two years following, he had successive duty as Radio Officer on the staff of Commander Cruiser Division Three and Commander Cruisers, Battle Fleet. From September 1939 to February 1942 he was Aide to the Chief of Naval Operations, Washington, DC.

In the early period of World War II he commanded the USS LANSDOWNE in the Atlantic and in the Southern Solomons Islands in the Pacific, and in 1943 put into commission and commanded the USS HUDSON, which participated in operations in the Northern Solomons Area. In January 1944 he was designated Chief of Staff to Commander Task Force 39, and Cruiser Division 12, and served as such during the consolidation of the Northern Solomon and throughout the assault and capture of Saipan, Guam, and Tinian, and the Battle of the Philippine Sea. In September 1944 he was ordered to the staff of Commander in Chief, U. S. Fleet, and served as U. S. Fleet Combat Intelligence Officer for the remainder of the war, and until March 1946.

For meritorious service during World War II, he was awarded the Legion of Merit, Gold Stars in Lieu of the Second, Third, and Fourth Legions of Merit, the Silver Star Medal, the Bronze Star Medal, and a Letter of Commendation with Ribbon. The citations to those awards follow, in part:

Legion of Merit: "For exceptionally meritorious conduct...as Commanding Officer of the USS LANSDOWNE during action against an enemy submarine on July 3, 1942...With superb judgment and accurate timing, (he) laid down an effective pattern of depth charges. After their explosion, oil slick and air bubbles appeared on the surface of the sea and the movements of the submarine indicated complete lack of control of the hostile vessel..."

This submarine was shown by German records after the war, to have been heavily damaged.

Gold Star in lieu of the Second Legion of Merit: "For exceptionally meritorious conduct...as Commanding Officer of the USS LANSDOWNE during action against an enemy submarine on July 13, 1942. With superb seamanship and sound judgment, (he) maneuvered his ship into a suitable position and launched a vigorous and accurate attack with depth charges...Oil slick and air bubbles appeared in large quantities...and the movements of the submarine seemed to be severely hampered..." This submarine was shown to have been sunk, by German records after the end of the war.

Gold Star in lieu of Third Legion of Merit: "For...outstanding services... as Chief of Staff and Operations Officer to the Commander of a Task Force and the Commander of a Cruiser Division during offensive operations against enemy Japanese in the Marianas Islands Area from June 15 to August 10, 1944..."

Gold Star in lieu of Fourth Legion of Merit: "For exceptionally meritorious conduct...as Head of the Combat Intelligence Division on the Staff of the Commander in Chief, U. S. Fleet, and Chief of Naval Operations, from October 12, 1944, to October 10, 1945...Captain Smedberg rendered service of inestimable value in the collection and evaluation of information which resulted in the continued prompt acquisition of extremely reliable intelligence service...(He) contributed in large measure to the effective coordination of other intelligence agencies and to the plans for the acquisition and prompt dissemination of intelligence, thereby materially furthering the prosecution of the war."

Silver Star Medal: "For conspicuous gallantry and intrepidity as Commanding Officer of a U. S. Warship during action against an enemy Japanese submarine off Guadalcanal Island. Although his ship was lying at anchor unloading ammunition when the submarine launched a surprise attack, Commander Smedberg successfully evaded an enemy torpedo. His cool and skillful maneuvering and the super functioning of his his entire ship's company enabled him to save his ship and complete an important mission."

Bronze Star Medal: "For meritorious service as Commanding Officer of a destroyer attached to a squadron operating in the Solomon Islands area from November 1, 1943 to December 28, 1944. During this period, (his) ship escorted troop transports to Bougainville, bombarded enemy installations at Cape Torokina, and took part in the repelling of two heavy air attacks against the task force. These engagements were successfully carried out, despite poorly charted waters and the determined resistance by the Japanese aircraft and shore batteries...(He) contributed materially to the defeat of the enemy in the South Pacific theater..."

Letter of Commendation from Commander in Chief, Pacific Fleet: "For meritorious action and distinguished service in the line of his profession as the Commanding Officer of a destroyer during the rescue operations subsequent to the loss of the USS WASP. His fine judgment in seamanship made possible the successful rescue of many officers and men in an area where enemy submarines were actively present. His skill and devotion to duty were in keeping with the highest traditions of the Naval Service.

In March 1946 he was transferred to the Office of the Chief of Naval Operations, and in May reported as Aide to the Secretary of the Navy, the Honorable James Forrestal. In June 1946 he assumed command of Destroyer Division Thirty-five. In July 1948 he was ordered to the Naval Academy for duty as Head of the Department of Electrical Engineering, and remained there until August 1951, when he assumed command of the USS IOWA.

He was awarded a Gold Star in lieu of the Fifth Legion of Merit, "For exceptionally meritorious conduct...in a duty of great responsibility as Commanding Officer of the USS IOWA, and as Commander of numerous task elements of Fast Task Force SEVENTY-SEVEN during operations against the enemy in the Korean area from 31 March to 29 July 1952..."

In September 1952 he became Chief of Staff and Aide to Commander Destroyer Force, Atlantic, and in April of the next year returned to the Navy Department, Washington, DC, as Director, Politico-Military Policy Division, in the Office of the Chief of Naval Operations. On January 4, 1956, the Secretary of the Navy announced his appointment as Superintendent of the U. S. Naval Academy to relieve Rear Admiral Walter F. Boone, and as such he had additional duty as Commandant of the Severn River Naval Command. On August 9, 1958 he reported as Commander Cruiser-Destroyer Force, Pacific Fleet. On March 21, 1959 he became Commander SECOND Fleet and Commander Striking Fleet, Atlantic, and on February 12, 1960 was assigned as Chief of Naval Personnel, Chief of the Bureau of Naval Personnel and Deputy Chief of Naval Operations (Personnel and Naval Reserve), Navy Department. "For exceptionally meritorious service...(in that capacity) from February 1960 through February 1964..." he was awarded the Distinguished Service Medal. The citation continues in part:

"Exercising dynamic leadership, keen foresight, and outstanding professional competence in meeting the challenge of manning a growing, complex, highly technical Navy during this critical period, Vice Admiral Smedberg initiated and vigorously pursued programs of far-reaching significance to improve the quality, standards, and morale of Navy personnel and to provide them with adequate compensation, benefits, and equal opportunity. In addition to the retention of far greater numbers of highly qualified personnel than heretofore, with concomitant savings to the Government in training replacement costs, these programs have made a positive impact on continuing efforts to maintain and increase the overall efficiency, effectiveness and stability of the Naval Organization. Through his exceptional administrative ability, sound judgment, and deep understanding of people and the importance of the role played by the individual in meeting the Navy's objectives and accomplishing its goal, Vice Admiral Smedberg attained a distinguished record of achievement..."

On April 1, 1964 he was transferred to the Retired List of the U. S. Navy.

In addition to the Distinguished Service Medal, Silver Star Medal, Legion of Merit with four Gold Stars and Combat "V," the Bronze Star Medal with "V," and the Commendation Ribbon, also with "V," Vice Admiral Smedberg has the Navy Unit Commendation Ribbon, the Second Micaraguan Campaign Medal; American Defense Service Medal; American Campaign Medal; Asiatic-Pacific Campaign Medal; World

War II Victory Medal; National Defense Service Medal; Korean Service Medal; and the United Nations Service Medal. He also holds the Expert Rifleman Medal, and Expert Pistol Shot Medal. The Order of the British Empire has been conferred upon him by the Government of Great Britain.

Married to the former Miss Claudia Stuart Barden of Washington, DC, Vice Admiral Smedberg has three children: Claudia Stuart Adams, wife of Captain Robert S. Adams, USN; Lieutenant Commander William R. Smedberg, IV, USN; and Lieutenant Edwin B. Smedberg, USN. His permanent home address is Paradise Point, Crystal River, Florida.

Navy Offie of Information
Internal Relations Division (01-430)
16 April 1964

# DECLARATION OF TRUST

The undersigned does hereby appoint and designate as his (her) Trustee herein, the Secretary-Treasurer and Publisher of the United States Naval Institute to perform and discharge the following duties, powers, and privileges in connection with the possession and use of a certain taped interview between the undersigned and the Oral History Department of the United States Naval Institute.

1. Classification of Transcript.

    (✓)a. If classified OPEN, the transcript(s) may be read or the recording(s) audited by the qualified personnel upon presentation of proper credentials, as determined by the Secretary-Treasurer of the U.S. Naval Institute.

    ( )b. If classified PERMISSION REQUIRED TO CITE OR QUOTE, the user will be required to obtain permission in writing from the interviewee prior to quoting or citing from either the transcript(s) or the recording(s).

    ( )c. If classified PERMISSION REQUIRED, permission must be obtained in writing from the interviewee before the transcribed interview(s) can be examined or the tape recording(s) audited.

    ( )d. If classified CLOSED, the transcribed interview(s) and the tape recording(s) will be sealed until a time specified by the interviewee. This may be until the death of the interviewee or for any specified number of years.

2. It is expressly understood that in giving this authorization, I am in no way precluded from placing such restrictions as I may desire upon use of the interview at any time during my lifetime, nor does this authorization in any way affect my rights to the copyright of my literary expressions that may be contained in the interview.

Witness my hand and seal this 27th day of June 1979

*[signature: R. W. Sundberg]*

I hereby accept and consent to the foregoing Declaration of Trust and the powers therein conferred upon me as Trustee:

*[signature: R. T. E. Bowler Jr.]*

Interview No. 1 with Vice Admiral William R. Smedberg III
U.S. Navy (Retired)

Place: U.S. Naval Institute, Annapolis, Maryland

Date: Thursday morning, 8 May 1975

Subject: Biography

By: John T. Mason, Jr.

Q: Well, Sir, this is a series I've anticipated with a great deal of pleasure. You had a terrific career in the Navy. Your name is mentioned so frequently even today after your retirement.

Admiral, would you begin a spoken biography in the usual way by giving me the place of your birth, the date of your birth, and then tell me something about your family background?

Adm. S.: I was born in a little, lonely Army post called Fort Grant in the Territory of Arizona, on the 28th of September 1902. My dad was stationed there with a troop of cavalry, the objective being to keep a rein on the Indians in the area. It was about 100 miles north of Tucson. When I was still under a year old, my dad was ordered to Jolo, in the Philippines, and we took an Army transport and spent, thirty-one days, I think it was, in passage. We lived in Jolo, Iloilo, in the Philippines for about two years. We lived behind a stockade while my dad fought the Moros.

Q: They're still proving obstreperous!

Adm. S.: Yes, they are. They're very independent people and in those days, when they would go "juramentado" (run amuk) they used to bind themselves with copper wire, their arms and their legs and their bodies, so that no matter how much they were wounded they could keep on after their objective without loss of blood, causing them to be faint or die. It was actually for that reason that General MacArthur introduced the 45-caliber automatic into the Army because that bullet was so heavy it would actually knock a man down. A Moro would bind himself up with copper wire and he'd come right at you, no matter how badly injured he was. You couldn't stop him, except with a .45, which would knock him down.

One of my brothers was born out there.

Q: How many brothers do you have?

Adm. S.: I had two brothers. One died of infantile paralysis in the big epidemic of 1914.

We had the usual Army life. My dad was a regular. He graduated from West Point in the class of '93, and, incidentally, my father in the class of '93 and my father-in-law in the class of '94 were both on the first West Point football team to beat the Naval Academy.

This is pretty much of a disgression, but when I was superintendent of the Naval Academy I had on the table there a picture of the first West Point football team to beat the Naval Academy, and whenever Army people would come in, they'd say:

"How come, Admiral, you've got this picture of a West Point football team?"

"Well," I'd say, "I'm very proud of that. That's the first time that West Point had ever beaten the Naval Academy and my dad, right there, was the quarterback and my wife's father was a halfback."

We generally got a laugh out of that.

During my early youth we were in and out of the Philippines. My dad served two tours of duty there before I was twelve and, as far as I can remember, I had no schooling, except from a governess who was a friend of my mother and was very good in languages and English, history, and things like that, but not so good in mathematics, and as a result I always had to struggle with mathematics.

Q: Was she an American governess?

Adm. S.: Oh, yes. She was a friend of my mother and she was a spinster. She traveled with us for many years.

Q: You were out there in the days of William Howard Taft, then, were you?

Adm. S.: We were there for two tours of duty between 1903 and

I think we came back from Camp Stotsenberg, which now is Clark Field, in April 1912. That was my last visit to the Philippines until some years later, of course, when I was in the Navy.

Because I had had no real schooling, my mother decided that I had to go to a good boys' boarding school and she being a New Englander, having been born in Newton, Massachusetts, thought very highly of Middlesex School. So I was put into Middlesex School; Concord, Massachusetts, when I was twelve years old. I was there until I graduated in 1921.

Q: Were you destined for the Army or the Navy?

Adm. S.: It was always assumed I would go to West Point.

Q: West Point!

Adm. S.: Yes, and after I graduated from Middlesex School, of course, my dad would be ordered here and there and I joined the family wherever they were for vacations, but I spent six years there at school. We had six forms there, from the sixth to the first form, and I graduated in 1921.

Q: How did you make the transition? Was it an easy one from no formal schooling to - ?

Adm. S.: I don't remember any difficulty at all. In later life, I realized that I'd never gone to school with a girl, ever. That may account for the fact that I never understood women very well! I like them very much, am very fond of them, respect and admire them, but I never really understood them. I think perhaps few men ever do really understand women. But when I graduated from Middlesex, I was going to West Point, and then we discovered that although I'd had four years of German, six years of French, and four years of Latin at Middlesex, I hadn't had enough trig and physics and chemistry to pass the exams, so I went to a prep school in Washington called "Shadman's" - We called it Shadman's, but it was the Columbia Preparatory School. That was the real name but old Mr. Shadman was the real brains of it. He and Paul W. Pool, who was the assistant headmaster, ran a prep school that got its pupils into both academies.

Q: On New Hampshire Avenue, wasn't it?

Adm. S.: No, it was on Rhode Island Avenue in those days. I went there during the winter of 1921-22 to prep for West Point. My dad had gotten me a principal appointment to West Point from old Senator Henry Cabot Lodge. His son, the current Henry Cabot Lodge, was at Middlesex with me, as was John Lodge.

Q: He was?

Adm. S.: Yes.

Q: I know John.

Adm. S.: John and I are very, very close friends, so are Cabot and I.

After about six months at this prep school and about a month before the exams for West Point, I came home one day and said:

"Dad, if you don't mind, I think I'll go to the Naval Academy."

Of course, my father was aghast and he said:

"Son, that's ridiculous. It's taken me two years to get you this appointment to West Point. I couldn't possibly get you an appointment to the Naval Academy."

"Oh," I said, "that's all right. I'll take the presidential exams."

In those days the president had thirty appointments for the two academies, fifteen to each academy, for sons of officers in the services.

Dad was dumbfounded. I took the exams and, because of the wonderful training and cramming that Shadman had given us, I stood high enough to come in on the presidential list.

Q: What made you make this shift?

Adm. S.: Well, I really hate to tell people now because, as I look back on it, it was so inconsequential. I had a girl in Washington at the time and I discovered that at West Point you got no Christmas leave your plebe year, and at the Naval Academy you got four days. That was one of the reasons. The other and really important reason was that the group of boys preparing for the Naval Academy, who included Admiral Leahy's son, Admiral Billy Leahy, and Admiral Charlie Buchanan, his father was a naval officer - that group, in my opinion, was a much more attractive group than the ones going to West Point. Incidentally, young Funston was preparing for West Point in that class of ours, Freddie Funston. I went to the Naval Academy as a result, and I think during the time I was at the academy I deeply regretted the fact I hadn't gone to West Point. I think it probably was an instinctive rebellion against my dad's assumption that I would go to West Point.

Q: The family mold.

Adm. S.: Yes.

Q: Did he get over it?

Adm. S.: Oh, yes. I think he was always disappointed that I didn't go to West Point.

Q: What about your mother?

Adm. S.: It didn't make any particular difference to my mother.

Q: Did you reveal your deep-seated reasons to them at the time?

Adm. S.: I think I said that I thought the group of boys who were preparing for the Naval Academy was a group that I would rather be with than the other group.

Q: Incidentally, what rank did your father ultimately hold?

Adm. S.: He was a brigadier general. He trained the 305th Infantry in Yaphank, New York, as a colonel, took it overseas, and was promoted while over there to brigadier general and went to the 32nd Division. My dad died while I was out in the Solomon Islands in 1942, and I think it was about six weeks before I learned that he had died, our communications were so scanty in those days.

I had the usual upbringing of a boy brought up in the Army who was constantly on the move. We would have about two years here and then two years back in the States, two year in the Philippines. We lived in Fort Ethan Allen, Vermont; the Presidio of Monterey; the Presidio of San Francisco; Walla Walla, Washington; Fort Sill, Oklahoma; Ethan Allen, Vermont; and, of course, several tours of duty in Washington when my dad was on the War Department General Staff, as they called it in those days.

Q: That really was fine preparation for a naval life.

Adm. S.: Yes, it was. Actually, I remember my dad's office was in the old State, War, and Navy Building and in that building were housed the State Department, the War Department, and the Navy Department, if you can imagine that. It's hard to believe, all of them in that one building.

So I did my four years at the Naval Academy.

Q: Tell me about those years. Give me a detailed picture, if you will, of the Academy at that time.

Adm. S.: I think I was rather an indifferent midshipman. I have the feeling now that I really didn't want to be at the Naval Academy. I did as little work as I could get away with and still stand about the middle of my class. I thoroughly enjoyed myself. I was in hot water a good deal of the time.

Q: You mean breaking rules and getting demerits?

Adm. S.: I got in bad with the upper class because they couldn't ever get to me with their hazing or their remarks and I enjoyed it.

Q: How were you able to escape it?

Adm. S.: I had whatever anyone else had, but it just didn't get under my skin. They finally gave it up, you know. For instance, in those days some of my classmates would be put under the table and then they'd have to hold their leg up and they'd pour a pitcher of milk down the trouser leg. I never had that happen to me, although the classmates at my table had it happen to them. I don't know why I was lucky enough to escape it.

I had several run ins with some of the upper classmen who came from Washington and who resented the fact that after Christmas vacation where they'd read about Midshipman Smedberg being at Rauschers or this party or that party. They would give me unmerciful hell when I got back.

Q: A certain amount of jealousy because of it.

Adm. S.: Yes, and they put me on report one time, 40 demerits for irreverent conduct in chapel because I'd whispered to a classmate. Of course, everybody does, but I got put on report. Another time, the same individual, whose father ran a hamburger stand in Washington and who used to work at the hamburger stand in the Christmas vacation, I would come in after a party at Rauschers at two or three o'clock in the morning - all of us would come in in tuxedos and have hamburgers, and when I went back to the academy he really let me have it. He put me on report once for "deliberate disrespect to the national colors." I was on the terrace over the messhall one time, talking to another midshipman, and way over on Farragut Field there was some drill going on. Apparently there were some colors over there. I had my back to them and was talking to this friend, a classmate of mine, and the first classman came up to me and said:

"You're on report for deliberate disrespect to the national colors."

I looked at him and he tried to point out the colors about half a mile away. I said:

"Sir, that's ridiculous." He said:

"What do you mean, ridiculous?"

I said: "I have more respect for the national colors than you will ever have. I was born and brought up in the Army. Every night of my life I stood at attention during Retreat. There isn't anybody who has more respect for the national colors than I have."

Of course, you don't talk like that to a first classman, especially one who doesn't like you. The commandant of midshipman dismissed the charge. I was hailed up there and I explained the circumstance. He laughed and tore it up.

Q: You bore a stigma, being an Army brat?

Adm. S.: Oh, yes. I was an Army brat and in those days there weren't very many Army brats at the Naval Academy. I had two or three classmates who were Army brats, but some didn't think an Army brat had any business being at the Naval Academy.

Q: I suppose that's one reason why you began to think you'd

made a mistake?

Adm. S.: No, I don't really think so, but I wasn't willing to just lie down and let them tell me there was something wrong with an Army brat.

I got in trouble when I was a first classman, also, because of a rather peculiar series of events. When we went on the midshipman cruise I was appointed one of the first mates of the deck, which was for the cruise a pretty important and responsible job. When we got to Panama on our way to the West Coast on that first cruise I was in the battleship Arkansas - I was detailed to the permanent shore patrol. We had a lieutenant commander, H.P. Sampson, as I remember, who was our shore patrol commander, so as soon as the ships arrived we went off on the patrol. Midshipman liberty, I think was up at six o'clock each evening. We were told that after midshipman liberty was over we could take off our duty belts and our brassards and we were on our own until the next morning when we went back on duty.

Well, that first night, I had been invited to a party at the home of Admiral Freeman. His daughter, Phyllis, I had known and they had a dinner party for the midshipmen, an early party. The midshipmen, I think had been granted special liberty until after the party was over, which was about nine or ten o'clock at night. All the midshipmen went back to the ship except me and, since I was on shore patrol, I went with the girls from the party, all of whom had late dates with the officers from the ship. I went to the Union Club with them.

While I was at the Union Club, one of the duty officers came over to the table where I was sitting with these young officers and the girls that I'd been with at dinner and said:

"What's your name?"

I told him and he said:

"Don't you know that the Union Club is out of bounds to midshipmen?"

I said, "No, Sir."

"Well," he said, "the notice was published on the ships."

I said: "We didn't know it, Sir. My shore patrol commander has said nothing about it."

"Well," he said, "you report yourself back to the ship under arrest."

So I went back to the ship, furious, burned up, and I was given 100 demerits, in spite of the fact that the notice had been posted after the shore patrol had left the ship. That was an injustice that rankled with me for a long, long time. Oh, I was restricted to the ship, too. As a result, in every port we came to I jumped ship. I got caught jumping ship in San Francisco.

Q: More demerits!

Adm. S.: More demerits. So when I arrived back at the Naval Academy I think I had about 200 demerits. The limit for first classmen was 150. Sinclair Gannon, the commandant of midshipmen, called me in his office and said:

"Smedberg, obviously you can't start the year with this number of demerits." Oh, and I lost my September leave, so here I was at the academy for my September leave.

Q: I wonder they didn't put you on the <u>Reina</u>!

Adm. S.: I'd had a pretty good record, so they made me the four-striper in command of all the plebes. No, it wasn't the plebes. I was in command of the "sub" and "weak" squads and all the people who had lost their September leave. At the end of two weeks, apparently I had done well enough so the commandant called me in and said:

"We're going to give you the next two weeks' leave." I think they left 100 demerits on because they recognized that I had been willful, which I had been. As a matter of fact, during that cruise I was so indignant about the injustice that had happened to me in Panama that I turned in my resignation from the Naval Academy.

Q: With the reason attached?

Adm. S.: Yes. The officer in charge of my group in the <u>Arkansas</u> was Lieutenant F. S. Crosley, whose father had been, I think, an admiral in the Navy, certainly a very well-known captain and whose brother Paul Crosley was in the class of '24.

Anyway, he called me in and talked to me for a long time and he tore the resignation up. As I remember, I submitted two or three to him and each time he talked to me and tore it up, thank God. I think the lesson that taught me was to try and never be really unjust in considering cases of midshipmen. I might mention that starting first class year with 100 demerits and only 50 to go for the rest of the year was difficult.

On one occasion, another midshipman and I frenched out - I think it was over Thanksgiving - and went up to Washington. His father was a member of the Chevy Chase Club, so we went up to a big dance at the Chevy Chase Club. We were in uniform, and we danced. During the evening Admiral Standley, who was then a captain on duty in the Navy Department and a close friend of Captain Buchanan, whose son was with me in this piccadillo, my close friend, now Rear Admiral Charles Buchanan, Retired, came up to me and said:

"Smedberg," - I'd been dragging his daughter, Helen, down at the Naval Academy.

Q: So he knew you?

Adm. S.: Oh, he knew me. He said:

"Do they give weekend leave from the Naval Academy now?"

I said, "No, Sir."

"Well," he said, "are you up here for some special reason? Is somebody in your family sick?"

I said, "No, Sir."

"How come you're up here in Washington, then?" he said, and I said:

"We just came up, Sir."

Then he went to Buchanan, whose father was his very close friend, and asked Buchanan the same questions, and Buchanan said:

"Well, we just came up."

We were pretty upset about that but, anyway, we got back to the Naval Academy about three o'clock in the morning, a civilian friend of ours driving us down.

Q: No trouble getting back in?

Adm. S.: Monday morning we found a notice when we got back from breakfast on our desks in our rooms saying to report to the commandant of midshipmen. The commandant was Captain Sinclair Gannon. He stood us at attention before him and said:

"Gentlemen, I don't know what you two have done but the superintendent wants to see you immediately."

So we went over to see Admiral Louis Nulton. We stood at attention before Nulton and he said:

"Gentlemen, I have heard the strangest rumor. I have heard a rumor that there were two first class midshipmen in uniform dancing at the Chevy Chase Club the night before last. I just hope to God I never find out who they are.

That's all Gentlemen."

Well, you know, we left his office in a daze. We never could get over that, and I want you to know that many years later when I was superintendent on two occasions I found out from hearsay what some of my midshipmen had been doing. I called them before me and I did exactly that same thing. I said:

"Gentlemen, I have the rumor and I just hope to God I never find out who it is. That's all."

So I passed on that wonderful experience of Louis Nulton.

Q: It was effective!

Adm. S.: Very effective, yes. But on the 22nd of February of my first class year, 1926, I left a hop early with the girl I was dragging, and in those days a first classman had, I think, an hour's hop liberty. They had to be back an hour from the time the hop was up.

Q: Presumably, you took her home and came back?

Adm. S.: Yes, or, if you left the hop early you had to be back an hour from the time you left. Of course, none of us ever paid any attention to that. I mean if you wanted to go home and do a little necking or something like that, you'd come back an hour from the expiration of hop liberty, which I did. Red McGruder had been watching me. He had seen the time I left the hop, which was about 9:30 at night, so when I came in -

Q: You were a suspect character!

Adm. S.: He had the duty. He said:

"Son, I just looked up and I see you've got 100 demerits. Now if I add up all the demerits for all the minutes you're over hop liberty, it's going to be an awful lot of demerits, so I'm just going to give you fifty. Now you get fifty demerits, and you now have 150 demerits. Let's see you get from here to graduation without one more demerit, or you're not going to make it, Son."

I made it from then until graduation without another demerit. I was the most regulation first classman you ever saw in your life.

Q: And you were a four-striper?

Adm. S.: No, no. That was just during that September leave period. I'd got no stripes at all because I had this bad conduct, 100 demerits to start the first class year with.

Q: Tell me about the courses. In retrospect, were they adequate?

Adm. S.: Frankly, except for the mathematical courses, they

were a breeze for me. For instance, in those days everybody took the same courses in French or Spanish. I had had six years of French before I came to the Naval Academy and I started in with "Je suis, tu es, il est" and so forth. I never cracked a French book the whole time I was here.

Q: You didn't take Spanish?

Adm. S.: Oh, no. Of course, I should have, but I was just taking the easy thing.

Q: But you obviously had background in Spanish, too, did you not, from the Philippines?

Adm. S.: No, not really. I used to know Spanish words as a kid and I still know some Spanish phrases. But I did well in history and government and geography and that sort of thing, which I enjoyed very much, and very poorly in the mathematical subjects, which I loathed.

I thought the course at the Naval Academy was very easy if you studied. There was adequate time then, which I'm not sure there is today, for studying for each recitation. How the youngsters do it today with all that they do, particularly those who take the overload courses, I don't know. I have great admiration for them. I would have a hard time getting through the Naval Academy today, I think. Certainly I couldn't get through it doing as little studying as I did when I was a midshipman. I think tremendous progress has been made at the Academy in the academic area.

We had a number of classmates who had gone to college or been in college and, of course, they had quite an advantage over those of us who hadn't been to college.

Q: Did they continue to have that advantage for all four years?

Adm. S.: Yes. I think they got off to a good start and just kept the momentum going. Although a number of late bloomers like, for instance, Bob Pirie, had no advantage like that. He was just a brilliant youngster and went right on up toward the top of the class. And P. D. Stroop was another classmate of mine, later a vice admiral. He was one of the youngest men in the class, about sixteen. I think Al Mumma - Albert G. Mumma, later chief of the Bureau of Ships and then president and chairman of the board of the Worthington Corporation, after four years as chief of the Bureau of Ships, he was another very young man who had a brilliant mind and still does.

But, as I say, I sort of coasted through the Naval Academy and, I'm ashamed to say, enjoying it pretty much and doing nothing of which I was particularly proud.

Q: What is your opinion of the greater emphasis on diversity and liberal arts now?

Adm. S.: I think it's been a good thing, but I'm not sure that it hasn't been at the expense of really selling the Navy to a youngster. I know that when I had the experience that I did for a number of years of being a member of the Secretary of the Navy's Academic Advisory Board to the superintendent, I took a very jaundiced view of the program, which they still have, where certain boys are chosen at the end of second class year for special projects in their first class year and they work on those projects -

Q: Trident?

Adm. S.: Trident, yes - because I felt that that was preparing youngsters for something other than the Navy. I'd really be interested in knowing how many of those brilliant youngsters have stayed in the Navy for a career. I would guess very few of them have. I don't know, I have no idea, but I know that during those meetings here of the Academic Advisory Board we always had dinner one night with the Trident Scholars, each of whom would get up and make a little presentation of the subject that he was pursuing, and the educators on our panel, college presidents and all, were absolutely amazed at the brilliance and the depth and the maturity of these midshipmen.

Q: Sort of incredible.

Adm. S.: It was incredible. I remember one time one of the college presidents said to me:

"Good Lord, this is postgraduate stuff at our university." They were very much impressed by that program. As I say, I kept feeling that this would take the kids out of the Navy rather than enabling the Navy to take advantage of the depth of study that they had pursued. Many of them, of course, didn't go to sea but went right on to postgraduate work. I always had the feeling that they should have gone right into the Navy, then gone on to the postgraduate work after they knew what the Navy was like, but many of them never even found out what the Navy was like until they'd had maybe six or eight years of study, counting the four years at the academy.

Q: What about the relaxation of marching to class and that sort of thing? Did you find that beneficial when you were here as a midshipmen?

Adm. S.: No, we disliked it. The only thing that was good about it was that you all got to class on time, you got back to your room on time, and you didn't loiter in between. You started studying as soon as you got back, then the bell rang and you fell into formation and went back to class.

Q: But wasn't it something that kept you close to the Navy, as such?

Adm. S.: I don't know that that was particularly true. I know the one thing we resented was that after we graduated about half of my class or a third, I forget which, was kept at the Academy for what was called aviation summer. We were ensigns and we were treated as plebes. We had to march to classes and keep quiet in ranks. The plebes would be marching down one walk and we'd be marching down the other, all ensigns. That was really an amazing thing. We called it plebe-ensign summer!

The other part of our class had done it the summer before. We did it the summer after graduation.

Q: Tell me about the summer cruises.

Adm. S.: I thought the cruises were very beneficial in that we learned how a sailor lives on board a ship, and we did the work of sailors, too. I think today the youngsters don't really appreciate exactly what living like an enlisted man is like. As you know, we were three months on each cruise, and they took half the sailors off the ship, so we actually replaced them body for body and did the same work they did.

Q: Where did you go on your first cruise?

Adm. S.: The first cruise we went to Copenhagen, Lisbon, a long, long cruise, that part of Europe, and England. The second cruise I guess we went back to Europe. The third cruise we went through the Panama Canal and up to San Diego, San Francisco, and Seattle, which was a fine cruise, except for me, because I was restricted all the time.

Q: That's where you got all your demerits!

Adm. S.: Yes. That's where I got in my deep trouble that really put me in a very bad frame of mind for first class year.

Q: In addition to getting to know how the sailors live on ship on these cruises, did it strengthen your resolve to be a naval officer?

Adm. S.: To be honest with you, as I look back, there were very few of us who had any thought but that we were going to be naval officers. And even after we went out into the service, almost nobody in our class ever resigned. You never thought of resigning. In those days we served at the pleasure of the president. We didn't have to serve for three years or four years or five years. We served at the pleasure of the president. If the demands of the nation needed officers, you had to stay in, and if Congress cut back on officers, then, a number were released. But very few of my classmates ever really thought about getting out. I shouldn't say that because a number did get out and started making money in 1929, before the crash. Then, of course, we were the suckers when we stayed in the Navy until the crash, and during the depression following the crash we were the lucky SOBs who still got a paycheck every month and our very wealthy classmates who no longer had jobs on Wall Street regretted the fact that they had gotten out then, many of them, except a few people like Gus Long, who later became president of Texaco.

No, while we were here most of us became imbued with the idea that we were going to be naval officers. Nobody ever questioned it. Of course, the fact that some got out after two years indicated that some had questioned it.

Q: This didn't prove attractive to them?

Adm. S.: Yes, but it really wasn't until I'd been out in the fleet that I began to appreciate and enjoy the Navy. I liked it then.

Q: As a midshipman - especially on the cruises, great emphasis was given to your status as a naval officer, you were honored and--

Adm. S.: Oh, yes. In those days when you went into a place like Bar Harbor all of society turned out to entertain you. You went into Newport and the facilities of all the clubs were made available to you and to the officers of the fleet when they came in.

Some years later, in 1952, when I went to Newport as chief

of staff of the Destroyer Force, Bailey's Beach was barred to naval officers, that is unless you had established yourself in Newport. The Newport Golf Club banned naval officers, and actually it was partially due to my efforts when I was chief of staff of DesLant that we got permission for commanders and above to again be accepted for golf at the Newport Golf Club.

Q: What you're saying underscores what I had in mind in the twenties -

Adm. S.: The status of the naval officer gradually dropped and dropped and dropped.

Q: And I suppose that in the twenties that was in itself an inducement to stay in the Navy?

Adm. S.: That's right.

Q: You were at the top of the heap, so to speak.

Adm. S.: Yes. I think the services were respected, or the Navy was, much more than the Army. I'd been born and brought up in the Army and in time of war people in the Army were great but between wars they were nothing. Just like today, or not so much today - I see the military profession has risen now - but a few years ago we were down with the garbage man and the mail carrier and so forth. But this is a sine curve throughout our history.

Q: Yes.

Adm. S.: Not long after a war the military appear useless and not needed, not necessary, not respected or admired. Forgotten.

Q: Going back to the cruises again. I would imagine that there was some practical application during a cruise of some of the things you learned in the classroom?

Adm. S.: Yes. Most, but not all, of the practical work was in the three summer cruises. We had nine months at sea on board ship to learn. However, we learned some of the details of guns, torpedoes, ammunition, boilers, naval machinery, et cetera, at the Academy in the Departments of Ordnance and Gunnery and Engineering, but we had much theory; we had to do these horrible interior ballistics formulae, which I think today did absolutely no good whatsoever. This was a tremendous formula you had to work out and if you were off by one decimal point you got a zero. You either got 100 or a zero. I never will forget that horrible thing.

Q: Tom Moorer was telling me that he learned how to make smokeless powder and he never did use it again!

Adm. S.: That's right. I really think that we got a pretty good grounding in basics at the Naval Academy, but most importantly we were "sold" the importance of sea power to this country. I left the Academy with the feeling that this country had to have a navy and it had to have a good navy.

Q: Did you get any training, direct or by implication, as to your role as a diplomat, the Navy being the arm of the military - ?

Adm. S.: Well, of course, we studied the influence of naval officers in our history of the past in foreign countries, and we recognized that naval officers, as they got more rank, would have an opportunity to exercise diplomacy for the nation in different places. We were encouraged to learn either French or Spanish well enough so that we could be interpreters and speak the language when we went to other countries, but I don't think there was any great emphasis on preparing us to be naval attachés or diplomats.

Q: Was it perhaps in a more general sense? I remember Admiral Tommy Hart telling me one time that when he was superintendent of the academy, his objective was to train the men as leaders and as gentlemen. Those were his twofold purposes.

Adm. S.: That's right. Well, we actually were constantly

told that a naval officer was an officer and a gentleman and we had always to live up to the principles of a gentleman.

Q: Did your father keep a watchful eye over your development here at the academy?

Adm. S.: No, not particularly. He was disappointed that I didn't stand better than the middle of my class.

Q: He knew you were capable of it?

Adm. S.: I think I was capable of standing a great deal higher in my class if I'd been willing to work but I wasn't. That's the fact of the matter.

Q: What about athletics while you were here?

Adm. S.: Let's just say I dabbled in athletics. I liked athletics. I enjoyed them thoroughly. I played class soccer and class baseball and class wrestling. I remember one time I was the inter-company wrestling champion in maybe my second class year and I was coxswain of the 150-pound crew in my first class year. I was in the Masqueraders. I remember the coach of the Masqueraders was Nancy Brereton, the wife of Captain Brereton, at the time. I was in <u>Bulldog Drummond</u> and was the female adventuress. Now Rear Admiral Charles

Buchanan was Bulldog Drummond. I had to wear a slinky evening gown and I remember Mrs. Brereton being very much upset because I was wrestling at the same time and I came with mat burns on my face and a shoulder. I was wearing an off-the-shoulder evening gown and my shoulder was all a horrible mat burn three or four days before the opening performance.

Q: Max Factor wouldn't take care of that?

Adm. S.: No! Well, I tell you, they put a lot of makeup on me before I came out on stage and they had to put sleeves in my evening gown to cover up this mess.

Q: It's surprising you didn't come out with a female nickname!

Adm. S.: Yes, it is. Well, I was the battleaxe type female, I think.

I enjoyed athletics very much. Plebe year there were two of us who were out for shortstop on the plebe baseball team. One was Jock Cooper, who later became captain of the Navy team. I was the other one. We played shortstop about the same but Jock was better than I.

I remember one time Dad came down to see a game that we were playing and that was the game the coach decided that he was going to play Jock Cooper the whole game. The game before he had played me the whole game. He was just trying to see which one of us was the better. So my Dad came and sat in the stands and I sat in the dugout the entire game. Later, when the coach found out my father was there, he said:

"My God, why didn't you tell me your dad was here? I would have put you in."

"Well," I said, "I didn't want to get in the game because my Dad was here."

My father had been shortstop at West Point and was an excellent athlete there; a little fellow but, as I said, he was quarterback on the football team and shortstop on the baseball team.

Q: Sometimes it's difficult to live under the shadow of a prominent father, isn't it?

Adm. S.: Yes. I think probably one of the reasons I went to the Naval Academy was because Dad had done so well at West Point. Probably one of the underlying reasons was also that I liked to go some place where nobody knew anything about me.

Q: What about your brother?

Adm. S.: My brother went along civilian lines. He kept moving with my family. They were in San Francisco a good part of the time when I was at the Naval Academy, at the Presidio in San Francisco. He went to Stanford.

Q: He didn't aspire to a military career?

Adm. S.: No, he wasn't interested in the military. He got imbued with a sense of drama. He went to Yale Drama School. He didn't graduate from Stanford because I think Dad was transferred to Washington or something. He's lived in California most of his life. He had his own lighting business for a while. He lives in Palo Alto, California, today. He's basically and primarily and essentially a civilian. He and I don't see eye to eye on many things such as the importance of having a very powerful Army, Navy, and Air Force in peacetime to make sure we don't ever have to go to war.

Q: Then he lives close to a university.

Adm. S.: Oh, yes, that's right.

Q: You mentioned aviation summer. Tell me a little about that.

Adm. S.: As I remember it, it was a very dull experience. We had some old flying boats. Our flying experience consisted mainly of about six or eight of us being put in the hull of a flying boat without any windows in it and we'd go out in the bay and taxi for maybe 15 or 20 minutes to get off the water. They would fly around a little bit, then we'd land again, and that was our flying experience. Of course, we studied things like weather and other aviation basics, but it was pretty much a waste of time.

Q: Not enough to whet your appetite to be an aviator?

Adm. S.: No. Later on, when we were ensigns, we were all required to take aviation indoctrinal training. Everybody on the East Coast had to go to Norfolk and all those on the West Coast had to go to San Diego, and we were given enough time up to the solo point - none of us soloed there, but we were either qualified to solo or not qualified. Those who liked aviation could then go into aviation after two years. It had to be two years, as I remember, before you could go to Pensacola. Those of my classmates who didn't like going to sea in ships or who really wanted to fly - I think a lot of them who went to Pensacola really wanted to get out of going to sea in ships because it was pretty dull in those days. In '27, '28, '29 -

Q: We weren't going to have any more wars.

Adm. S.: No, there were going to be no more wars. The Navy's funding was very low. Then, of course, it got worse and worse as we went into the depression.

Q: And we had the limitation on armaments.

Adm. S.: Yes, that's right. And we were limited, I remember, to 11 knots as the maximum speed we could make at sea because of fuel limitations.

I remember going as an ensign in the destroyer <u>Mullany</u> (DD-325) from Bremerton, Washington, to Corinto, Nicaragua, at the time of the insurrection of the bandit down there.

Q: Sandino?

Adm. S.: Sandino. We had to go at 11 knots and it just seemed like forever in a destroyer at 11 knots, all by ourselves from Bremerton, Washington, to Corinto, Nicaragua.

Q: And to keep busy all the time.

Adm. S.: Well, of course, there was no way you could keep busy. I think we had five officers. We had the captain, the exec, and five officers. Then we lay at anchor in Corinto Harbor for I don't remember how long, several months. It was an interminable period. We got mail once a month and our outgoing mail went out once a month. We'd go ashore and go on hunting trips in the jungle, go to the little local cantina and drink a beer at night, and fish. That's about all, and go to the beach, run up and down the beach and swim. But I tell you it was a dreary existence.

Q: That was an inducement to get out of the Navy as soon as possible!

Adm. S.: Yes, it really was. Of course, it was easy to get a job at that time because this was in 1927. This was before the real depression.

I enjoyed destroyers, although I had an unfortunate thing happen to me when I was an ensign. I suddenly developed asthma. I used to be a very enthusiastic golfer.

Q: You now are today!

Adm. S.: Yes. My friends and I used to play golf whenever we'd get off Saturday and all day Sunday we'd play golf. We'd play thirty-six holes of golf.

Q: Where did you play?

Adm. S.: We played in Coronado, at the old course in Coronado, which is now covered with houses.

I used to come in from my golf games with this terrible asthma, which I'd never had in my whole life. I remember the first real attack I had. We were married, my wife and I, and I came home from golf and thought I was going to suffocate. She rushed me out to the dispensary. I couldn't breathe. The doctor took one look at me, gave me a shot of adrenalin, and in thirty seconds I was fine. He said:

"How long have you had this asthma?" I didn't know what it was. I had no idea what was the matter. I said:

"I didn't know what it was. I've never had it in my life."

From that time on it got worse and worse and worse and, by 1929, I was sent before a medical survey board and recommended for retirement. I would have been retired, except that I refused to be retired. I sent a telegram to Captain Buchanan, who was on duty in Washington, the father of my very close friend and classmate, and he got the Navy Department to say that if I would pay my own way and that of my family to the East Coast, they would give me a month's leave to get over it. I could report into the Naval Hospital in Brooklyn, and if I was all right then, then maybe they wouldn't retire me.

So I was put on the train almost on a stretcher and, after twenty-four hours on the train, I was just as healthy as I am today. I played golf in El Paso where my dad was at that time in command of the Eighth Cavalry, went on to New York, stayed on Governor's Island, where my wife's father, a colonel in the engineers, was on duty, and I reported to the hospital in New York just as healthy. They gave me a clean bill of health and I was ordered to the cruiser <u>Northampton</u>, which was fitting out and building in Quincy, Massachusetts, put her in commission, never had any problem.

Then, when the trouble with Japan was developing, we were ordered out to the West Coast and it came back again.

But I was able to fight it. I didn't have it at sea. They found out later it was from pollens.

Q: It was an allergy?

Adm. S.: It was an allergy.

Q: That was in the time when they weren't thinking in those terms.

Adm. S.: That's right. Anyway, I gradually outgrew it. I had a period of about eight or ten years when it was very tough for me to climb up to the bridge. I'd be gasping when I got up to the bridge, especially at general quarters when everybody had to go on the dead run. If you're got four or five flights, not being able to get your breath is pretty rough. But I was determined I wasn't going to be retired.

Q: Let's go back to your graduation. You succeeded in carrying those 150 demerits until graduation without any missteps and then what?

Adm. S.: You mean what after graduation?

Q: Yes.

Adm. S.: I went out to the West Coast and reported to the New Mexico. I spent my month's leave at the Presidio in San Francisco, where my father was stationed. Then I reported to the New Mexico, which was in the Navy Yard in Bremerton.

Q: How many of your classmates were with you?

Adm. S.: There were about sixteen of us. Almost everyone went to a battleship. We had a JO mess, and you had two classes in the JO mess, the class ahead of you and your class, and there were twenty-five to thirty of us in each battleship.

I remember my skipper in the New Mexico was Admiral Leahy and the executive officer was John Sidney McCain.

Q: So you had some excellent officers?

Adm. S.: Oh, yes, and that delighted John Sidney McCain, who had a wonderful sense of humor but a wry one at times, I thought, called me in to his cabin when I reported and said:

"Son, what would you like to do when you're on this ship?"

"Well," I said, "Sir, I don't know really. Anything that I'm told to do."

"What do you particularly like?" he said. "Do you like navigation, do you like gunnery, do you like engineering?"

I said: "I'd like gunnery more than anything, Sir, and navigation, but I really dislike engineering."

"Fine," he said, "you'll be an assistant in the main engine room."

For one year I went all through the engineering department! He had apparently looked at my record and he said:

"I see that you were coxswain of a crew at the Naval Academy."

I said, "Yes, Sir."

"Well," he said, "starting tomorrow morning, and every morning when we are in port at four or five o'clock you will take out the enlisted race boat crew, and then when you come back you take out the officer race boat crew, because we are going to win the races."

So while my classmates were going up to LA and coming back at six o'clock in the morning, I was getting up every day at four and taking out the enlisted race boat crew and then the officer race boat crew, and we won both races that year. We won the officers' boat race and we won the enlisted boat race.

Q: He believed in proper indoctrination, didn't he?

Adm. S.: Yes, Sir, he sure did. But you know in those days, in the JO mess particularly, there was practically a continuous poker game going all the time, all night. You'd go on watch at midnight, you'd come off, you'd get out of the poker game and go on watch, come off at four o'clock and get back in the poker game. This was when you were in port, quite often.

Q: What kind of stakes?

Adm. S.: You could lose forty or fifty dollars. They were pretty high. We used to play a game called Red Dog, too, which was a horrible game. I haven't seen it played for many, many years. This was a perfectly horrible game. You could bet the pot, you know. It was just a simple game where you had four cards in your hand and if you had four aces, of course, you could bet everything because the next card turned up you had beat. But if you had a couple of kings and a ten and a nine, you had a pretty good hand. If you had a ten of diamonds and they turned up the jack of diamonds, you'd lost.

Those days were very different from today when everybody on board ship is working pretty darned hard.

I've stayed close to the Navy through the fact that both my sons are Naval Academy graduates. One has just been selected for admiral and the other on the 30th of this month is going to be the skipper of VS-29, the first jet ASW aircraft squadron in the Pacific Fleet. I'm going to be out there to see him take over. Just like next week, we're going down to Norfolk to see my son relieved as Commander Destroyer Squadron 10, after which he puts on his admiral's uniform and then goes to duty in BuPers.

Q: This was a good basic experience, wasn't it, in the New Mexico?

Adm. S.: Yes, it was. I was there one year. Generally, you had two years, but across the dock from us was the destroyer Mullany. She'd been ordered down to Corinto, Nicaragua, because of the Sandino insurrection and about two days before she was to sail one of her young officers, an ensign, an ensign, got sick and they had no replacement, so the New

Mexico was ordered to send an ensign over there. I was a makee-learn assistant engineer and they put the finger on me and I was ordered. Two days later we sailed for Corinto. That began three years in destroyers.

Q: By that time had you developed an aptitude for the engineering profession?

Adm. S.: No, I disliked it intensely.

Q: You didn't get over that?

Adm. S.: No, I did get over it. I knew enough about engineering to know what was down below and what I could and should expect of the engineering department, and I knew where to look for the dirt and the carelessness in upkeep. And I knew enough to look for the valve threads and see if they had paint on them, look for leaks and other things. It was a good experience because I spent three months in auxiliaries, three months in main engines, three months in the electrical department, and then three months as oil king.

Incidentally, that was a sad experience because in those days the engineering competition was so keen that the expression originated that you won the competition by the sharpness of your pencil, the way you figured out your oil consumption, and everyone was always sort of cheating on the oil consumption, trying to get more oil that didn't show on the books.

One of the jobs I got first of all, and which was extremely distasteful to me, was when a civilian tanker would come alongside. I would go over to see the skipper taking with me a five-gallon can of alcohol which, in those prohibition days was just like fine gold, and let the skipper know that if he could give us any extra oil that wouldn't go through the meters the five-gallon can of alcohol was his.

Q: A bribe!

Adm. S.: Yes, and we generally managed to stow away quite a lot of extra oil so that we appeared to be burning less oil than we were actually burning, and that year we won the engineering "E".

Q: Not exactly in keeping with the code of ethics of a naval officer.

Adm. S.: No, and I tell you it really made me sick at times; that business. Now I think we just had an engineer officer whose ethics were not very high and I don't think the exec or the captain knew anything about it. They were proud of the fact that we were steaming so economically, but a lot of that economical steaming was on oil that we had obtained and never accounted for.

And, speaking of oil, some years later I was on the staff of Admiral Vernou in the <u>Concord</u>. We were up in the

Aleutians, in Dutch Harbor, Alaska. I was on the bridge of the Concord when we were ordered alongside the New Mexico in this tight little harbor to fuel. The engineer officer of the Concord was a Scotsman named Angus Sinclair, who was in the class of '24. The assistant engineer in the New Mexico was Hyman Rickover, who was a young lieutenant.

Everybody was dressed in whites in those days. We all had our white uniforms on, and this is fueling ship.

Q: Up in Alaska!

Adm. S.: In Alaska, yes. Our admiral was Admiral Walter Vernou, who was a stickler for etiquette in dress and a magnificent seaman, a man I loved and admired very much.

It turned out that we were only going to take fuel forward because our engineer had shifted a lot of the fuel to the after tanks so, in order to expedite, we were just going to take the forward hose. So the New Mexico had the after fuel hose stopped up over the quarterdeck, over her beautiful shining quarterdeck. When the order came to commence pumping, down in the engine room they opened the valve to the after line, instead of the forward line, and it blew the plug and a great geyser of oil came all over that beautiful quarterdeck and all over the exec in his whites. And then the funniest thing you've ever seen happened. It took some time before they could get that oil shut off, but Angus Sinclair, whose mind was just as keen as could be, had his whole engineer force over there with buckets, dustpans, and squeegees, and they were squeeging the oil off the deck, putting it in buckets, carrying it back, and putting it in the tanks because that wasn't going through any meter. It was all spare, free oil.

And then Rickover came up, saw what was going on, and ordered them off the ship because we were getting his oil free! I'll never forget that as long as I live. I wasn't ever going to tell that story until old Rick had died. He was jumping up and down and ordering Sinclair to get his men off that ship. Then he started squeegeeing the oil and putting it back in his own tanks, a few bucketsful, you know, that hadn't gone into the scuppers.

For months and months they scrubbed that quarterdeck and never did get it back to its beautiful pristine whiteness.

Q: Nor the uniforms, I take it!

Tell me a little about this annual competition in the fleet. This was almost their main occupation, wasn't it?

Adm. S.: That's all we did.

Q: Was it a salutary thing to do?

Adm. S.: Yes, it was, because we were constantly, in gunnery for instance, striving to improve our accuracy and the methods we used for our fire control.

I remember we had a young commander who came to the New Mexico, a gunnery officer, about the time that I got there. His name was W. H. P. Blandy. He introduced methods we had never heard of before. I was in the engineering department so I wasn't actually carrying them out, but it was the talk of the wardroom and the JO mess. He was so meticulous he made us measure in caliber every shell and every rotating band was shaved so that every one was exactly the same thickness, and in the drills every shell had to be seated exactly the same amount. Every powder bag had to be rammed exactly the same place so that there were never any gaps between the powder bag and the breech, or if there was a gap it was the same in every gun.

We won the long-range battle practice that year through that kind of attention to every little detail that went into the firing of the big guns. We had stood in a rather mediocre position in the battleship competition the year before. Blandy came aboard and announced that we were going to win it, and we did win it. That's the kind of brilliance that began to show up among certain officers who later went on to be flag officers, and you could spot them. You could spot people like Corky Ward and Rivets Rivero when they first came out into the fleet. Immediately you could see favored people who were going on and on and on, whereas others were just in a rut. I think most of the present-day flag officers when they were young showed a lot of spark in one direction or another, so they began to be marked.

Q: And initiative, on their own?

Adm. S.: Oh, yes, tremendous initiative and tremendous willingness to accept responsibilities and an eagerness to tackle a new problem. I think that's the thing that I always looked for in my young officers in my ships, their willingness to accept responsibility, and then I watched them to see how well they carried it out. Did they slough it off? Did they carry it out well? The officer I liked best was the one who would come to me and say:

"Captain, I've got this job you gave me, but frankly I haven't been able to crack it. I need a little more help."

Sometimes you'd find an officer who couldn't do it and he'd give up without saying anything to anybody about it. Of course, that's the fellow you really have to watch out for. But the officer who honestly tries to do the job and finds he can't do it and comes for more help, that's the kind of officer to have, too.

Q: How much latitude is there within the fleet for a young officer with initiative and imagination to exercise these talents in the purview of the regulations?

Adm. S.: I think there's great latitude in small things. The way an officer handles his division, the way his men view him. Pretty soon it becomes apparent that the men in a certain division think the world of their division officer, and you find after a while that he knows every man by name and he knows about their families and he knows their capabilities. He pats them on the back when they do a job well and gives them hell when they don't. The first thing you realize is that that is one of the top divisions in the ship and you begin to look at the young man more and more favorably, and when a vacancy comes some place you recommend him for it, whereas some officers just sort of coast along with their petty officers running the division more than they are.

I think the officer with initiative and ability makes his own opportunities and it begins to come to the attention of senior people that he is a sparkplug. Once you find a sparkplug, you load more and more onto him and the good officer gets better and better the more work he has loaded onto him. I think that's the way it is in all of life. I had two officers who were sparkplugs in each of the two ships that I commanded in World War II, the two destroyers I put into commission, trained the crews in Casco Bay, and took out to the Solomon Islands; one in 1942, the other in '43. In the first one, the Lansdowne, I had only two other officers who had ever been to sea before, my exec and my gunnery officer. There were only 32 of the enlisted men, out of a crew of 282, who had ever been in a ship before. That's quite an experience.

Q: And to go into a war zone!

Adm. S.: That's right. We trained in Casco Bay in miserable weather, then convoyed in the Atlantic for a little while, and then went through the Panama Canal and straight nonstop, except for fueling, out to the Solomon Islands.

Q: Let's go back, Sir, to the Mullany.

Adm. S.: DD-325?

Q: You went down to take care of Sandino?

Adm. S.: Yes, and it was a very deadly, dull affair. The Marines were taking care of whatever was taken care of, and as far as I could see we served no useful purpose except to have an American presence in Corinto. We were the only warship there. The Navy had another warship or two in Bluefields, on the other side is the isthmus. Well, it was a deadly, deadly period - deadly. As I look back on it, I wonder how we got through it, or why we ever stayed in the Navy after it.

Q: After that mission, what did you accomplish on her?

Adm. S.: The Mullany?

Q: Yes.

Adm. S.: We began to get active in fleet problems, fleet exercises. We had a very aggressive skipper, who was a magnificent shiphandler, a tough disciplinarian, a Prussian named Hans Ertz, who is still alive today. He's a class of 1912. He lives in Santa Barbara. But he was a fine skipper because he believed in letting his officers handle the ship. After he'd shown us his skill, and he was very skillful, he pretty much let us younger officers handle the ship in maneuvers.

In those days, you know, we used to run without lights. Of course, we had no radar. We'd run at 30 knots, blacked-out ships, black nights, 250 yards apart - actually, the standard distance was 300, but we tried to close up to 250, six destroyers all making 30 knots on a black night.

Q: Shades of Honda!

Adm. S.: Looking for the enemy battle line, and then we'd launch a torpedo attack. On several occasions we launched our attack and then turned away, but on one or two occasions we went right through the battleships in the black of the night without a light, they didn't have a light, and we went right between those battleships at 30 knots.

I tell you if you don't think that's hair-raising. Sometimes you couldn't see the battleships. You could hear the whine of their blowers. Suddenly they'd loom up and there you were going right through the column. They're making 12 or 15 knots, and you're making 30. That used to be hair-raising. When we did that the skipper always had the con.

He was right out there, hanging out that open window on the bridge.

We had some wonderful fleet problems in those days and we had some very fine -

Q: These were all off of San Pedro or something?

Adm. S.: Yes. We operated out of San Diego, and off San Clemente. We did our shore bombardment on San Clemente.

We had at one time as our squadron commander Husband E. Kimmel, and I tell you Kimmel was one of the finest officers in the efforts he made to get us prepared for any eventuality.

I was the signal officer and communication officer, among other things, in the Mullany; that is radio officer, signal officer, communication officer, stores officer, and commissary officer at one time. Kimmel, when he came to the squadron, required every communication officer to take his typewriter over to the tender every day in port and practice codes for two hours a day. And he required us to sit in on the circuit and actually operate the radio circuit. No one had ever done that before, and that was tough, learning that. We had to sit there in that tender and listen to codes and copy the circuits, then go back on board ship. We had certain drill exercises at night and we would have to be there on board ship when these drill exercises came in, and when you're married and you're in port, that's tough. We had blinker drills every night. We had to copy the blinker messages and turn them in the next day to the tender for the squadron commander's communications officer to look at. We used to beat the system somewhat. I was married and had a youngster. I would go ashore and, of course, I had to go back to the ship for this drill at eight o'clock at night, or nine o'clock, depending on the darkness of the season.

My wife and baby and I would go down to the bay in the car and I would sit there and read the blinker coming off the tender and write it all down and turn it in the next day. I wouldn't go back to the ship. A lot of us started doing that. But for the radio circuits, we finally complained to the point where they eased up a little bit on us.

He also established a rule that whenever two or more ships were nested together one radio or signal or communication officer, and it was always the same officer, had to be on board with the nest communication duty.

Q: What irony that a man like that -

Adm. S.: Yes. He was a man who was always preparing us for tough times, and he was the guy who got caught. In the minds of the general public, he was caught with his pants down, but he wasn't. The very fact that the fleet reacted as it did and was able to get the ammunition to the guns and start shooting as quickly as they did with the Sunday crews on board -

Q: This was at Pearl Harbor?

Adm. S.: Yes - was evidence of the fact that he had kept that up. He just is a fall guy in history, but he was a magnificent officer.

Q: While you were on destroyers, were you involved in a course at the war college? Did you take a correspondence course?

Adm. S.: No.

Q: This was a practice then, was it not, in the fleet?

Adm. S.: Yes. Now wait a minute. Maybe I did. I think I did take a correspondence course. Yes, I did. Then, of course, at the end of three years we had a very comprehensive series of examinations we had to take, and we studied for those very, very hard, and all took the exams for JG. In those days we were ensigns for three years and then took the exams for JG.

On battleships, our first year, we had to keep journals. We had a navigation journal, an engineering journal.

Q: Who inspected them?

Adm. S.: Well, the navigator inspected the navigation journals and the engineer inspected the engineering journals. You had to turn them in, keep them up to date. Every ensign at the end of his three years was supposed to have gone through every department in the ship and had at least three months in every department of the ship, in which department he kept a journal. I only had one year in the battleship instead of the two because of this sudden emergency transfer to a destroyer. We didn't have any program like that on the destroyer. We were supposed to have, but there were so few officers and you were generally busy enough so that you didn't have that kind of school work. We were pretty busy.

Another thing that was difficult in our destroyers was that there were restrictions on fuel so that we'd have to get underway very early in the morning and go out to the operating area and do our exercises. Of course, during the exercises you could make full speed, if it was an exercise calling for full speed. As soon as the exercise was over, you had to go back to your eleven or twelve or thirteen knots, whatever the order was at the time. You'd have to go back to port at slow speed and would sometimes get back at ten o'clock at night and off again at five or six in the morning. So your nights in port were pretty bad. I used to get home some nights at ten o'clock and off at four or five o'clock in the morning. These were our in-port periods.

Q: For purposes of this story, you neglected your personal life and you didn't tell me when you got married.

Adm. S.: Oh, I got married on December the 10th 1927 on Governor's Island in New York Harbor. Actually, while I was in the New Mexico I had gotten engaged to a girl who was then in the University of Washington and whose father was an Army colonel in the engineers. He was district engineer for the Engineer Corps in that whole area.

Then I went off to Nicaragua suddenly, and they were transferred back to Governor's Island while I was in Nicaragua. We had gotten engaged and she had set the date as December the 10th in New York City. That was very interesting because we wrote each other every day. Once a month I'd get thirty letters and I'd mail thirty letters. When I got back to San Diego, which we did about, as I remember, in September or October, here was December coming up and I was slated to get married on December 10th in New York City. The Fleet commander just issued an order saying that no officer could have over ten days' leave because an officer who could be spared from the ship for longer than ten days could be spared indefinitely. That was the wording of the order. This came out just a few weeks before I was going to put in for my leave.

In those days it took five days by train to get to New York from California and five days to get back. There's ten days. I went to my skipper and told him my problem and he said:

"Well, you don't have a chance. She'll have to come out here."

I asked him if I could talk to the squadron commander

and he said okay. So I talked to him. He was Lewis Cox.

"Oh," he said, "Smedberg, with this order I don't think there's a prayer."

So I said: "Sir, may I have permission to talk to the Commander, Destroyer Force?"

I talked to the admiral and he was sympathetic but he said:

"I don't see how you can do it. This order is from Commander, Battle Force," who was Admiral Kalbfus, I think. So I asked permission to go and see the chief of staff of Admiral Kalbfus, Commander, Battle Force. I went to see him and he was Admiral Harris Land. He was extremely sympathetic but he said:

"Smedberg, I don't know, but I'll talk to the admiral."

You'll never believe it, but I was given thirty days' leave because it was obviously impossible for me to get to New York and back and get married in ten days. I got an awful razzing for getting this thirty days' leave. It was unheard of.

I went to Governor's Island, we got married, we came back to the ship. Then I started my tour of duty as a young married officer in San Diego, and it was rough. We generally operated two weeks at sea and two weeks in port. And every now and then we'd cruise reserves on two or three-week cruises. Sometimes we'd be gone for six weeks, and of course, we always had the fleet problem once a year for about three or four months.

We had seven years of sea duty after graduation, and my

last year I got a letter from the Naval Academy saying that they had noted that I starred in French and would I be interested in teaching French at the Naval Academy. I wrote back and said that I would be delighted because they said "If you're interested we will send you for the whole summer to France with your family. You'll live in a little pension and you'll learn the French language thoroughly, conversationally."

I was so excited about that, I accepted with gratitude, and I was so happy.

Q: Your wife probably was happy?

Adm. S.: She was delighted. Then came my orders for me to report to the postgraduate school. I wrote a letter to BuPers and said that I hadn't requested postgraduate school. You had to request it in those days, and everybody was requesting it, but I didn't want it. I wanted to go down and teach French at the Naval Academy. BuPers wrote back that they didn't care what I wanted, I had been selected to go to postgraduate school and I was going to postgraduate school.

I wrote back again and said there must be some misunderstanding, I hadn't applied for postgraduate, I didn't want postgraduate, and I'd been asked if I wanted to teach French at the Naval Academy. It took me a little while to catch on that BuPers had decided that I was going to postgraduate school. I went to the postgraduate school, but in those days they didn't have any money for transportation, so we were all ordered to go in the USS Chaumont with our wives and our children from Long Beach and San Diego to Norfolk.

We had two little babies at that time. My wife had a father who was on duty at Governor's Island in New York, a colonel in the Army. He wrote her and said:

"I'll pay yours and the kids' way east by train if you'll come with us while your husband's on the three or four-week trip, or whatever it is, through the Panama Canal on the Chaumont."

We thought that was a pretty good idea because we knew the transport was going to be pretty crowded. So I put her on the train and I sailed in the transport. On the Chaumont we were so crowded that we had staterooms of eight - eight wives and kids in one stateroom and the eight husbands would be in another stateroom. That's the way we made that trip. I was a bachelor on board, so I wasn't particularly put out, but we used to make little arrangements so that seven of us would vacate one of the rooms so a man could have his wife in, you know, for a little visit and the other seven would get out for a period. That's the only way a husband and wife could ever get together on the whole trip.

I'll never forget another thing on that passage. We were in San Juan for one day and a classmate of mine, of whom I was very fond, had two little girls, two and three. He and his wife wanted to go ashore in San Juan but they had the two little girls, so I said I'd take care of them during the day. They went ashore about nine o'clock in the morning with everybody, and the ship was going to sail about five in the afternoon. Well, everybody came back but John and his wife. They didn't come back. So I'm standing up there with the two little girls waiting for their mother and their father, and the order comes to take in the gangway.

I rushed up to the exec and said:

"Sir, Lieutenant and Mrs. Doe are not back on board yet. I have their two little kids here and they've got to get back to the ship."

He said: "Well, we can wait a few minutes," and he got word to the captain.

Pretty soon a taxi drove up to the dock and the taxi-driver and Mrs. Doe between them drag on board this almost unconscious classmate of mine, who is the father of two little girls.

I helped put him to bed and we got things settled down, but for a while there I thought I was going to be the father of the two little baby girls all the way back to Norfolk!

Q: That's going more than one mile!

Adm. S.: I'd rather not mention that officer's name. I have called him John Doe. Some years later he was dismissed from the Navy for drinking.

Q: You glossed over the fact that you were in Quincy, Massachusetts, to fit out the Northampton. Tell me about that.

Adm. S.: Yes. I was the fourth officer ordered in connection with the fitting-out and commissioning of the USS Northampton. She was one of the first of the 10,000-ton treaty cruisers, a wonderful ship. I think we were the first one to be launched, maybe the second. Maybe the Chester beat us.

Anyway she had the first integrated fire-control system, whereby we controlled the main battery from the plotting room. We could shift the guns from one director to another director. We had nine 8-inch guns in three turrets. We had the first automated telephone system on any ship in the Navy, a dial system, which turned out to be a terrible headache because from any place in the ship a sailor could dial the old man and say, "You son of a bitch", call him any name he wanted and hang up.

Q: And this happened?

Adm. S.: It happened all the time, and one of my jobs was to stand a watch down there with my people, my electrician's mates, as they called them in those days, behind the automatic switchboard and try to follow that bug. We could see the bugs running in the back of the board, the little electronic bug, you know, would search out a circuit, and try and pinpoint where the calls were coming from. We'd stand watch back there and then as soon as we'd located it we'd send someone down quick to the area that we had plotted and every now and then we'd catch somebody. But generally they'd just call up quick. They got onto the fact that we were monitoring it.

That used to burn the old man up. He was a very strict disciplinarian. That was Captain Walter N. Vernou, a magnificent seaman. He was later aide to President Roosevelt, when he was an admiral.

Q: This must have been quite an interesting experience for a young officer? To be involved in the fitting-out of a new ship?

Adm. S.: Very. That's right. We got to know the ship intimately because everything that went into it we watched being installed. Then we went on a perfectly wonderful cruise -

Q: Let me ask you, was there any feed-in by the officer personnel as to what was being installed on the ship? Was there any possibility of this?

Adm. S.: I think not. The installation had all been approved by the various bureaus in Washington. We watched the installations. I will say this. I was sent to the Ford Instrument Company on Long Island.

Q: Oh, yes.

Adm. S.: To learn about the main battery computers and the AA battery computers that had been installed in the ship, brand new.

We went then on a cruise through the Med to Europe to show the flag and show off this brand-new 10,000-ton treaty cruiser.

Q: And it was a shakedown cruise as well?

Adm. S.: Shakedown cruise, a wonderful three months' cruise. We went all through the Mediterranean. We had a wonderful time. We'd spend two weeks at anchor in Villefranche, Nice, and Monte Carlo, and all through that part of the world where we showed the American flag.

Q: Here was the navy and obviously in operation.

Adm. S.: Yes. Oh, it was great. We spent two weeks anchored off the campanile, in the Grand Canal in Venice. I remember being all dressed up one time in my whites and going ashore as boat officer to escort some dignitary, and as I got out of the boat to go up the slimy, slippery steps, I slid down the slimy steps in my whites and right into this stinking, dirty canal. So when the VIP arrived, here I am in a dirty, soaking wet suit of whites!

Q: Did the foreign navies show real interest in the Northampton?

Adm. S.: Oh, yes. We had many, many visits. We were very proud. Of course, there were certain places we couldn't take them - the plotting room, for instance - but in the main we showed them our ship. Everything was very new and very modern. Our engineering spaces were beautifully designed. Our gun turrets were magnificent, the powder-handling and the hoists and the ramming equipment - everything was beautiful. It had all been developed at Dahlgren. We were a good shooting ship.

Q: This was in 1930?

Adm. S.: This was - we put her in commission in 1930, and I was in her '30, '31, '32, '33, when we were ordered back to the West Coast. We stayed out there and I was detached in June of 1933 to come back to the postgraduate school. Then the postgraduate school was in Annapolis.

We were based in Long Beach.

Q: Were there any particularly interesting experiences or significant experiences when you were on board her?

Adm. S.: To be perfectly honest with you, I can't right now think of anything that stood out particularly.

I told you about the incident when we fueled - no, that was in the <u>Concord</u>. In the <u>Northampton</u>, let me see. We had a division of treaty cruisers out there. We finally had the

Chester, the Salt Lake City, the Pensacola, and the Northampton. I was shipmates with people like Admiral Wat Tyler Cluverius as our division commander, a wonderful man, a fine seaman, a great naval officer, a thorough gentleman. He's the man who stood out most in my mind in those days.

Q: All under the overall command of Joseph Reeves, were you not?

Adm. S.: Yes.

Q: Tell me a little about him.

Adm. S.: Not when I was in the Northampton, but later on I was on the staff of Commander, Cruiser Division 3, and Commander, Cruisers Battle Force, who first was Admiral Walter Vernou and then was Admiral Harold R. Stark. That's when I first met Admiral Stark, with whom I was to spend many years.

It was during that period, which was 1935, '36, '37, '38, in San Diego that Admiral Reeves began to make his presence felt, particularly on one Friday afternoon at three o'clock when he ordered the entire U.S. Pacific Fleet to sea - "immediately". We didn't believe it.

Q: This broke all the rules, didn't it?

Adm. S.: Broke every rule. I'll never forget. In Coronado

there was a wedding that day and, of course, the groom never showed up.

Admiral Vernou and I - he was my boss, I was on his staff - were leaving our flagship to play golf. It was about three o'clock in the afternoon. We had gotten back to port an hour earlier. The admiral had gotten into the boat, I followed when the officer of the deck called down to me. I ran back up the accommodation ladder to him. He said:

"Here's a priority that's just come in. An urgent priority." Then he said: "You don't understand. It says 'From Commander in Chief, U.S. Fleet to U.S. Fleet. Get underway immediately and proceed to sea.'"

I looked at this message, and I was so long up there that the admiral stuck his head out of his gig below and said:

"Come on, Smeddy, what's the matter with you?"

I went down the gangway and showed the admiral this dispatch. He didn't turn a hair. He got out of the boat, went up the gangway, and said to me:

"Get all of the captains over here immediately. Send a dispatch to each ship to report when they're ready to get underway. We will proceed to sea within one hour."

I looked at the admiral and I said:

"Admiral, this must be a joke or something. This must be a drill."

He said:

"Smeddy, do you read any word drill in there?"

"No, Sir."

He said: "This is no drill."

I couldn't believe it, and I want you to know we got underway whether the skippers were on board or not. Many of our officers and men were ashore. We all went out. Some ships were towed out. Got every ship out of that harbor.

Q: Wasn't there some sort of a vague threat of war or something?

Adm. S.: If so, it was so high above us that it didn't seep down to me. No, I think he wanted to test the readiness of our fleet in case we did have a threat. To me, it was very impressive. Here we all were, the cold iron watches, we were all swinging around the buoy. This was Friday afternoon, everybody was going off on their weekends and only the weekend watches were going to be on board.

We had come in about an hour before from a week at sea and the people who had things to do like the commissary stewards and all those people had gone ashore. Preparations were made to get the fuel barges alongside. Of course, we never got them, we had to go to sea without them. Nobody had time to fuel.

That opened my eyes to the fact that maybe some day there might be an emergency. In those balmy days of peace we really didn't ever think much about the possibility of war, even though the Northampton had sat out there and we were uneasily aware of the Japanese threat in the Far East. Nobody ever really thought of war. When I say "nobody" I'm talking about the people around my rank. Perhaps the senior officers did, I don't know.

Q: It just wasn't an actuality.

Adm. S.: No, but we got a long way with the Northampton. The Northampton was in the '30, '31, '32, and '33 area, and this other was '35, '36, '37, '38, after I came back from the PG school.

Q: Inasmuch as the Northampton was one of the treaty cruisers, did you have any opportunity to see one of the Japanese treaty cruisers?

Adm. S.: No.

Q: They didn't let you near?

Adm. S.: No. We didn't see them and they didn't see us.

Q: Tell me about the installations at Pearl Harbor in the early thirties.

Adm. S.: I really can't tell you much about the installations, except what a person would see from going in in ships. I had been many times into Pearl Harbor and there was nothing that seemed impressive to me at all, that I could see.

Q: There were repair facilities?

Adm. S.: Oh, yes, we had repair facilities, we had good dry dock facilities. We had tremendous oil storage and, of course, the big mistake the Japs made was not hitting those oil tanks. Had they done that, they could have really done a lot toward crippling us and then, had they been able to sink the tankers resupplying the oil from the mainland.

We were aware in those days that we didn't have enough patrol planes to keep a proper surveillance around the islands. There was a general peacetime attitude that it can't happen here.

Q: In the early thirties you were mainly concerned with your yearly competitions.

Adm. S.: That's right, or solely concerned with that.

Q: How important were athletics to the fleet in that time?

Adm. S.: They were very important because that was one of the few ways you could keep the men occupied, and particularly in the years to come were athletics more and more important. At least I always felt they were important. Now, to jump ahead a little bit, I had a destroyer squadron from about

June 1947 till August '48. It was at a time when we were pinched for funds, had very little money. We had three types of destroyer squadrons: the fully operative one, the semi-operative one, and the one that could only get one ship underway once a week by taking the crews off the other ships and putting them board. They'd go out and steam for four hours and come back.

I happened to have DesRon 3, which was a fully operational squadron. We were restricted as to speeds, but we did carry out all of our exercises, and I required a very strict and stringent athletic program for my ships. We had competitions among the men and the officers in everything you can imagine. We had baseball - we didn't have football, of course - ships were too small, we had officers' golf, officers' tennis, officers' pistol teams. We didn't have a rifle team only because we didn't have a rifle range.

Q: Did you have wrestling?

Adm. S.: No, we didn't have wrestling as a squadron sport. Of course, we had soft ball and hard ball. We had bowling, we had boxing. We had good facilities in San Diego.

The point I'm getting at is that in this period of almost depression in the Navy when we had very little money for fuel and very little money for anything else, the fact that this athletic program really paid dividends was illustrated by the fact that in my division and my squadron of two divisions the ship that stood No. 1 out of something like 56 ships in the class was my flagship, the Keyes, and the ship that stood No. 2 in battle effiency was the Hollister, Corky War's ship. And we stood 1 in athletics, not only in the squadron, but in the division, and our ships stood something like 1, 2, 4, 5 in that, all of our ships were up at the top in battle efficiency, and I think it was a result of the ships being made to feel like teams, the officers and men. For instance, I did all I could to see to it that the officers went to the ships' baseball games with their wives in the afternoons. I didn't say they had to go but I always remarked the next day that I'd seen Ensign and Mrs. or Lieutenant and Mrs. So and So at the ball game and I sure was happy to see they were supporting the ship's team or something like that. Pretty soon it got to be sort of a habit. We'd take our wives and our kids and go over to see the ship's baseball game or basketball. We had basketball teams, too.

I have a letter which I'll send you sometime. You can make a copy and send it back to me. It's a letter of commendation about the standing of the ships in my squadron of the Pacific Fleet in 1947-48. I also would like to locate, although I have temporarily mislaid it - I haven't lost it, I never lose anything, but I sometimes can't find something. I've got a file cabinet full of stuff. There is a letter that I wrote after being detached as squadron commander telling the Commander, Destroyer Force, Pacific, what was wrong with the way he was operating the Destroyer Force. I had quite a few pages of real blasts against the way our destroyers were being operated, things like our operating from Monday till Friday and getting into port at four o'clock Friday afternoon with every single facility closed in the port. We needed provisions, we needed fuel oil, we needed everything, and we spent hour after hour after hour trying to get somebody with a key to open up things, that sort of thing. And the fact that the mail would come on board about five or six o'clock, and our mail orderly would come back with it, and in the mail were all the operations orders for Monday's exercises.

Q: And you were completely immobile over the weekend?

Adm. S.: Yes, and we had to get underway at six o'clock Monday morning in order to get out to the operating areas, and frantically trying to read the operation orders on the way out to find out what the hell was going on.

As a result of that letter that I wrote, I remember the chief of staff - I think Savvy Forrestal was commander of the Destroyer Force, to whom I wrote the letter, and Vice Admiral Sabin, later - Lorenzo Sabin - was the chief of staff. I was on leave in Carmel for a couple of days before I came east. They sent for me and I thought I was really going to catch hell. The admiral said:

"Smedberg, this is the best thing I've seen in a long time. Why in Christ's name didn't you bring this to our attention sooner?"

"Well," I said, "frankly, we were all so beaten down and all so busy and all so tired when we'd get into port and there were so many things that were wrong, I didn't think we ever had a chance to really air them before. But after I was relieved I said, now I'm going to sit down and put everything in writing that I could think of that has been wrong in the way you've been operating."

Immediately, they changed a great many things. Nobody was permitted to get underway before eight o'clock in the morning. Nobody was permitted to be kept at sea after noon on Friday. No fuel facility was to be closed. No commissary. These things were all put in proper perspective. It did a lot of good.

Q: A bit of clairvoyance?

Adm. S.: No, it was just an officer who was so frustrated he put down every feeling that he had. He'd been pent up for a long time. I mean you hate to go to the boss and complain about one little thing, when in the sum total these things were absolutely unconscionable and they were wrong, and the people sitting on the staff in the tender had no idea.

Later on, I was commander of Cruiser and Destroyer Force, San Diego, Pacific Fleet, and I used to say to my staff:

"Look, we're sitting here on this tender and we really don't know what's going on. Get out into those destroyers, some of you, and find out what's going on.

Q: Was golf a part of the competitions?

Adm. S.: Yes, that's right. We had officers' golf, officers' pistols, officers' tennis, and we awarded medals and trophies. As a matter of fact, at that time there was a lot of money available in the Navy for athletics - not appropriated funds, but ship's service profits - and very few people were availing themselves of it, so we had nice trophies for every single thing, and we'd get almost every man who participated in anything some kind of a trophy or a medal. I thought it was very worthwhile.

Q: This is not true today, is it, in the Navy?

Adm. S.: I don't think they have much time. Everybody is so busy and so shorthanded. Of course, I'm not quite as far removed from today's active navy as some of my contemporaries due to the fact that I have a son who's a destroyer squadron commander, who's had three commands, and another son who's executive officer of an aircraft squadron and is about to get command of one, and a daughter who's been married to a jet fighter pilot, a naval aviator, who's just retired as a Navy captain. Through those kids I have really seen a great deal of what the Navy is doing today.

When my son was the surface operations officer of the Sixth Fleet, we went over and followed the Sixth Fleet right around from port to port. I expressed many times my shock and dismay and disgust over the appearance of our officers and men when they went ashore in European ports in shoddy civilian clothes, most of the sailors in a pair of dungaree pants and a sports shirt, and beards and mustaches. In the old day in Europe every man left his ship in a uniform that was immaculate and the appearance of our men was commented on by everyone. During the last few years over there every sailor from every nation in the world that has a navy looked better than our American sailors did. I used to go in and talk to Admiral Zumwalt about it, and he used to ask me whenever I was in Washington to come in and talk to him about the things that I thought about the Navy. I said:

"You know, Admiral, I vowed when I retired that I was never going to offer a suggestion and I've never done it, unless someone like you has asked me what I think about something. When you ask me what I think about the relaxation of some of your standards in dress and conduct, I have to say that I think it's doing great damage to our Navy. If a man can't feel proud of himself in his personal appearance, then everything else is going to start suffering. That's my feeling, just my personal feeling."

I got way off the track and digressed there.

Q: That's all right.

Adm. S.: Let's go back to where we were.

Smedberg #1 - 74

Q: Interesting digression.

Well, we're on the Northampton still. Some of the innovative installations on the Northampton, how did they prove out in operation in the fleet?

Adm. S.: I think they proved out very well. Our main battery consolidated fire-control system, of course, was carried on into all the rest of our ships, improved, and proved to be the best way to fight a ship's battery.

Q: Did people from Washington keep a watchful eye over the operations of the Northampton?

Adm. S.: Yes, I assume they did. I sometimes wonder what happened to all the voluminous reports that went in year after year. We're all familiar with the story about the chief engineer who sent in his report and he put a 10-dollar bill in the middle of the report, and years later when he went back to the Bureau of Engineering of the Bureau of Ships, he looked up this report and there was a 10-dollar bill still in it.

Q: I hadn't heard that story.

Adm. S.: Oh, yes, that's supposed to be a true story.

Q: It's possible.

Adm. S.: Nobody ever read it back in Washington.

Q: What about developing importance of the airplane in the fleet in the early thirties?

Adm. S.: I think that those of us who were not aviators began more and more to appreciate the value of the airplane. I know that in one fleet problem, in which Admiral Vernou was in command of the cruiser forces, or some of the cruiser forces, the Lexington and Saratoga were enemy ships and we learned throughly the tremendous advantage they had through their long-range reconnaissance abilities, and how hard it was for us to track them down because they knew where we were all the time and they could always keep out of our range. We had no radar in those days, you know. They could be over the horizon from us. They knew where we were all the time and we didn't know where they were.

We developed some pretty good tactics with our own observation planes, our "Kingfishers" that we carried on our cruisers. I remember that it was a matter of great pride among the officers and men of our ship that our captain got in the rear seat of the first launch from our catapult, the first time an airplane had ever been fired from our ship. We thought, boy, that takes guts. Here's the captain of our ship in the rear seat with a young, junior lieutenant, pilot going off that catapult. That's the way Vernou was. He was a leader in everything and the greatest shiphandler I've ever known in my life. Once he demonstrated to our satisfaction and his that he knew all there was to know about shiphandling, we did the rest. He stood there and let us conn the ship, do the conning, landings, et cetera. He felt, and he used to tell us many times, that his job was to teach us as much as he could, to pass on to younger officers all the experience he had learned in the Navy.

He was a magnificent naval officer. A lot of people felt that he wasn't progressive enough. For instance, he was always against good officers going to PG school. He said what you learn in the fleet is what you need as a naval officer. You don't need to go to PG school and learn it out of books. So he was not progressive in that area. He didn't understand the necessity for advanced education, but he was a great seaman and a great naval officer with the highest moral standards.

Q: From what you say about him, he seems to reflect many of the characteristics of Admiral Nimitz?

Adm. S.: Yes. He and Nimitz were very close friends. And he and Ernie King were duty officers together at the Naval Academy many years earlier when they were lieutenants. They were known as two strict martinets when they were company officers. He and Ernie had been contemporaries, although they were not classmates but they were close. He had great respect for Ernie and Ernie had great respect for Wally Vernou.

I remember one time when Wally had an operation order in connection with a fleet problem. He prepared the operation order, asked me to take it over to Admiral King's flagship, which was then the <u>Langley</u>, at North Island at the time, and get Admiral King to approve it so that he could get it written up. I got over there about on o'clock in the afternoon and asked to see Admiral King. I was told by the flag lieutenant that the admiral couldn't be disturbed. I said:

"This is important. Admiral Vernou says I must come back with the answer within half an hour."

He said: "But the admiral can't be disturbed." Then he said, "Confidentially, he's taking a nap and when he naps he can never be disturbed."

So I said: "Well, could I talk to the chief of staff?" Pretty soon I was taken down to the chief of staff. The chief of staff said:

"I understand that you've been told that Admiral King doesn't want to be disturbed but you still want to disturb him?"

I said: "Yes, Sir, I'd just like to take this paper in to him from Admiral Vernou and just get his initials on it."

He said: "You've been told that the admiral is not to be disturbed. That's enough. He's not to be disturbed."

He didn't know that the flag lieutenant had told me why he couldn't be disturbed. So I went back to see Vernou and he said:

"Is it okay with King?"

I said: "Admiral, you won't believe this, but Admiral King is taking a nap and can't be disturbed during his nap."

Vernou blew his top.

"Taking a nap!" he said, "At one o'clock in the afternoon of a working day?"

He never did get over that.

Well, I really disgressed again.

Q: The carrier was beginning to be noticed?

Adm. S.: Oh, yes, and carriers carried out bombing attacks on the Panama Canal, successful ones. We were all very much impressed by the things that the carrier-based planes could do. We had one incident there that was historic and has been written up, I'm sure, and talked about many times, when the attacking planes got mixed up and torpedoed their own battle line. The details of that are rather hazy in my mind but I never will forget seeing these friendly planes who were supposed to be on our side coming and torpedoing all of us! A lot of us got hit, too. They dropped torpedoes, with dummy heads on them, that hit you.

Q: There were variants on that in World War II?

Adm. S.: Oh, yes, that's right.

Q: What was your attitude toward the flyers on the cruiser?

Did they stand watches? What was their role?

Adm. S.: We watchstanders were very much aggrieved because they couldn't stand watch the night before they were going to fly the next day, but they could play poker all night on board ship. That used to irritate the devil out of those of us who were standing regular watches. In fact, we used to accuse them of going into aviation to get out of standing regular watches! We used to have some rather bitter arguments about that in the cruiser force.

We felt that the reason they weren't to stand a night watch was so that they could get some sleep and they shouldn't be playing poker all night.

Q: That's reasonable enough.

Adm. S.: Yes. We'd be playing poker with them and then we'd have to go on watch, but they stayed in the poker game because they were flying the next day and they didn't have to go on watch.

Q: Did you have a plane or two on the New Mexico?

Adm. S.: No. I don't believe we did. Not in 1926-'27.

Anyway, during the period I was in the Northampton, 1930-1933, we developed this recovery by sea sled while underway, you remember?

Q: Yes.

Adm. S.: We used to practice that by the hour. The ship would be making 10 knots into the wind, the seaplane landed and taxied right up onto this sort of cargo net. Then he's towed by the cargo net with his wing fairly close to the side of the ship. The crane lowered a large ring which the man in the back seat had to get up and hook the plane on - a tricky maneuver. The plane was hoisted out of the water. Every now and then as the hoist started, a pontoon would go under, and the plane overturn. We had some terrible moments when some of these planes would tip over.

Q: A hairy career, wasn't it?

Adm. S.: Yes, it was a hairy career, and we had a great deal of admiration for those young people, young flyers. As a matter of fact, I remember the time when one of the young flyers was circling the ship, preparing to land, and I was officer of the deck. He was being smart, you know. He dipped his wing over, thumbed his nose at me on deck, hit his wing tip on the water and went crashing. The plane was lost. He lived. I guess it was just a smart alecky thing that used to happen now and again.

But in the main we had great respect for them and as the years went on and I operated in the Solomon Islands I used to bless those pilots, without whom we could have done nothing in the South Pacific.

Q: Well, in that transitional period, in the early 1930s, the aviator was beginning to be viewed as someone of more importance than he had been in the late twenties?

Adm. S.: That's right. There was a feeling, as I said before, in the early days that the aviators were just people who didn't want to take the drudgery of standing watches and this was a more flamboyant carefree sort of life which they chose.

Q: And the line officers cautioned against pursuing such a career, didn't they?

Adm. S.: Yes, some did. I wanted to go into aviation but the admiral talked me out of it two or three times.

Q: You did have an urge?

Adm. S.: Oh, yes, I had an urge.

Q: You didn't tell me that.

Adm. S.: Well, I had two factors. One was my wife who begged me not to do it, and the other was that Admiral Vernou was constantly against it. During the three years I was in the Northampton, the first two years when he was my skipper, I had great admiration for him and his advice and his opinions.

Q: When did you begin to develop an urge to be an aviator? Your aviation summer at the academy was such an unsuccessful one that you seemed to be turned off. When did you develop an interest in it?

Adm. S.: As I saw my aviator classmates and heard their stories and saw what a pleasant life it was.

Q: Not theory, for instance?

Adm. S.: Yes. Of course, I didn't see the horrendous landings they often had to make on the carriers or the times they were lost in the fog and some of them didn't come home. We had one period out there when a whole squadron from the carrier was lost.

Q: Just didn't find their way home?

Adm. S.: Never found the carrier and just disappeared. Occasionally we'd find a lot of them in the water and go pick them up. They'd run out of fuel, trying to find the carrier. They didn't have any TACAN in those days to get home. How they got home I don't know. I certainly hand it to them.

Q: Did you ever reach the point where you made application to go to Pensacola?

Adm. S.: No, I never did apply to go to Pensacola. At one time, though, I was on the point of applying for lighter-than-air, after I'd been in surface ships for a long time. My wife said: "If you put in for lighter-than-air, I'll divorce you. That would be the final straw."

I don't know that that was the reason I didn't put it in, but it was just sort of a change of duty I wanted more than anything else.

Q: You anticipated a future for lighter-than-air craft?

Adm. S.: Yes. At that time we had a great big dirigible with us on the fleet problem and we were quite impressed with its ability to scout long range. Of course, we didn't appreciate the fact it could be shot down by any of the carriers' aircraft, any time. It could have been.

Q: And weather would be an impediment?

Adm. S.: And in some of our big fleet anchorages, down there in Panama, for instance, this big oiler was converted with a mooring mast would have the dirigible there. We'd look over and see this thing. It was quite a fascinating life to contemplate. But I was never really very serious about it. As I look back on it, I had no great urge to go into lighter-than-air. I just wanted a change of duty. I'd been in this one ship two years and that seemed long enough.

Q: Then you indicate a certain adventuresome spirit.

Adm. S.: That's right. I just learned a lot about seamanship and handling ships under fine seamen. I know that Admiral Vernou was relieved by a captain who, in my opinion, was a milque-toast. He was scared to death to handle the ship. When he found out that two or three of us were excellent shiphandlers, we handled the ship all the time. He never did. We'd bring it in to port. We'd do everything. We'd pick up the buoys, we'd pick up the sleeves. That used to be a neat trick. You'd shoot a sleeve down and you had to get it before it sank so you could count the holes in it to get your score. We'd come up at full speed, back down full right alongside, and pick it up.

This new skipper of ours was really impressed the very first time we did that. I remember he said, the first time our A. A. guns shot down a target sleeve: "You've got to slow down, you've got to slow down.'

I said, "Captain, we've got to get up to that sleeve."

"Slow down," he said, "I tell you to slow down. I paid no attention to him, got up there, backed full, and caught the sleeve right under the leadsman's platform with a grappling hook. The captain stood back and said:

"Well, I guess you knew what you were doing." I'd been

disobeying orders all the time.

Of course, some of the arguments used to be over accusations that we put holes in the sleeve with the grappling hook getting it up and, of course, you're not supposed to count those. I think every now and then there's be a grappling hole counted as a shrapnel hole.

Q: All of that indicates, (your expressed ability in this area,) indicates the value of Vernou's training?

Adm. S.: Oh, yes. I've always been proud of the fact that I'm a good shiphandler, and during my two destroyer commands, after I had handled the ship and made a number of different kinds of landings alongside tankers or docks or picking up buoys, then I let my officers handle the ship thereafter. In fact, I made a practice to go up on the flying bridge, over the bridge, stand there and grit my teeth and let my officers make mistakes. I remember one time I let the young gunnery officer bring the ship alongside a concrete tanker out in the Solomon Islands. I could see he was going to do damage. I just stood up there and grit my teeth, and he wiped out all the stanchions along the side of the tanker. He was red-faced, choked up and said:

"Oh, Captain, I'm terribly sorry."

I said: "That's all right. You've learned how not to do that again. Now get over there with the repair party and tell the tanker we'll repair all the damage done. Get over there and you're in charge. You see to it that everything's repaired."

It takes a lot of determination to keep from having your officers feel that you're breathing down their neck and you're going to rescue them every time they get in trouble. My skippers, starting with Captain Ertz in the Mullany, who was a wonderful shiphandler, had confidence in us and we justified it. Captain Vernou did exactly the same thing. He couldn't stand a timid skipper. When he had a cruiser division in 1935-36 in San Diego; he had the light cruisers, the old Concord class, the four-stackers, you know?

Q: Yes.

Adm. S.: 7,500-tonners. He used to make his ships do all kinds of unexpected things. He'd called the captains and say:

"Some of the things I'm going to require you to do will make you think I'm a madman sometimes, but if I run up a signal to stop and send a fried egg over to the flagship in a boat, that's what I want done, and I want to see who's going to get here first with a fried egg."

Then, suddenly he could call a ship alongside and make us have megaphone-to-megaphone communication. In those days everybody was scared to death to get close to another ship, and this captain would come along about a quarter of a mile away and try to establish megaphone communication. Up went the signal "Close this ship" and he would come over maybe an eighth of a mile, so timid and scared. In those days, if a captain made any kind of a mistake with his ship, and there were endless mistakes he could make, his career was in jeopardy.

Q: Exactly!

Adm. S.: Yes, because the people who made mistakes were passed over. Very often they were among the best officers. They were the ones with initiative. I think there was a tendency in the old days to promote the cautious fellows that never got in any kind of trouble, didn't exercise much initiative, and didn't take any chances.

Q: That seems all right for peacetime, doesn't it?

Adm. S.: Fortunately, a number of people like Ernie King, Kimmel, and Wally Vernou didn't feel that way. They wanted to see the ones who had gumption enough to take some chances, and if they made mistakes they'd forgive them.

Q: Is there any noticeable diminution of that kind of training in the modern Navy?

Adm. S.: It's hard for me to say. I can't really comment on the modern navy because I'm so far removed from it. I get, vicariously, stories from my kids and their contemporaries.

I think the longer we are from war the more cautious people will become. A lot of our officers today have had commands of destroyers and ships in the Korean War and in the Vietnamese War. They've taken all kinds of chances. They've been on their own pretty much. We've got some very fine officers with initiative and courage and daring in our Navy. We have some very fine young officers who won't get out because they believe in the Navy, they believe that the Navy has to be, and has to have a future. I'm always sorry when a very fine young officer says he's getting out because everybody else is making more money than a naval officer. That isn't really a good reason today because the Navy officer is well paid today. In comparison with many of his civilian contemporaries, some say that he's overpaid in peacetime.

I know that he is not overpaid, but in comparison with what the salary of a naval officer used to be in the old days, he's extremely well paid.

Q: Together with the emoluments that go with it.

Adm. S.: That's right.

Q: One other question occurs to me about that period in the Northampton and that has to do with ammunition. This was the depression time. How restricted were you in ammunition?

Adm. S.: Believe it or not, we in the treaty cruisers, and

I think in the fleet as a whole, always had ammunition for a lot of practices. And to best illustrate that I'll tell you that in the Northampton when we were firing these 8-inch shells, in most of our practices we would fire ten rounds per gun - 90 8-inch shells in a single, long-range battle practice, at a time when my brother-in-law, who's a West Pointer, was in command of a 3-inch battery in the Army and was allowed to fire two or three live rounds a year per 3 inch gun. He used to be bitter.

I know that on one or two occasions when we visited him in Fort Bliss and I would tell him about our long-range battle practice and our short-range battle practices and other AA shoots, and the ammunition we were firing, he would get so damned mad over the fact that we had enough money for ammunition and he had to go bang, bang most of the time.

But I believe it was probably due as much to Carl Vinson and a few of our far-sighted congressmen on the Naval Affairs Committee that we got enough money for ammunition and for exercises at sea. I think the nation and its naval adherents in the Congress appreciated the fact that we had to keep control of the seas and they supported the Navy to a far greater degree than the Army was ever supported in peacetime.

We were most fortunate. Very little restriction on our use of live ammunition.

Q: That was a very potent committee of the House.

Adm. S.: Oh, yes, Vinson, and old Senator Walsh.

Q: He was in the Senate.

Adm. S.: Yes, Walsh in the Senate, but particularly Vinson in the House.

Q: Vinson and Fred Britten and Colgate Darden.

Adm. S.: That's right. Way back in 1939 when I first became the aide to the chief of naval operations, I always accompanied the boss to all the hearings in the Congress, 1939, '40, '41, and then, of course, when I was aide to Forrestal I went again to all the hearings, and as Chief of Naval Personnel I had for four years to go up and defend my appropriations before the Senate and the House committees. So I spent a lot of time in the Congress listening to presentations and to the manner in which various congressmen received our presentations. in the main, the people on the Armed Services Committee, and the old Naval Affairs Committee were pretty dedicated people. We had a few sad characters but most of them were pretty solid U.S. citizens who were determined that our fleet was to be a good fleet, fortunately. We have a lot of people in Congress today who worry me because they are actually cutting into the bone of our armed forces.

Q: They don't seem to have that determination that we should have an invincible fleet?

Adm. S.: No, and the idea that we now talk with Russia seems to have made some of them feel that this is a protection, when in fact the real threat is always behind "detente".

Q: Well, Sir, I think we're about ready to leave the Pacific and come back at last to Annapolis and to the postgraduate school?

Adm. S.: As I told you, when I was ordered to the postgraduate school I was quite upset because I had been offered this job of teaching French at the Naval Academy and after seven years of sea duty I could think of no nicer way to spend a tour of shore duty with my family than teaching French at the Naval Academy.

Q: Tell me, how did they fill that billet?

Adm. S.: I think they probably ordered in someone who had taken French at the Naval Academy, but I don't think they had time to send him abroad. I don't remember now.

When I finally arrived at the PG school, I was called in to see Captain van Meter, the executive officer. He said:

"I notice that you haven't expressed a preference for any PG."

And I said: "No, Sir. Frankly, I didn't want to come here."

He said: "You didn't want to come here?"

"No, I didn't." I told him about having been offered a job at the Naval Academy doing something that I would have enjoyed very much.

"Well," he said, "what would you like to have a PG in?"

I said: "It doesn't make any difference to me."

He said: "How about Applied Communications?"

I said, fine, so I took the Applied Communications course for two years and that stamped me immediately as a communicator.

Q: Changed the direction of your career, didn't it?

Adm. S.: Yes, it did, but it put me in line for lots of very interesting jobs. I went from the postgraduate school to the staff of Commander, Cruiser Division 3, in the Pacific, who had requested me. That was Admiral Vernou.

Q: Would you, perhaps, stop and talk about the direction communications were taking at that time, and what new ideas you acquired at the postgraduate school?

Adm. S.: There were two types of communications postgraduates. One was the engineering postgraduate and mine was applied communications. In other words, we who took the applied communications course were the users of the equipments that were designed and improved by the engineers, you might say. The officers who took the engineering communications course had one year at Annapolis and then went to either one or two years at a university where they got their master's in communication engineering. They were the people who went on later to be the radar experts and the ones who made tremendous contributions to our communications equipment, our signal equipment, radio equipment, and so forth.

Q: What were you trained in using in the operational field while you were at the postgraduate school?

Adm. S.: We had to learn to type, we had to learn to receive radio, we had to learn to read blinker, we had to learn semaphore, we had to learn every single thing that a signalman and a radioman had to know in the fleet. We had to learn circuit design, not so that we could design a circuit but so that we could understand it, although we were not supposed to get in and fix anything. We were not engineers. We were the people who used the equipment and disseminated information.

Of course, we had to learn the signal book from A to Z. And then we got a lot of instruction on staff work, the function of the admiral and how we on the staff helped the admiral to do what he had to do. Many of us went to Flag Officers' staffs from the postgraduate school, as I did.

Q: You were groomed for that particular function?

Adm. S.: Yes, we were groomed for that. In a way, it was quite narrow because it was hard to get out of. This was sort of a new thing, this applied communications specialty.

They had had the engineers, but senior officers were so delighted to get communication officers who were knowledgeable in the use of the signal book, in radio and communications and could read the signals on the bridge, go down and sit in on a radio circuit down below and actually know how well the circuits were being handled, could sit in and monitor the circuits, radio and visual and so forth, that it was hard to get out.

As I say, I went with Admiral Vernou. He was Commander, Cruiser Division 3, first, then Commander, Cruisers, Battle Force. I went with him there, and he promised me that after these two years I could be executive of a destroyer, which I wanted; that's what my contemporaries were doing and I wanted to do. Some day I wanted to be skipper of a destroyer.

When Vernou was relieved he had it all set with the Bureau of Personnel for me to go as executive officer of a destroyer, but his relief, the new admiral, requested that I be retained, because he didn't know anything about communications. The new admiral was named Harold R. Stark. He came out as Commander, Cruiser Division 3 so that I went down from being the Cruiser/Battle Force communicator to being just a division communicator. A year later Stark was promoted Commander, Cruiser, Battle Force, and I went back to the job I'd been in before. From there he was ordered as Chief of Naval Operations. He had promised me that I could go to a destroyer, after one year with him.

Well, after one year, he wouldn't let me go; made me

stay a second year. When he received his orders to be Chief of Naval Operations he asked me to go as his flag lieutenant to Washington. I said:

"No, Sir, nothing doing, Admiral. I've been on a staff so long that I think my career is completely ruined, if I don't get out and do the nitty gritty stuff you're supposed to do in the Navy. I feel that I have to have my chance to be executive officer of a ship."

He and Charlie Wellborn, who was his operations officer on the staff, and "Ching" Lee, who was our chief of staff - put sufficient pressure on me to cause me to "see the light". Incidentally, did you know the admiral and we were called "Snow White and the Seven Dwarfs," do you know about that?

Q: No, I don't.

Adm. S.: Admiral Stark had snow white hair and there were seven of us on his staff, so we were "Snow White and the Seven Dwarfs"; known as such to everybody. They all worked on me and finally I reluctantly said, okay, I'd go. Admiral Stark was pretty burned up because he thought he was offering me a tremendous opportunity, which he was. He thought I was not dry behind the ears, trying to turn him down to be exec of a destroyer.

So I went with Stark and did three years in Washington, which gave me seven consecutive years on a staff.

Q: It really didn't hurt your career?

Adm. S.: No, of course not, and I learned more about the Navy from the office of the Chief of Naval Operations than I could ever have learned any place else.

Q: There are exceptions –

Adm. S.: That's right.

Q: Let's go back to that period in the middle of the decade of the thirties because it seems to me that that is something of a watershed in terms of communications.

Adm. S.: Yes, it is. One of the things that bothered us in communications was the fact that we had never developed the radio-telephone between ships. We had a telephone in our ship but nobody ever used it, the idea being that it wasn't secure. We didn't have a good one, anyway. It had a tremendous amount of static in it and great skip distances so that sometimes you could be heard in the Philippines, for instance, on a band that's only supposed to carry to the horizon. And very often our harbor frequency in San Diego was completely blotted out by the voice communications of the fleet in Manila, the destroyers in Manila. The skip distance would just come down exactly right and we would get loud and clear, Force 5 or 6, and hear conversations and orders and communications from the destroyers in Manila.

Q: Did you understand that at the time, the reasons why?

Adm. S.: Well, we knew about the Heaviside layer. We didn't know as much about it as they know today and we didn't know how to get really good short-range radio that was secure.

What we started doing by having officers who knew about radio and visual and could read both, was to sit in and monitor the circuits. The enlisted men used to chat back and forth on the radio circuits. They had little radio discipline because there rarely was any officer qualified to sit in on the circuits. Occasionally, you'd find someone like Cy Rumble, who was a fine communicator, who himself had been, I think, a radioman once. He came up from the ranks. He was Admiral Courtney's communicator. When I was ComCruDes 3 he was DomCruBatForce communicator. But in the main officers were never privy to what was going on in the circuits, and most of the officers couldn't read blinker, so the signalmen were always PVTing, and you know a PVT is a private message. Back and forth all over San Diego Bay there'd be "How's your girl? I was at a great dance last night," all this kind of stuff going on all the time.

We managed at least to dampen it, not stamp it out, and leave the circuits clear for proper traffic. And, as I say, some of our seniors like Kimmel insisted that we turn in copy on these circuits.

Then, another thing, we knew what we wanted in communications and were able to write back to the Navy Department giving specifics of what should be developed. I'm sure that that got the Bureau of Engineering started thinking along lines of developing what we in the fleet, the operators, thought we needed.

Q: What were you envisioning as necessary for development?

Adm. S.: One of the things was a fairly secure method of communication by voice. That was one of the developments. And, in that connection, every officer who ever stood watch wanted some kind of device that could see through a fog. I remember one time when we were cruising reserves, I had a young reserve lieutenant, a physicist in civilian life, standing on the bridge with me when I was on watch in a thick fog, and I said:

"You know, if we had some kind of a device that could tell us if there's anything ahead of us within a mile or half a mile, it would be the most invaluable thing."

And he said: "Hell, that's not hard to invent. I can invent a heat-seeking device that would pick up the heat from the smoke and gases of a funnel maybe a quarter of a mile or half a mile. Would that be useful?"

I said: "If you could invent something like that you'd be a millionaire. It would be absolutely invaluable if we knew that there was another ship out there, out of fog-signal range, sound range."

So he said: "Well, Lord, that's not too difficult."

It was a constant insistence of those of us who were at sea that we had to have something that would enable us to see ahead of us or around us when it's black or fog, mainly fog. We were mainly concerned about fog.

Q: Did this young man go to work on something like this? Was his name Tuve?

Adm. S.: No. I never heard any more from him but he did give me enough confidence in the idea for me to be able to say in the company of experts that there was possible, and should be developed a system of detecting either heat or something ahead of us within a range of up to three or four miles. I never conceived of anything up to forty or fifty.

When I first came into Admiral Stark's office as aide to the chief of naval operations, and this was after four consecutive years of being a communications officer at sea, the very first secret that Charlie Wellborn and I were let in on was when we were taken down to Bellevue, the naval research lab, and shown a radar that was being developed down there by Dr. Taylor. He showed us the airplane that he was tracking as a target, he showed us a ship on the river. Charlie Wellborn and I came back from there tremendously impressed. Of course, we were sworn to absolute secrecy -

Q: This was in 1939?

Adm. S.: '39. This was top secret. It wasn't too long after that that they put a big mattress antenna on one of the ships. The director of naval intelligence came in to Admiral Stark furious. He said:

"Admiral, do you know that your two aides have been briefed on one of the greatest secrets that we've got in the Navy today?"

Stark said: "Why shouldn't they be? They've got to keep me informed and there isn't any secret that they can't know about in the Navy today."

At the time, the director or chief of naval intelligence was Walter S. Anderson. He was a very positive character and he didn't believe that any young officers should know about a big thing like radar. He used to go in with a folder under his coat so that Wellborn and I wouldn't know that he was carrying in some "magic." We weren't ever supposed, according to him, to even know that there was such a thing in the Navy because the fewer the people who knew about it the better.

Q: Maybe this is the appropriate place to get you to comment on classifications in the Navy and secrecy. It can be overdone, can't it?**

You said that King did some amazing things and that everybody was afraid of him, afraid of his shadow, actually!

---
**Note: At this point in the interview some material was deleted for it proved to be repetitious in the light of other interviews following.

Adm. S.:  They stayed out of his way pretty much.  At the time I was head of combat intelligence, I was running the war room in which we kept the locations of all our ships and our plans and so forth.  That room was generally filled with admirals, senior captains, and a very few commanders.  King would walk in there and there might be six or eight people in the room.  After three or four minutes, there wouldn't be one soul in there but me.  I was always there when King came in because my watch officer would immediately push a buzzer in my office, and the minute King was in there I was up there, and King would ask questions about various things we had posted.  But every other admiral on his staff would just evaporate when King was in that room.

It wasn't that they were afraid of him as much as they - well, I don't know what to say.

Q:  I know!  I saw him in the corridors of the Navy Department and I know what you mean.

You used that as a very apt illustration of the bad effects sometimes of super secrecy in the Navy.

Adm. S.:  That's right.  In my opinion, the single most valuable weapon we had in the war was our code room, our ability to read the other person's intentions.  And, of course, all of us took an oath that we would never discuss it again.  I feel a little bit relieved from that, although I don't discuss the details, ever, but since so much has been published I feel that I can say certain things about it.

Q: The codebreakers took care of much of that.

Adm. S.: That's right, but that was so vital to our success that you can't blame them for not wanting very many people to know about it, because it only required one little leak like that one to the Chicago Tribune that pretty near gummed up the whole works. We just barely recovered from that in time to know about Midway, in time to take advantage of the information we got about the coming attack on Midway.

Q: When you were at the postgraduate school there was no thought at all of the development of radar, as such?

Adm. S.: No.

Q: We had no knowledge that the British were working in this field?

Adm. S.: If there were such knowledge, it never percolated to a JG. I was a junior lieutenant at the time in the PG school. It never got down to me, nor did it get down to any of the instructors who tried to instruct us, to pass on to us what they knew.

I'm sure that in the technical bureaus there were people who were aware of what the British were doing, but I'm also aware of the fact that when the British were in the war and we started sending one or two observers over - I remember Admiral Gus Wellings - young Gus was sent over to the British and he, I think, rode the King George V - he rode some British battleship and I think he was present when the Bismarck was sunk. Anyway, he sent back the first account I ever saw of the British radar, which, to me, was unbelievably impressive.

I know that the technical people must have known about this but it never got down to us younger officers in the Navy.

Q: This is jumping close to our period, but it has to do with communications?

Adm. S.: Yes. After the war ended it was decided on a very high level that there should be a permanent agreement between the United States and Great Britain on the military level to exchange you might say information obtained from "magic" sources - exchange high-level intelligence, put it that way. And a group of us from the United States went over and met with the British for about six weeks in Grosvenor Square. We had a great big house there with guards all around it, three lumps of coal in the fireplace to keep us warm in the frigid atmosphere. There was Joe Wenger from the Navy, who was a great man, as you know, in the cryptographic field. There was Preston Corderman, who later was chief of the Army Signal Corps and head of Arlington Hall.

Q: Was Friedman there?

Adm. S.: No, Friedman didn't go with us. There was Carter Clark, who was the intelligence fellow for the Army headquarters in Washington. There was a man from OSS, and I'm not sure there wasn't somebody from FBI. Anyway, we were a very small group and we worked with a like group on the top-level agreement that I think we're operating under today. Of course, my knowledge of what we're operating under today is purely a guess. But we do have a good exchange of information with Great Britain, as far as I know. We did up to the time I retired.

Q: It probably would have been most fruitful if we'd had one before World War II?

Adm. S.: Oh, yes, no question about it. As you know, Admiral King was extremely distrustful and mistrustful of the British and it was very difficult for the British to get any information out of Admiral King or any of his subordinates.

Q: Well, Sir, let us go back to the first assignment you got after you were in PG school and learning something new about communications.

Adm. S.: I told you I went out to the staff of Admiral Vernou in Cruiser Division 3.

Q: Yes, but tell me some of the details of that duty assignment.

Adm. S.: My job was to see that the communications in our division improved. I gave all of the radio tests to all the radiomen, all the officers in communications. I gave all the visual signal tests, all the communication tests, I graded them all. I established drills and followed what I had learned from Admiral Kimmel in making the officers sit in on the circuits. We'd sort of gotten away from that since I was a younger officer and had my nose rubbed in that kind of nitty-gritty.

I wrote the communications plans for all the exercises we had, and I was also the force athletic officer in addition to being communications officer.

Q: In your spare time!

Adm. S.: Yes, and I think in port I spent more time on athletics than I did on communications.

Q: Did the new developments in communications techniques entail rewriting the regulations in any way?

Adm. S.: Yes, but frankly there were not many new developments in communications during that period. That was a dead period, in the thirties. We had no money and the Navy was existing on a bare-bones budget. We got no new equipment. We had to make the old equipment work. We couldn't buy a new typewriter. I remember you had to take the paperclip off a piece of paper because you knew you wouldn't get another paperclip. You weren't allowed a new pencil unless you turned in the stub of the old pencil, and you couldn't get a pad of paper unless you turned in the cardboard back of the old pad of paper. That's how stringent our funds were in those days.

I think there were very few real developments in communications during that period. We just tried to improve and do the best we could with what we had.

Q: That in itself is a -

Adm. S.: That's what you try to do between wars all the time. Hold the team together so that it can be mobilized quickly in case in war.

Q: By that time you were thinking more about the possibility of a conflict, weren't you?

Adm. S.: Not really. In the long range, yes. I think all of us thought that some day we probably would have to go to war with Japan.

Q: But it still wasn't imminent?

Adm. S.: No. And here we were when Admiral Reeves sent us all to sea, of course, it was a shock to all of us because our mentality was completely a peacetime mentality, and we couldn't understand that the old man apparently felt that hostilities were close enough to start doing some strange things that we didn't do in peacetime.

Q: The Naval War College was more cognizant of this, was it not?

Adm. S.: Yes, I think so.

Q: And the men who received training there were much more aware of an imminent conflict?

Adm. S.: I think so, but, you know, it's very difficult for the military to be thinking about the possibility of war when the entire country is apathetic and complacent and nonsupportive of the military.

I remember when Admiral Joe Taussig made a statement in a speech that he made - and this was in about 1940 - that there was a possibility, in his view, that within a few years the United States would be engaged in a war against Germany and Japan and, perhaps, Italy. The headlines came out "Warmonger." Roosevelt called Stark on the telephone and said:

"Betty, I want that man Taussig fired right away. I want him retired from the Navy and put on half-pay."

Admiral Stark argued and argued in favor of Taussig. When Stark first came out with his request for a two-ocean navy, they blasted him as a warmonger, and Stark said it would very easily be that we would find ourselves at war in both oceans at the same time. He was laughed at and jeered at and mocked. We were alarmists in the military. This was in '39, '40, and '41.

Q: So we talk about the Congress as being representative of the opinion of the people. I never thought of the military as being exactly reflectors of the attitude of the public as a whole.

Adm. S.: I think the military has to be affected, if not infected, by the attitude of all the people around them.

Q: It's a potentially dangerous state, isn't it?

Adm. S.: Yes, but at the same time you can't live by yourself in an atmosphere that's solely pertaining to the military. After all, you have lots of civilian friends and you have to listen to them when they express their views. They don't listen to yours, mainly, because they don't agree with them. There is a great danger when the country is apathetic that the that the military will get complacent and apathetic, also. Fortunately, there are enough military people in all the services who are gung-ho enough and have a sense of responsibility for the requirement that they do the best they can with what they've got to keep a nucleus of a defense force together during the most desperate days of economy when the funds are cut.

Today we're seeing the old situation where our ships are not getting enough fuel, steaming enough hours at sea for proper proficiency. Our aviators are being cut back on their fuel so they can't get enough flight time to maintain their proper proficiency. We don't have enough money in the Navy for spare parts to keep our ships properly operating. You don't find our top people in the Navy saying these things because they can't say some of them. They go before the Congress and they do the best they can to get as much money as they can for what they've got to have and it's always cut.

That's about all I can say now. I no longer have any responsibility whatsoever, so it's easy for me to say more than I would say if I had the responsibility.

Q: Tell me about going as radio officer to Cruiser Division, Battle Force under Admiral Stark.

Adm. S.: That was no different. That was just a continuation of what I had done previously under Admiral Vernou. You know,

I was with Cruiser 3, then CruBatForce, then back to CruDiv 3 for another year, then back to CruBatFor another year. It was just writing the communications plans for all the fleet exercises, overseeing the communications efficiency of all our ships, visiting the different ships and seeing how they kept up their equipment, how they operated their equipment, and how proficient their operators were. We had quarterly tests that we gave to test the efficiency of our signalmen and our radiomen, all our communications personnel.

Q: Did you begin to see improvement in this area as you served in the same role all these years?

Adm. S.: I have to say that the improvement went up or down, depending on the initiative and energy of the officer who was supervising. One of the things that was saddest to me, and this is that old competition again in peacetime, was that when I was giving the tests to the ships of Commander, Cruisers Battle Force, and I was the communications officer for Cruiser Division 3, a part of Cruisers, Battle Force. I was designated to give all the radio and visual tests to all the cruisers in the Battle Force, and I gave all the tests. But the marks were not good marks for the senior admiral's own, personal division. I was ordered to redo the tests because the marks were not high enough or to change the marks. I refused always to change the marks. I then had the alternative of making a whole new tests and giving all the tests over again.

Q: How could any officer in command in good conscience ask you to change the marks?

Adm. S.: If you knew the officer in question, you would know that he always ended every command he ever had with the statement:

"When I came here, this and this and this and this existed. When I left, this improvement, this improvement, this improvement," every one of these conditions had improved. So he had to build up during the time he was there a record of the radio tests having been at this level when he came in, signal tests, communication tests, gunnery tests, everything - every one of them had to be much higher when he left.

Q: He thought this would be reflected in his own file?

Adm. S.: I think so, because I was ordered to raise the marks. I went back to my own admiral and said:

"Admiral, I'm not going to do this. I've been ordered by the admiral to do it."

He said: "Don't do it, Smeddy. I'll stick by you." Then I got word that if I wouldn't raise the marks I would have to give the tests all over again and they would have to be higher, I made up new tests, I gave the tests all over again, and they were damned little higher, very little higher, and the admiral didn't like it.

It was just the way when I was Chief of Naval Personnel.

I was told by the civilians in the Pentagon, my civilian bosses, that we had to lower the standards for admission to the Naval Academy in order to take in Negroes, and I said that I would not go along with that, because we will not lower our standards to take in anyone. If anyone can meet our standards we're delighted to have him, but we're not going to lower our standards, and have one standard for the whites and one standard for the colored. I never did agree to do that. And, you know, it's pretty hard when you get someone who gets his back up and says he will not do it, it's pretty hard for them to insist on it without firing the fellow, and they're a little afraid when they fire somebody that he'll talk.

Q: The publicity on it would be detrimental?

Adm. S.: Yes.

Q: In the light of your future service, when you went to BuPers, would you say that this particular officers' concern for his record would reflect the fact that there was constant improvement under his surveillance? Could you say that this was important in terms of his selection?

Adm. S.: He never went higher than where he was. He had hoped to get command of a fleet or a force. He never did. It was important to him and I think that possibly it helped him on the way up to become a rear admiral, because it showed in the record that everything he'd had always was improved during his incumbency. But I happen to know, from the way he operated, that lots of this was not honest.

We younger officers very often know these things that the seniors don't know. We see it going on, just the way some enlisted men are aware of the deficiencies in an officer that the senior officers aren't aware of in that officer.

Q: Would a record of that sort cause any suspicion in the minds of the board of selection?

Adm. S.: Yes, I think so. It's hard to say because when you talk about a selection board you're talking about nine individuals and each individual makes up his own mind concerning every individual on whom he votes. There is no such thing as telling a board who they have to select. Lately there have been a number of efforts and I know that the boards have been directed to do such things as pick at least two or three prisoners of war, or something like that.

Q: They narrow the category so that they have to be picked?

Adm. S.: Yes. In the past we have been directed on occasion, to so narrow the category that there's just one officer who really could meet all the particulars that the secretary of the navy had said must be in there. I've even had one Secretary of the Navy say to me:

"If so and so isn't selected, I will not approve and forward to the President the results of the selection board. It's up to you to see that he's selected."

And I said: "Mr. Secretary, I say nothing to the selection board except what their duties are. When the results of the selection board come out, if that officer's name is on the list, fine. But I can assure you I will have said nothing to the selection board about him."

"Well," he said, "you'd better see that his name is on there or else I will not approve it."

In this one instance, his name happened to be on it, to my great surprise. But it was on there because six members of that board felt he deserved it, not because they had had a directive to do it.

You take these selection boards in the Navy; there are nine individuals who vote according to their own consciences, and I am convinced in my mind that that's about as fair a system as a human can devise. They're all capable of errors, and when a good man is passed over in favor of one who is not quite so good, it's generally because we've got one or two strong supporters on the board who tell about all the fine things he has done for them, and the others don't know him well enough to be able to counter. So, quite often, a few of the best officers are passed over for selection.

I can name in my own time officers who, in my opinion, were far superior, in their performance, to me. I consider

I have been extremely fortunate to be selected. It's like lightning striking, really, because when you can only select, say, twenty people out of a field of 400, there are at least fifty people in there who should be selected. You can't really pick twenty out of that number and be certain that they are the head and shoulders people.

Q: I suppose one of the outstanding examples of a man being passed over temporarily was Arleigh Burke?

Adm. S.: Yes, and, of course, Rickover finally got selected because the board was ordered to select him.

Q: Yes!

Well, when you came to serve on the staff of Admiral Stark you established some kind of rapport with him, didn't you?

Adm. S.: Yes. He was a wonderful man to work for, really, and the thing I liked about him was that he let me run my job and almost everything I did he agreed with. That's a wonderful feeling, that you can run the job the way you think it ought to be run and it meets with your superior's approval.

I ran the whole athletic program for the Cruiser Force, I ran the communications competitions in all of the communications. He approved my communications plans.

Q: Certainly, by that time, you were a very great expert in that field?

Adm. S.: I was, yes. I feel that I was pretty expert in communications. After four years, if I hadn't been I should have retired or turned in my suit. I could spot a ship that had good communications and could spot the reasons why it had good communications, could spot poor communications in another ship and find the reasons for it and generally set about corrective action.

That's the whole story, really, of the Navy. If you have individuals who are willing to work on a problem and are expert enough to know what the problem is, you have a good group that you're working with. And if you have an individual who is willing to accept everything the way it has been going and isn't forceful in his requirements for good performance, excellent performance, everything slides.

Q: In your case, there was continuity over a period of several years in that particular job.

Adm. S.: That's right.

Q: This doesn't always happen in the Navy.

Adm. S.: No, that's right.

Q: I mean a good man is yanked out and sent somewhere else?

Adm. S.: That's right, that happens too often in the Navy.

Q: Is that not a waste in one sense?

Adm. S.: The Navy's main problem, as I finally decided after four years as Chief of Personnel, was that when our officer personnel was set up originally we got exactly the number to man the fleet at sea with the supporting shore establishment. As the Navy grew, the shore establishment grew way out of proportion to the fleet. Lots of new concepts were introduced, such as the increased education of officers. In the Army and in the Air Force, their officer pools have always taken account of a large number available for schooling. In fact, in the Army, in peacetime, education is about 50 percent of what they do. Housekeeping is the other 50 percent.

When the Air Force was set up, they set up a great pool of excess officers who could spend a lot of time in postgraduate training and in schooling.

We never did that in the Navy. Originally, our basic officer plan was based on manning the ships at sea and having proper sea-shore rotation, and keeping the people ashore who could service the fleet. Everything was for the service of the fleet. As the different requirements came in - for instance when the Secretary of Defense's office was set up - immediately he siphoned off a great number of officers, flag officers and captains, the best of them all, to work for him. That, of course, causes a thinning-out in our ships and in our shore establishment.

Then, we've had our flag officers drawn into the State Department as advisors and scattered all over the world in things like MAAGs, and various other places - assistants to NATO, all over the place. So we keep being diluted to the point where we don't have enough officers to be able to leave them. We have to keep either having gaps or moving our people too rapidly to fill things we have to fill.

If the secretary of defense says, "I have to have a flag officer in this billet here to support the assistant secretary for ISA," for instance, we have to furnish a flag officer, and he has to come from some place. We have to move him even if he's only been in there six or eight months. This is the kind of thing that's happening all the time, and the bigger the civilian pyramid over the military, the more the military talent is drawn into that area and the more diluted becomes the talent that is available to the service itself.

It's like an inverted pyramid, in a way.

I remember Forrestal when he was against the single department of defense. You know, originally, he didn't approve of it?

Q: No, I know he didn't.

Adm. S.: He never did approve of it.

Q: And he wanted it to be small, didn't he?

Adm. S.: That's right. He said to me one time:

"You know, if the secretary of defense would keep his staff to the 100 officers that are provided for in this initial legislation, it would not be so bad. But in order for the secretary of defense to be properly advised and informed, he's going to have to build up a staff so large that the Defense Department will soon be bigger than any one of the services."

And, of course, the staff of the secretary of defense is today many, many thousands of people. Forrestal foresaw that. He said:

"If the secretary of defense would continue to solve only those problems and make decisions on which the services can't agree, that would be all right. But you'll find he'll soon be operating. He's going to get into the operating field," which he is all the time now.

During the Cuban missile crisis, the secretary of defense was practically calling all the shots that John F. Kennedy wasn't calling from the White House. They had to know every time a plane landed on a carrier, what they saw, what they did. We had to tell them every time a plane took off.

Q: Poor Corky learned that when he took command some of his ships were being ordered by the White House!

Adm. S.: Yes, that's right.

Q: This is empire-building in a sense.

Adm. S.: That's exactly what it is. I sat beside Bob Dennison one time in his war room during the Cuban missile crisis and I listened in on the circuit. Bob was listening in, too. He was the Supreme Allied Commander and also the Commander in Chief, Atlantic Fleet. He was listening to all the orders coming out of the White House and going direct to his units out in the operating area. He was the most frustrated man I've ever seen.

I don't know what he says in his. I'd like to read it. I hope he's frank and honest.

Q: He is. Tell me more about that tour with Stark at sea. This was not a command that drew him, as a man, to the attention of the powers that be in Washington, was it?

Adm. S.: No. I really think he was probably a compromise. He was jumped over the heads of a lot of people, you know, over the heads of a number of senior admirals. I think he must have been a compromise and acceptable because nobody had anything against him. He'd been a very good Chief of the Bureau of Ordnance and was well thought of.

Another thing. I think Roosevelt felt that he was a man that he could direct without any difficulty. He and Stark were friends.

Q: He had a certain cultural background with similarities -

Adm. S.: Well, sort of, and Stark when he was a young officer had command of a destroyer and was ordered to take Roosevelt some place when he was assistant secretary of the navy. The two formed a pretty good rapport and friendship and Roosevelt wanted to be his own secretary of the navy. He would call Stark direct and give him orders all the time without ever referring to the Secretary of the Navy. When I left the office I destroyed all the wax cylinders that I had kept of all the conversations between the president and Stark. I tell you, they'd be worth a million dollars today if I had some of them. But if Mr. Nixon had destroyed all his tapes he'd be in a lot better position today than he is!

Q: Stark also knew Secretary Swanson, did he not?

Adm. S.: Very well. He was the naval aide to Swanson, as I remember, and Swanson was sick most of the time he was secretary of the navy.

Q: Yes, in a sense he was a figurehead.

Adm. S.: Oh, yes, he was a figurehead. Many times he'd be sick, he'd be in bed. He'd come to the office but he'd be in a little back room on a bed, on a cot, and his signature was very often signed by the chief clerk - I can't think of his name but he was a very famous character in the Navy

Department. He could sign Swanson's name better than Swanson could.

Those were the days when the secretary of the navy was a very ineffective person, not like the rigorous ones we've had since then like Forrestal, and Frank Knox was a pretty vigorous secretary of the navy.

Q: In spite of the fact that Roosevelt was such a Navy buff himself?

Adm. S.: Yes.

Q: That was exceptional. Stark was selected from this particular command where you were communications officer -

Adm. S.: That's right, but I don't think he was selected because of what he had done in the command. He was selected because, of the list of people who were in the approximate rank and age bracket, he was the least controversial and the fellow that Roosevelt probably thought he could get along best with.

Q: Who are some of the others who were possibilities at that time?

Adm. S.: Ernie King was one, Chester Nimitz was one, Joe Richardson was one. There were many, many who could have been selected. If I had the list I could give you the names of probably ten who we all thought in the Navy, the younger officers, had a far better chance. It was a big surprise to everybody in the Navy when Stark was made CNO.

Q: And this was to succeed Admiral Leahy who was retiring because of age?

Adm. S.: Yes, that's right. Wellborn and I preceded Stark to Washington and we were with Admiral Leahy all that summer.

Q: This was a kind of a break-in period?

Adm. S.: Yes, kind of a break-in period.

Q: Because you both had been designated to Stark's staff?

Adm. S.: Yes. He was to be Stark's flag secretary and I was to be his flag lieutenant.

Q: How did Stark take the news that he had been selected?

Adm. S.: He was flabbergasted. He could hardly believe it. But he had quite a bit of ego and it didn't take him very long to feel they'd made a good choice. He was a dear old man and I loved him very much, but he's not the man that I would have chosen as chief of naval operations.

Q: As he prepared to assume this command, what were his thoughts about the possibility of conflict in the Pacific?

Adm. S.: I think he felt that there was a very strong probability that a war would come in the next few years. I know he was concerned about the few ships we had in the Navy. He knew we didn't have enough ships to really do the job if we had a showdown, and he started working to get the President to approve more men, more money for equipment. The President himself, personally, would approve every additional man added to the Navy. Stark would call up and say: "I've got to have 500 more men, Mr. President," and the president would say:

"Okay, Betty. You can tell Dave Walsh," or whoever it was up in Congress, "that I said it was okay." They'd agree to get the authorization for 500 more men or 1,000 more men, and gradually built it up.

Q: This was also the period when the president was using every means of getting funds, rather than direct appropriations, from Congress, which were not possible. He was using every means to use other funds for naval purposes, was he not?

Adm. S.: I really don't feel that I'm competent to comment on that. I've read all the material and I think that's probably the case. President Roosevelt was not a man to worry about how he got funds as long as he got what he felt he had to have to do what he wanted to do. The only thing I'm certain of in my mind is that he did not plan or know about Pearl Harbor in advance, despite some of my friends who feel that's not true.

Q: So you came in advance of him to Washington.

Adm. S.: That's right, and frankly that whole three months was spent in being briefed in every office of the chief of naval operations and all the bureaus. We went to every bureau, found out what everybody was doing, what all the projects were, even the most secret ones, so that we would be able to keep Admiral Stark advised of what was being done in the Navy. The man at the very top is pretty shielded from the specifics of what's going on every place.

I remember when I was Chief of the Bureau of Personnel I would often read in <u>Navy Times</u> what we were doing in the Bureau of Naval Personnel that I had never heard of. It used to infuriate me. I'd send for the section head who would say:

"Sir, we've been working this thing up and are going to bring it up for your signature when we get all the bugs out of it. This reporter was down there the other day and was asking us a few questions, and we said, yes, we were going to bring this up to you pretty soon."

So I'd read that the chief of naval personnel was about to do something that I hadn't heard of. They hadn't even told me about it yet. It was an idea they were going to bring to me.

Q: Your period of indoctrination along with Charlie Wellborn, was this an innovative thing for an incoming CNO to undertake or was this the normal procedure?

Adm. S.: I don't know. I think we had a little longer period of indoctrination than the average person gets, and we were most fortunate in having that opportunity. We came in in about June, as I remember it, and Stark didn't relieve until the fall.

Q: Until September, I believe.

Adm. S.: Yes, I think so.

Q: You were relieving a man named Freseman?

Adm. S.: Bill Freseman, yes, and I'll never forget him. He said:

"The first thing you have to get is a pair of striped pants and a frock coat."

I looked at him and I said:

"If that's what you have to do as aide to the CNO, I sure as hell don't want it!" I never did get a pair of striped pants and a frock coat. Freseman had them.

Q: The war relieved you from that, I guess?

Adm. S.: No, not really, because we were there in '39, '40, '41 before the war came along. When war broke out, I went to the admiral and said:

"Admiral, please, I'd like to get command of a destroyer and get to sea."

"No, Smeddy," he said, "I want to take you to London with me."

I said: "No, Admiral, no way. I've got to get out in this war."

So we said a tearful farewell. He felt, I think, for a long time that I'd deserted him in his hour of need because he had been disgraced at Pearl Harbor and was being sent to London, where he did a fine job, as a matter of fact.

Q: Let's concentrate on that time of indoctrination. Your knowledge of the Navy was fairly extensive before that, wasn't it?

Adm. S.: Only the sea part. I knew nothing whatsoever about how the Navy Department operated. I learned there just how the Navy is run from Washington and who were the men who made the Navy tick in Washington. There are generally just a few people in each group who called the shots. Kelly Turner was one of our people. He was in planning, and Kelly Turner was calling the shots for most of the things that went out to the fleet. He was the one who wrote the war plans. He was the one who got Admiral Stark to agree to the war plans he wrote. He was a very brilliant and a very forceful and persuasive man. A good naval officer.

Q: Walter Anderson was there.

Adm. S.: He was the intelligence man and Roland Brainard was the operations fellow on the staff, a very fine gentleman, but with nothing like the decisiveness or the forcefulness of Kelly Turner, for instance.

Charlie and I soon got to know to whom we should go if the admiral wanted something done in a hurry. The way the admiral operated was whenever we had something to do, Charlie and I would go to the people whom we knew had to get the thing initiated, then tell Admiral Stark that the ball had been started rolling, tell him whom we had notified, and he might say:

"Well, see that so and so and so and so get in on the act, also."

But our job was pretty much to get things started and keep the admiral advised of what was going on. I kept a wax cylinder record of everything the president said to the admiral because often Roosevelt would call up and say:

"Betty, I want this done right away," and he'd give five or six things in rapid-fire order. The admiral would say:

"Yes, Mr. President, yes, Mr. President, yes, Mr. President."

"Have you got that, Betty?"

"Yes, Mr. President." And he'd hang up.

The buzzer would ring and I'd go in and he'd say:

"Did you get all that, Smeddy?"

"Yes, Sir."

"Well, get going on it."

Q: This was an attachment on his telephone, was it?

Adm. S.: Yes. I monitored every conversation he ever had with anybody, and I made a record of almost all of them. Every now and then, when it was a personal thing, Stark would tell me to destroy the record. But I kept most of them, and I had them all destroyed when I left, to the disgruntlement of some people.

Q: I'm sure.

Adm. S.: But I said, "I made them and I'm going to destroy them."

Those three years with Stark were probably the most interesting from the point of view of learning about the Navy that I ever had. I learned of its shortcomings, how you got things accomplished in the Navy, who the really up-and-coming officers were. I mean you'd spot a commander down the line some place who was really the sparkplug in that whole organization, and he's marked right away. You know that he's a fellow you can always go to to get something going. You knew other individuals you'd avoid because you knew that nothing would happen when you got to them with a project.

Q: So it boiled down to the fact it wasn't a collection of titles that ran the Navy -

Adm. S.: Individuals. Individuals with the sparks. People with the initiative and the intelligence and willingness to take responsibility and action.

Q: Some of these people with sparks clashed with each other?

Adm. S.: Oh, yes, sure, but I think wherever you find individuals with great initiative and good intellectual capacity, they're going to clash because they're not always going to agree. And I think it's very healthy to have good, hot arguments.

Q: For instance, Kelly Turner and Walter Anderson were strong people and I'm sure did not agree on many things.

Adm. S.: That's right.

Q: Of course, you were in communications. Were you amazed

at the development of communications in Washington? The naval communications setup?

Adm. S.: No. Our communications setup in Washington was terrible.

Q: Was it?

Adm. S.: Yes. We had no communication with our commander in chief in the Pacific. We had to use Army communications, for instance.

Q: But the fact that the Navy, as an independent service, as it was, without a department of defense, was relying on the Army for its communications is somewhat appalling.

Adm. S.: That's right. Stark and Marshall agreed that some message should be sent - I've forgotten which one it was now - to Kimmel and Short, and the Army agreed to send it. It never got out there until after hostilities. And yet it was the day before that the message was to go. That was typical of what was happening in those days. Nobody felt anything was very important. Everyone was apathetic. The country was apathetic, so was the military, to a lesser degree but no one in the military thought war was anywhere near imminent.

Q: What was Admiral Noyes like as Director of Communications?

Adm. S.: I would say he was all right. I liked Admiral Noyes personally. I knew him very well as an individual. I was with him when he was torpedoed in the Wasp out in the Solomon Islands and picked up some 500 of his men from the Wasp. Later on, I sank the Wasp —

Q: You did?

Adm. S.: Yes. I was left behind to sink her.

Q: Tell me about what you discovered in communications in terms of codes and so forth when you arrived in Washington. Joe Safford was there, wasn't he?

Adm. S.: To be perfectly honest with you, this was so secret that Wellborn and I were not — well, let me put it this way. Wellborn was cut in to some degree and I was never cut in, because Wellborn was the flag secretary. He had to see all the papers. I didn't. I was flag lieutenant. You didn't see anything unless you had a need to know. Even Charlie was not cut in fully, I think. What Charlie has told you, I don't know, but all he would know quite often was that Anderson had gone in with this under his coat, showed something like this to Stark, and Stark wasn't able to tell us about it, or he wouldn't say anything about it.

Q: It's incredible!

Adm. S.: Yes, that's right, but that's how secretive these intelligence people were, and really for good reason because if word ever leaked out that we were doing this thing we never would have had the success we had in World War II.

Q: Was the knowledge abroad in the highest circles of the Navy that we had sort of mastered the Japanese diplomatic code?

Adm. S.: No, that was not common knowledge.

Q: That was not common knowledge?

Adm. S.: No. It was very closely held knowledge, very closely held. As a matter of fact, you know that the communications people had such a grip on this intelligence that they put a special officer with each admiral in the Pacific and in the Atlantic, who was an intelligence officer and had his own code that nobody else could read, and he was the one who gave the admiral the information.

Q: When you came to Washington with Stark there wasn't much in the way of a civilian hierarchy over the CNO, was there?

Adm. S.: No.

Q: There was the Secretary and one Assistant Secretary, and that's all?

Adm. S.: That's right.

Q: Was that why there was more direct communication with the president?

Adm. S.: Yes, I think so, and during our period, you know, we had Mr. Edison as our Secretary for a while. He was deaf. And Frank Knox. I forget whether Swanson was there when we first came in or not.

Q: I believe he was.

Adm. S.: I think he was, too. But he was completely - nobody even thought of him because they knew he was almost non compos mentis.

Q: He'd been there for -

Adm. S.: A long time.

Q: He came in originally with the cabinet in 1933.

Adm. S.: That's right, and they kept the old gentleman on just to keep from cutting him off the payroll. That's what it amounted to. But the CNO in those days ran the Navy.

Q: He directed the actions of the fleet.

Adm. S.: That's right. He ran everything. Then, when Knox came in, he, of course, took a very energetic part in controlling the Navy. He began controlling Stark, the CNO.

Q: What about Edison?

Adm. S.: He was more interested in the technical bureaus, I think, than he was in the operations of the fleet. An awfully nice man. Is he still living?

Q: No. He died about two years ago, I think.

Adm. S.: An awfully nice man but not particularly interested in operations, as I sensed it. He had no problems with the CNO at all.

Q: Ghormley was there when you first came, too, was he not?

Adm. S.: Yes, Ghormley was there, and he was succeeded by Royal Ingersoll.

Q: What was Ghormley like as a -

Adm. S.: He was a very pleasant, easy-going man who, in my opinion, was not over-gifted with intelligence or initiative. One of the nicest men you ever knew. Ingersoll, who relieved him, was a very fine, thoughtful, very intelligent man with lots of decisiveness, ability to make decisions quickly. He never had a paper on his desk. He'd take action on it or send it back if he didn't like it and wanted this done to it, whereas Ghormley was the type who would let things sort of pile up. Kind of easy-going, you know. You'd have to go in sometimes and get papers out of his basket and say, "We've got to do something about this, Admiral." But he was a perfectly delightful, charming person.

When he was down there in the South Pacific, I had my first destroyer command in the Solomon Islands under Ghormley when he was ComSoPac. There was a tremendous change as soon as Halsey got in there. We began to feel the boss at the top, at the helm. Halsey made each one of us feel that he knew we were right there and he knew what we were doing, he was grateful for what we were doing, he was backing us up. But, poor Ghormley, he didn't have many resources. We started getting a few more when Halsey got out there. Ghormley was really ineffectual, that's all I can say. I loved the man, he was a wonderful person.

Q: What was the nature of his mission to London, when they sent him over as SPENAVO?

Adm. S.: He was just supposed to pick up everything he could from the British and send it back. He was a special naval observer. He had as his right hand, I think, Count Austin - Admiral Bernard L. Austin.

Q: But we had a perfectly good naval attaché there in Charlie Lockwood?

Adm. S.: Well, you know, the attachés communicate through the Office of Naval Intelligence, and this special naval observer was supposed to communicate with OpNav. In other words, he was the CNO's liaison over there, as opposed to the ONI liaison.

A naval attaché is really an intelligence-gatherer. That's not his prime thought, but he picks up intelligence on everything that has to do with the Navy and passes it back to Naval Intelligence.

Ghromley's function was to tell Admiral Stark everything that the British were doing that was superior to what we were doing or any new thing they had, how they operated, did they have anything that was better than what we had - that sort of thing. It was most important and the sort of thing that we have to do if we ever get in trouble ahead of time is start building up our connections with the operating forces of the other nations, so that when the time comes that we're in it we're not neophytes completely.

Q: You say that SPENAVO was an observer put there for the chief of naval operations and, in a sense, bypassed ONI. Does this say something about the status of ONI in the Navy at that time?

Adm. S.: Well, you know, I was a lieutenant in the Navy and

for me at this late stage to try to think what I thought when I was a lieutenant! All I knew was that ONI collected intelligence and received it and gave whatever they thought was necessary to the CNO. And SPENAVO was over there to find out how the British operated their fleets, their navy department, and what they did that was better than ours, what new developments they had that we were behind in and so forth.

Q: When you say that ONI was a collector of intelligence, do you mean in terms of monographs and that kind of thing?

Adm. S.: Yes, that kind of thing.

Q: It was a repository, a library, wasn't it?

Adm. S.: Sort of, yes. Of course, a naval attaché is supposed to pick up information about the operating forces, also, but in those days he was pretty much a social character. He had to go to all the parties. He didn't get out to sea very often with the forces, and our SPENAVO was there just to see how the forces operated and to see what they were producing in the way of equipment and weapons and other essentials that we didn't have, to see how we could benefit from their wartime experience.

Q: I judge from what Count Austin has told me that SPENAVO also drew upon his social abilities to collect some of the data that he got.

Adm. S.: Oh, yes, there's no question about it.

Q: He was acceptable.

Adm. S.: If you made a good friend out of another naval officer, over drinks, you can learn more from him than you can learn in his navy department or the Admiralty ever. He trusts you after a while and you become to feel that you're working for the same purposes. It's hard to do it until you get to know each other.

I remember when Russia came into the war, at the end of our war with Japan, immediately a Russian naval captain was assigned to me as my liaison and to tell me everything about the Japanese that the Russians knew. King said I could tell him nothing about us. He actually came to me and he gave me all the information on where the Japanese mines were in Tokyo Bay. The Russians had all of them located.

Q: They did?

Adm. S.: Oh, yes, and they gave it to us.

Q: He really was giving you information freely, then?

Adm. S.: Of course, we never had that tested out. I can't vouch for the accuracy of it.

Q: Or how much he was giving you?

Adm. S.: Yes, but he seemed to know a great deal about the Japanese that we didn't know, and I was giving him nothing except what he could have read in the newspaper. I'd give him a lot of information but there wasn't anything that he couldn't have found out other ways.

Q: I suppose that wasn't lost on him?

Adm. S.: I don't know whether it was or not. I think he felt he was picking up information. Perhaps when he got back home they didn't think it was very hot stuff!

Q: It looks as though you've been on hot spots many times!

Adm. S.: Yes, and it hasn't always been enjoyable, either.

Interview No. 2 with Vice Admiral William R. Smedberg III
                                    U.S. Navy (Retired)

Place: The Naval History Center, Washington, D.C.

Date: Thursday morning, 2 October 1975

Subject: Biography

By: John T. Mason, Jr.


Q: Admiral, it's certainly nice to see you this morning. I was hoping that I could latch onto you when you came up for this foundation meeting and the game, so I've been lucky.

Last time, we broke off during your tour of duty with Admiral Stark in Washington, prior to Pearl Harbor. You made one statement that perhaps you would elaborate upon. You said that during 1939 and 1940 Stark was constantly begging for funds in order to build up the Navy and, because of his almost heroic efforts in this area, we were at least partially prepared when war did break out.

Would you tell me in what way he succeeded in building up the Navy? What did he do?


Adm. S.: It's hard to pinpoint the various things he did. He was constantly on the telephone to the president asking for every sort of insignificant little bits and pieces here and there. For instance, he'd ask for 1,000 more men to fill a shortage in a new ship that was building, a class of ship.

What the admiral would ask was permission to go to the committees of the House and Senate, naval affairs committees, in those days, and ask them for the additional men.

In those days, of course, you couldn't do that unless you had the president's okay.

The president would often very grudgingly say:

"Okay, Betty, okay," and the hardest thing really to get from the president were men. The admiral finally got so he'd get men in maybe jumps of 1,000 or 5,000 from time to time. We were always short of personnel.

Q: Why was that more difficult than other things?

Adm. S.: People cost more. They're continuing costs.

Q: But we had all sorts of Public Works projects and so forth to employ people.

Adm. S.: This was in 1940 and '41, and the depression was pretty well over by that time. I don't remember, frankly, how long the PWA projects lasted, but it seems to me it was in the mid-thirties to maybe 1938, '39 before the recession really started receding.

Then, of course, the admiral led the fight to build what we then called a two-ocean navy. On occasion, headlines would come out and accuse him of being a warmonger, or some of the other admirals who were thinking along the lines that

Admiral Stark was espousing, like Joe Taussig. He made a statement one time, and I think I mentioned this before, in which he said he could conceive of the possibility that we might be at war at the same time between Germany and Italy in one ocean and Japan in another. Tremendous headlines came out following that. The next morning there was one of the biggest headlines I ever saw in The Washington Post calling him a warmonger. The president got furious, called Admiral Stark, and told him to fire him. He said:

"I want that fellow Taussig fired."

Admiral Stark argued and argued and begged to the president to reconsider, to sleep on it, and gradually he got the president - or, rather, the president grudgingly agreed that Stark didn't have to take positive action right away. He even said:

"Well, put him on furlough, on half-pay." Stark fought against that. He said:

"After all, Mr. President, the admiral is expressing his views. He's a great historian, he's a student of history, and the things that he talked about are not impossible."

Q: So did he finally win the battle as far as Taussig was concerned?

Adm. S.: Well, old Carl Vinson and some of the others pitched in and we got a lot of money for a two-ocean navy, which was starting to take shape at the time of Pearl Harbor. This was a buildup that I think Admiral Stark had more to do with than anybody else.

Q: Somebody told me that he was concerned also about some of the minor craft and transports.

Adm. S.: He was very much concerned over the fact that we didn't have enough oilers, we didn't have enough transports, we didn't have enough supply ships, we didn't have enough ammunition ships, because if we had a war in the Pacific we would have to have a lot of these train ships to service the fleet that would be operating a long, long way from any base.

Q: Did the president see this need?

Adm. S.: Yes. He was a very perceptive man, but, of course, his politics came first and he had to play his politics. There was no shrewder politician, probably, than Franklin D. Roosevelt.

Q: How adept was Admiral Stark with the congressional committees?

Adm. S.: I think he impressed them with his honesty. He was a very simple sort of man, you know. He was not devious in any way. He was honest. I think he got as much from these committees as any man could have done in those days.

Q: Did you go with him to the congressional committees?

Adm. S.: Sometimes. Well, no, that's not true either. Admiral Wellborn was always with him. He was the flag secretary. I was sometimes. I got a little mixed up because years later when I was the aide to James Forrestal I always went with him when he went before the Congress and the different committees. But with Stark, no, it was generally Wellborn who was with him. I was with him enough times to see that congressmen listened to him.

Q: Can you recall any specific instance of that nature?

Adm. S.: No. It's awfully hard to recall that far back and to disassociate what you felt at the time from things you've read since. I hesitate to give views advanced by others as my own at this late date.

Q: Yes. I've been told that Admiral Stark insisted upon fleet exercises in the Pacific, sometimes when it seemed somewhat inconvenient to deploy the ships in that way. Do you recall that?

Adm. S.: I don't recall anything particular. He was constantly trying to improve the state of readiness, and when our fleet was kept in Hawaiian waters it was kept there really for political reasons, not Navy reasons. He did his best to get more reconnaissance planes, long-range PBYs, so that we could protect that base because we had nothing like the number of planes that we had to have in order to fly proper reconnaissance.

Q: That's precisely what Admiral Richardson wanted, isn't it?

Adm. S.: Oh, yes. Of course, Admiral Richardson felt so strongly about the fleet being out there at Pearl Harbor. He was removed from command of the fleet because he insisted to the president that it was foolhardy to keep the fleet in Pearl Harbor under the inadequate protection that was then in existence.

Q: That removal was somewhat precipitate, as I remember, because he had been told that he was staying on for another year, then, bingo.

Adm. S.: That's right. I think the president just removed him because he got irritated with him. That's my own feeling.

Q: Much in the same fashion as he wanted to remove Taussig?

Adm. S.: Yes, that's right.

Q: Very impulsive.

Adm. S.: He was a very impulsive man. You know I used to keep recordings of every conversation that my boss had with other people outside our department and many within the department. The reason being, particularly in the case of President Roosevelt, that he talked so fast. He would call up and say:

"Now, Betty," he always called the admiral Betty, "I want this and I want that and I want you to do this, and do that, and this and this and this." I was trying to copy it down and Admiral Stark, of course, in his office was trying to copy it down - I monitored every conversation. I had a little switch under my desk and I threw the switch. That started the machine that recorded the conversations on a wax cylinder.

As soon as the president hung up Admiral Stark would ring for me and I'd go in and he'd say:

"Did you get all that?"

I'd say yes, Sir.

"All right, get action started on everything." Then I'd get the cylinder and listen to it, gradually get every single thing, make certain I had the entire list, and farm out the things to Admiral Brainard, who was Fleet Readiness in those days, and Kelly Turner, who was Operations, as I remember. I'd tell them what the president had said had to be done.

Q: These requests on the president's part by telephone were

never followed up with written memos?

Adm. S.: No.

Q: So there was no record?

Adm. S.: No. That's right. It was the most informal way of running a government. I don't know how it was in the Army. I suppose it was the same thing, except that I think Stark had a closer and more intimate relationship with Roosevelt than did General Marshall.

Q: Did that seem to be a deliberate policy on the part of the government, or simply his spontaneous way?

Adm. S.: I think it was spontaneous. And, you know, he felt it was his navy. He'd been Assistant Secretary of the Navy years before, you know. He felt he knew all about the Navy. It was a great thing, really, for us that the president did like the Navy and did feel the need for the Navy because we got more than we would otherwise have gotten.

Q: Yes. He had to resort to various ways of getting the funds, didn't he? I mean other than outright appropriations.

Adm. S.: Well, generally appropriations followed appearances before the Congress, but in every case the president had okayed it first. In those days you didn't go to the Congress and start making requests unless the president had said okay first, and never in writing that I know of. Just little informal things.

Admiral Stark would get from the president: "Okay, Betty, you can have 800 more men," and that meant that Stark would go before the naval affairs committees, make his request, and let them know on the side that the president said it was okay.

Q: The president must have had an awfully good memory to recall the fact that he'd given approval?

Adm. S.: I doubt very much if he remembered it. I'm sure he didn't remember all the times that he had given in.

Q: Back in November of 1940 the British made a raid on the Italian fleet at Taranto. This made a great impression on Admiral Stark. Do you recall that?

Adm. S.: Yes. As I remember it - I think that was the time the British employed torpedo planes, wasn't it?

Q: Yes, and really did a lot of damage.

Adm. S.: That's right, and we were interested at that time in trying to find out whether our torpedoes would run in shallow water or would go to the bottom. I've always felt that our experts, and I certainly was not an ordnance expert at the time or since, really, felt that torpedoes would not run in Pearl Harbor. Of course, the Japs had their torpedoes modified so they would run very shallow, and they were very effective in Pearl Harbor.

I don't think we followed up on all the lessons we could have learned from the Battle of Taranto.

Q: Walter Ansel told me, and he was in War Plans as a very junior member of the team there, that he prepared a letter for Admiral Stark's signature to the secretary of war on this whole episode. I believe Admiral Stark also notified Pearl Harbor of this.

Adm. S.: I know he did, yes. I know that there was considerable correspondence about it with Kelly Turner. Kelly Turner, I guess, was War Plans -

Q: Yes, he was War Plans.

Adm. S.: I can't give you any of those details because I just don't remember them.

Q: Do you recall anything about the development of the plans known as Rainbow V?

Adm. S.: I was on the fringes. Admiral Wellborn was the man who knew most about them. Have you talked to Admiral Wellborn?

Q: Yes.

Adm. S.: He was the one who actually worked with Kelly Turner and Admiral Stark. Wellborn was the one who explained to Admiral Stark the various features of the war plans. I wasn't because at that time it was very secret and they let as few people as possible into those secrets.

For instance, Wellborn was reading excerpts from the codes that were being broken. I wasn't. I was aware of the fact that we were breaking them. I was aware of the fact that Admiral Anderson, who was Director of Naval Intelligence, would come in with a folder under his coat, go into the admiral's office, and show him this very secret stuff that he didn't want anybody else to know about.

Q: He was calling attention to it by covering it up, wasn't he?

Adm. S.: Right. Admiral Wellborn and I used to get a big kick out of the Director of Naval Intelligence going in thinking that he was fooling everybody into think that he didn't have anything special.

Q: I'm interested in the development of those plans and

wondered if you had any knowledge.

Adm. S.: No, I don't. I have no knowledge that would be useful in the development of any of the Rainbow because, as I say, I was just on the fringes.

Q: I know that Admiral Hart and Admiral Stark were close and had a lot of correspondence, and Admiral Tommy told me that it was largely in his own handwriting that he wrote to Admiral Stark. I mean this, again, was very secret so it couldn't be passed on.

Adm. S.: Many of those letters that went back and forth between Stark and Kimmel and Stark and Richardson and Stark and Hart were written in longhand.

Q: Were they preserved?

Adm. S.: I don't know. That's a matter of history. If they were, I'm sure somebody has them some place, but I don't know whether they were or not.

Q: There was a committee in existence called the Joint Liaison Committee, which had to do with State, War, and Navy, and Admiral Stark attended those meetings. Did you go with him to those?

Adm. S.: No, I didn't - very infrequently.

Q: They were very informal.

Adm. S.: What was it called - the State, War and Navy Co-ordinating Committee, or something like that. It existed on paper more than it did in fact, really. They had meetings. Admiral Wellborn, I'm sure, went with the admiral. I didn't. Wellborn was the paperwork man, the administrative, executive assistant. I guarded the door, made the appointments, and saw to it that the admiral got where he was supposed to get on time, the usual flag lieutenant.

Q: You were the organizer for those things?

Adm. S.: Or disorganizer!

Q: Tell me about some of those duties.

Adm. S.: I told you, I think, about the time I scheduled the Starks to be guests of honor the same night at both the British Embassy and the French Embassy. That was one of the great blunders on my naval career. And we discovered it the morning of the day they were the guests of honor at the two embassies, and we discovered it because Mrs. Stark called me on the phone, as she always did each morning when she got to her desk in her house, Admiral's House, and said:

"Smeddy, let's check the admiral's calendar today," and she said, "I see that we're going to the French Embassy tonight for dinner."

I said: "No, Mrs. Stark, you're going to the British Embassy."

"No," she said, "we're going to the French Embassy."

"Well," I said, "I'm sure, Mrs. Stark, it's the British Embassy."

What had happened actually was the invitation to the French Embassy had been sent directly to Admiral's House. I don't think I had seen it. The invitation to the British Embassy came to the admiral's office. I saw it, I checked with the admiral, I checked with Mrs. Stark, and she thought I was referring to the French Embassy apparently. It was a failure of communications, and this was four, five, or six weeks ahead of time that these invitations went out. They didn't come in on the same day, but maybe within a week or two weeks of each other. So when I said, "You're going to the British Embassy," she got the word "Embassy," checked her calendar, and said yes, "in five weeks we are going to be guests of honor at the embassy."

So it wasn't until that morning, and when the enormity of what had happened dawned on me I went in to Admiral Stark and said:

"Admiral, I don't know whether you're going to send me to Siberia or have me shot, but I've made the most terrible blunder."

"What did you do?" and I told him:

"You and Mrs. Stark are scheduled to be the guests of honor of the British ambassador and the French ambassador tonight." And I distinctly remember he looked at me with a twinkle in his eye and said:

"Well, Smeddy, what do you propose that we do about it?"

"Sir," I said, "I think you'd better tell me which one you want to go to and I'll go over and crawl at the feet of the other ambassador and explain that I made the mistake."

So the admiral called Mrs. Stark and called in a lot of his advisers. I forget right now, but it seems to me that he knew the British ambassador fairly well and didn't know the French ambassador well. We were having difficulties with the French at the time.

Q: The British one was Halifax, wasn't it?

Adm. S.: I think it was Lord Halifax, and he and Stark were pretty good friends. The State Department wanted very much to have him go to the French, so I went over and groveled at the feet of the British ambassador, explained that I had made the mistake, it was entirely my fault. He was pretty burned up about it, of course, but that's what happened.

That was one of the terrible blunders of my life.

Q: I would think it would be an embarrassing one! What else happened of that nature?

Adm. S.: It's kind of hard to think.

Q: Did you go with him to any of these official dinners?

Adm. S.: Yes - well, not to many dinners. We always went with him to the various receptions. Sometimes, the Wellborns went, but we always went, the flag lieutenant and his wife always went with him, Claudia and I, and Mrs. Stark.

Another thing that I enjoyed about being aide to the chief of naval operations was that he loved football. He and I went to every Navy football game that we could get to, including all the Army and Navy games. Charlie Wellborn, who was not as avid a sports fan as I, was perfectly happy to have the admiral and me go off early on Saturday morning and he'd have Saturday to either get the papers straightened up in the office or take a morning off, which was very unusual for us to have.

We used to thoroughly enjoy our football Saturdays. We always went with Admiral and Mrs. Stark.

Q: What was his relationship with the Japanese Embassy? Nomura was the ambassador.

Adm. S.: Yes, he was, and I'm sure that I told you the incident -

Q: No, you didn't mention it.

Adm. S.: When I had a phone call from Ambassador Nomura. No, I didn't either. A young Japanese naval officer from the embassy in civilian clothes came over to my office and said the ambassador had a very personal message for Admiral Stark, very private, which he could not tell me; no one but Admiral Stark and I were to know about it. The Ambassador felt it was most important that he have a private meeting with Admiral Stark that nobody knew anything about. I can't really remember just when this was, but I think it was in late November of 1941. I should have some papers to help me check my memory, but I don't have them.

As a result, Admiral Stark had me go over to the Japanese Embassy. I met with Ambassador Nomura and we arranged a little scheme whereby the next afternoon I would be driving in my personal car up Massachusetts Avenue and I would stop and offer a lift to a gentleman who was walking along the way who happened to be Ambassador Nomura, who happened to be in civilian clothes. I would drive him into the Naval Observatory, the Admiral's House.

We arranged this and the next day I did exactly that. I took him to the admiral's house, we went in, he and the admiral were closeted together for quite a long time and I sat outside. When they came out, Admiral Nomura had tears in his eyes. I got him in my car, took him back to Massachusetts Avenue, and dropped him off, just as though he were going for a walk.

What the admiral told me afterwards was that Nomura was

extremely worried about the possibility of the war party in Japan making some drastic decisions. He said the Japanese Army - and, of course, the war party was headed by the Japanese Army at that time - don't understand the power and the potential of the United States. He said he had tried in vain to tell them that Japan could never win in a war against the United States. "But," he said, "Admiral, if the United States doesn't ease up on these sanctions against Japan, the military in my country are going to be driven to do something desperate, in my opinion. I know that my country can only come out second best in any war with the United States."

That's the best recollection I have, and Admiral Stark was deeply impressed. I think it was as a result of that that he and Marshall got together and went to see the president. Marshall, and Admiral Stark, I think at this meeting, at which both Stark and Marshall said that under no circumstances could the United States accept a war in the near future. We were so unprepared. We were doing our best to get better prepared, but we needed a long time, many, many months. We had more planes on the way to Pearl Harbor, for instance, and things like that.

The president had Hull read the proposed answer to the Japanese request for an easing of sanctions.

Q: This pertained to scrap iron and all that sort of thing?

Adm. S.: Yes. And Hull's proposal was a very strong

resistance to any easing of any of the sanctions. Both Stark and Marshall said:

"Mr. President, we think if you send that it could be disastrous."

This is third-hand information. I mean this is what Stark told Wellborn and Wellborn told me. Stark told me some of the things himself.

As a result of that, the president said:

"Okay, take it back and modify it. We will ease up on the Japanese."

Several days after that, our little group who were breaking codes, the Safford group, and who were practicing on the State Department codes - I'm sure I'm not violating my oath now because I'm sure this has been revealed before - broke a long message from the State Department to our ambassador in Japan, which contained the harsh provisions that had been read initially by Hull to the president, General Marshall, and Admiral Stark. There was no modification whatsoever, as had been directed by the president.

When this came to Admiral Stark's attention, he and General Marshall got together. I'm not sure whether they both went to see the president or whether Stark called the president on the phone. But they got the president to admit that after Hull had gotten back to the State Department, all his advisers, one of them being Stanley Hornbeck, I think -

Q: Yes, he was the Far East expert.

Adm. S.: — had impressed on him the fact that the Japanese respected firmness and if he gave in we would lose face and so forth and so on. So Hull called the president up and apparently said; in effect:

"Mr. President, my people are absolutely against weakening this position paper of ours, and we want to send this dispatch just as I read it to you." And the president said okay and never notified the Army or the Navy that the position had changed.

That to me had the greatest potential for disaster of many of the things in our history.

Q: Well, it certainly did spark things, didn't it?

Adm. S.: And we only found out — you know, later on that message was called the ultimatum. At the time, I never heard it referred to as an ultimatum.

Q: No, in its aftereffect it was the ultimatum.

Adm. S.: Yes. After the president had admitted to General Marshall and Admiral Stark that he had changed his mind without telling them, he apparently called Hull and must have said to him:

"Didn't you tell the Army and the Navy about this?" Because Hull called Admiral Stark on the telephone somewhere around the second or third of December, I would guess, — a few days before Pearl Harbor - and said:

"Admiral, I'm afraid the fat's in the fire. It's up to you military fellows now."

I heard that conversation. I used to have all these wax cylinders and I just wish I hadn't destroyed them all when I left my office. When I left my office, I broke them all up.

Q: That certainly was a significant event.

Adm. S.: A tremendous event, and if we could just document it with all the material that we did have, it would be very significant. The real significance is that we should never get into that kind of a position again. Of course, in those days, State rarely talked to Navy or Army.

Nowadays, I hope, through the Security Council that we have completele knowledge by everyone about everything.

Q: Much more structured now.

Adm. S.: Yes. I hope it isn't over-structured. I hope it isn't so structured that the word doesn't get to where it should go. Although I sometimes wonder how much the Army and the Navy really know about what Kissinger really told the Egyptians and the Arabs in his latest dealing. I recognize that you have to have secrecy in diplomacy and we can't hear everything that Kissinger said to the two leaders or he won't get very far in his diplomacy in the future, and I don't really think that the people have a right to know all about all the secret talks of our diplomats in conducting their business. I don't need to know, as a taxpayer, and you don't need to know, neither does the farmer out in the field. The only people who *say* we need to know are the press people who want the sensation.

Q: The Japanese had sent a special ambassador, Kurusu, also. Did Admiral Stark have any contact with him, do you recall?

Adm. S.: No, he didn't. But Admiral Nomura, whom I got to know and like very well in the years to follow, and incidentally, he personally delivered to me a copy of the book he wrote about Pearl Harbor, in which my name appears.

Q: He died not too long ago.

Adm. S.: Yes, I know. He was a wonderful gentleman. He was a good friend of the United States, and an especially good friend of old Admiral Pratt. I remember Admiral Pratt telling Admiral Stark once that "You can trust Nomura. He's a trustworthy Japanese, and you can trust him."

Nomura told me in Japan after the war when I went to see him that he didn't know Kurusu's mission when he arrived. He was kept completely in the dark. He didn't know anything about the plan that Kurusu divulged at the time of the attack on Pearl Harbor. He was sent over and instructed, apparently, to keep Nomura in the dark. They didn't trust Nomura. His government felt that Nomura was so close to the Americans he might leak it.

Q: I suppose Nomura is an example of that bond of fraternity, naval fraternity, which is -

Adm. S.: That's right, the world over. I think most career Navy people have a very solid bond due to the fact that they have all shared the rigors of the sea. Anyone who has spent a lot of time at sea knows what an awesome creature the sea is, and we've all seen what can happen in a hurricane and does happen. So I think all Navy men have a very common bond and feeling. In the Navy everyone in a ship either stays afloat or goes down together, and the navies all over the world, I think, feel pretty much alike. We have a very fine rapport with naval officers the world over.

Q: Would you turn your attention to the events that immediately preceded the attack on Pearl Harbor?

Adm. S.: Contrary to what we read in retrospect, there was no great excitement. We worked long in our office. As a matter of fact, the night of the 6th of December, which was Saturday evening, we had been watching, through our intelligence, Japanese warships and transports that were headed for the Kra Peninsula. I remember leaving the office that night at about seven o'clock, between seven and eight, with Admiral Wellborn and John McCrae, who was a special assistant, later Vice Admiral John McCrae - he was then a special assistant to Stark and the man Stark had sent to the Philippines with a personal message to Hart, not too long before, that he didn't even want to trust to the mails or the wires or the codes. When we left the office that night, we said:

"Well, the British are sure going to catch it tomorrow in Singapore."

This was the eve of Pearl Harbor. We didn't have the slightest suspicion that there was any threat to Pearl Harbor. Of course, a lot of people like Kemp Tolley, he's one of the ones today - he's a good friend of mine - he's absolutely convinced that Roosevelt planned this whole thing and purposely brought it on and that he had information he didn't share with us people. I'm certain that he was just as much caught unawares as were the rest of us.

Q: I think Kemp believes that Admiral Stark, Marshall, and all the others were gathered at the White House that night, waiting for the event.

Adm. S.: That's right. As a matter of fact, you know, the next day - and he thinks the fact General Marshall was out on a horse Sunday morning when the attack took place, when we heard about it, had been planned. It just happened that

Stark went to the office that morning but he let Wellborn and me off. He said: "I won't need you in the office tomorrow."

I was flooring my attic in my house in Arlington, Virginia, when my daughter called from downstairs and said:

"Daddy, the radio says the Japanese have bombed Pearl Harbor."

"Oh," I said, "don't be ridiculous."

"No, really, Daddy, come on down here." So I went down and listened to this thing, put on my uniform and rushed to the Navy Department. I got there just as Charlie Wellborn got there. Admiral Stark was there, and then all the natives began to gather.

Q: Well I remember it. Ed Layton says that it might have been different if all the intercepted messages had been transmitted to Hawaii.

Adm. S.: Yes, it might have been.

Q: But they were not?

Adm. S.: I think I've told you this before. At the time that Admiral Stark was called back for - I was going to say "trial," but it wasn't really a trial -

Q: Congressional hearings, you mean?

Adm. S.: Yes, when Hart was conducting the investigation. I was brought back to Washington to help act as one of Admiral Stark's assistant counselors, and the job that was given me was to go through all the incoming decoded, decrypted, Japanese messages and pick out all those in which the Japanese requested or reported ships in harbors around the world. The reason being that those who were after Admiral Stark were trying to pin this disaster on him. I took all the messages that had to do with Pearl Harbor and when you read all those by themselves it was obvious that something was going to happen to Pearl Harbor. I produced a series of messages about Singapore, Manila, Panama, San Francisco, they were getting these same reports from these harbors all over the world, and they were all coming in together, you see. There would be a little bit about Pearl Harbor, then something about Panama, and something about San Francisco, something about Singapore, ships leaving and entering and the locations of ships in the different harbors. So that, before the fact, it would have taken a very astute man.

Even Ed Layton, he was smart, but even Eddie - of course, since he was at Pearl, he would be particularly alert to anything that had to do with Pearl. And he may be right that they may have suspected something.

Q: That is, of course, what he said and he referred in particular to one dispatch that apparently didn't get there and that had to do with instructions to the Japanese consul in

Pearl -

Adm. S.: To burn his codes?

Q: No, henceforth to divide the island into sections and to report on the different sections. That didn't get to Pearl. It was a part, as you say, of the bigger picture, sandwiched in between others.

Adm. S.: There's no question but that, after the fact, you can assemble data that point definitely to Pearl Harbor, which we should have known about - that people say we should have known about.

Of course, I wasn't reading any of those messages at the time. I was only privy to the fact that we were reading parts of the Japanese codes. Wellborn shared Admiral Stark's knowledge of it, but I didn't. All I knew was that this material was going in there. It was very secret and I wasn't one who had a need to know, so I wasn't cut in on it. I never saw anything until I started my investigation, long after Pearl Harbor.

Q: Layton makes another point, to the effect that he thought Washington was preoccupied with the Atlantic at that time.

Adm. S.: That's true. Washington was preoccupied with the Atlantic.

Q: Where the submarine menace was.

Adm. S.: That's right, and that's where Great Britain was fighting for her life and the President was doing his best to help all he could within the laws of this country, and violating them in many cases, like the Neutrality Act. We used to have our ships follow German warships and broadcast their positions in plain language.

Q: As a neutral ship!

Adm. S.: Yes.

Q: Admiral Hart had some problems with General Wavell at one time, who was the commander in chief out there, in terms of the use of U.S. naval units to convoy ships to Singapore. Do you have any knowledge of that?

Adm. S.: I only know what I've read since then, that Admiral Hart felt he should keep his ships available for the purposes for which they were designed and trained, and that's war, not split them all up in little bits and pieces convoying all over the ocean out there. He felt that he should keep a force in being, a fighting force. Once they started scouting, he would have had nothing. I think he was absolutely right. As a matter of fact, Hart was one of the smartest people on our side before Pearl Harbor.

Q: He certainly had the confidence of Admiral Stark?

Adm. S.: Yes, he did, but in a way it was kind of like the blind advising the blind, because we didn't have any information in Washington, any good solid information. We were just caught with our pants down. And really the whole attitude of the country affected the military. I couldn't conceive of our going to war in the peacetime atmosphere we had then, almost a pacifistic atmosphere.

Q: It was almost violent and pacifistic in turn, wasn't it?

Adm. S.: Yes. I remember taking a group of students from Princeton University who'd come down to Washington as part of their political-military course they were taking, or whatever they called it in those days, through the Navy Department. There was a young professor and eight or nine Princeton boys, and they laughed and said:

"What the hell are you guys doing? There isn't any need for a Navy. What do you do in peacetime? Just sit around on your duffs all the time?"

It irritated me to the point where I wanted to slug them. And afterwards I referred to this professor as a pinko. He was a pacifist. This was the prevailing opinion at the time, that we didn't need an Army and a Navy any more, the wars were all over, and we were just a drain on the taxpayer.

Q: You were talking off-tape about the destroyer deal with Britain and you began to express the attitude of some naval officers.

Adm. S.: Yes. I was an old destroyerman myself and I hated to see these destroyers of ours being given away. We desperately needed them in the Navy, I thought, and I particularly resented the fact that we were ordered to fill every destroyer up to its maximum level in provisions and ammunition. We stocked them before we turned them over.

Of course, it was a magnificent gesture to the British, and I think Roosevelt struck a hard bargain in getting the bases that he got.

Q: Yes, he balanced one against the other.

Adm. S.: That's right but I, as a young officer, couldn't see that. All I could see was that we were giving away fifty of our desperately needed destroyers.

Q: And, as a matter of fact, many of them were just old cans. They hardly made it over there, didn't they?

Adm. S.: They made it over there. They were old cans, that's true, but we were operating all the time. We operated hard and we operated at 30, 32, 33 knots, night and day, at night with no radar, no lights, attacking an enemy battle line -

33 knots right into the battleships at night, darkened ship. Sometimes you didn't know that there was another ship until you could hear the whine of her blowers. It would be that black and that tough.

Many's the time we've gone into battle line and torpedo attack and actually had to run between the battleships, steaming at 12 to 15 knots. We were doing 30 knots and we just ran between the battleships after we fired our torpedoes.

Q: You're talking about the old four-stackers?

Adm. S.: I'm talking about the old four-stackers, yes. These were four-stackers that they gave away.

I spent the years of 1927, '28, and '29 in DD-325, the old Mulany, based in San Diego, with cruises all over the place, including down to Corinto, Nicaragua, where we stayed for four or five months, making the world safe for democracy in Corinto. We were the only U.S. naval ship there. We got mail once a month. It certainly was a sad existence.

The Navy had so little money that on this mission we went from Seattle, Washington, to Corinto, Nicaragua, at the maximum allowed speed of 11 knots to conserve fuel. We were only allowed to make 11 knots between ports in those days.

Q: You were consuming a lot of food in the process!

Adm. S.: We didn't have much food to consume. We didn't

have any real ice boxes, you know. We had a terrible time. I think it took us pretty near a month to get down there.

Q: Going back to the pre-Pearl Harbor scene in Washington, how did Admiral Stark react to this whole thing?

Adm. S.: He, like most of the people there, was stunned. I think the man who was least stunned was Admiral Ben Morreel. The admirals were all sitting around in Admiral Stark's office when Admiral Ben Morreel walked in. Bouncy is the only word I can use to describe him. He was always on his toes and just full of vim and vigor, pep and energy. He said:

"Well, gentlemen, I've lined up every heavy contractor in the United States ready to go to Pearl Harbor to start raising those ships."

This was within twenty-four hours of our getting the word about the damage that had been done out there. Ben Morreel was right on the ball. Everyone else was sitting around in a state of shock, practically everybody else.

Q: Admiral Morreel, prior to that, had been very alert to building up naval bases and that sort of thing?

Adm. S.: Oh, yes. He was a magnificent man. Ben's dead, isn't he?

Q: He's still living.

Adm. S.: Is he? I've lost track of him, but I was very fond of him and a good close friend of his. I'm a great admirer of his.

Q: One of the controversial points that's been referred to a number of times is that before the actual attack on Pearl Harbor, because of the difference in time Admiral Stark had started to telephone Kimmel and then didn't?

Adm. S.: Well, in those days our telephone wasn't secure, you know, and I think that's what deterred him. Not only that, but our telephone communications were terrible. Trying to talk to Hawaii in those days was very, very difficult, and I think that's part of the reason why he didn't.
    Yes, he did start doing it. As a matter of fact, had we sent the message that didn't reach Kimmel before Pearl Harbor by Navy radio, I'm sure he would have had it. But it was sent by Army - you know the Army was not as good as the Navy - so it didn't get there, the message that would have given Kimmel some warning.

Q: The Army was actually charged with the defense, anyway, wasn't it?

Adm. S.: Yes. The Army is charged with defense of the fleet in port.

Q: And some of the people who take an opposite point of view claim that perhaps it was because General Marshall had been designated as the sole authority to notify Pearl of anything.

Adm. S.: I don't know. I can't comment on that.

Q: Tell me about when the news came to Washington, to Stark.

Adm. S.: Well, as we began to get the details of the ships that were sunk, the lives that were lost, and the planes that had been destroyed, as I say, everybody was stunned.

Q: How soon did that start coming in?

Adm. S.: It's pretty hard for me to remember now. We all stayed down there day and night for several days. Maybe Wellborn and I relieved each other to go home and get a few hours' sleep occasionally, but I don't seem to remember. We started rushing everything we could out to Pearl from other places in the United States.

Q: Were Stark and the President in communication very frequently at this time?

Adm. S.: Yes. And Secretary Frank Knox got into the picture very firmly. It seems to me Knox flew out to Pearl.

Q: He did.

Adm. S.: And came back and gave the first real details we'd had, at least that I heard, of what had happened out there. Of course, it was some days before we had more than just fragmentary accounts of what had happened. People out there weren't sure what had happened for a while, you know. They didn't know how many people had been lost or what the situation was.

I can't add too much to that from my own memory now because I've heard so much about it since then. I can't remember my own reactions too well.

Q: Say something about Secretary Knox as secretary of the Navy, prior to Pearl Harbor. What were your dealings with him? What was your impression of him?

Adm. S.: I thought he was a pretty forthright man. I thought he was tremendously interested in public relations. In those days the secretary of the Navy did pretty much what he was told to do.

Knox started to take charge after Pearl Harbor. But up to that time, we'd had a very ill Claude Swanson, then we had Edison, who was deaf, but awfully nice. Frankly, the secretary did pretty much what the admirals advised him to do. The first real secretary who took charge was Forrestal, and he started telling the admirals what to do. But Knox -

Q: He was a pretty positive man.

Adm. S.: Yes, he was, and he got very much on the ball after Pearl Harbor.

Q: Why was that? Why was there a contrast between his actions before Pearl Harbor - ?

Adm. S.: I don't know. I really don't know. I can't say. I don't think my guesses would be worth anything. You see, it wasn't long after this that I left the office. Admiral Stark was told he was going to London and asked me to go with him, and I said:

"Admiral, I'm sorry, if you don't mind I've got to go to sea. I want to go to sea, and I'm told that I can get command of a new destroyer."

"Well," he said, "I don't blame you. I understand how you feel, but I just feel that you're deserting me, and I need you."

I said: "Admiral, I've been with you five straight years, five consecutive years."

I was with him when he was Commander, Cruiser Division 3, as his radio and signal officer, communications officer, when he was Commander, Cruisers, Battle Force, the next year as his radio and communications officer for a big force of cruisers and destroyers. I had three years with him as chief of naval operations. That was five consecutive years, and

I didn't want to go into the aide to the chief of naval operations job, in the first place, because I'd been promised that I could be exec of a destroyer.

I first went out as communications officer for Admiral Walter Vernou as Commander Cruiser Division 3. I went with him right out of the PG school, where I learned to be a communicator. I had two years in flag communications. Then, when Vernou was relieved by Stark, Vernou said: "Now, I'll get you that exec of a destroyer that you want." I said thank you. The Navy Department had a different idea. They said the new admiral didn't know anything about communications and he insisted that I remain as his communications officer, although he didn't know me from a hole in the ground. I was a communications postgraduate, I'd had two years in the job, and he wanted me to stay. So when he arrived he promised me that at the end of that year, I could get my destroyer.

At the end of the year, he was promoted to Commander, Cruisers, Battle Force, and he insisted that I stay and when that was over, then I could get to be exec of a destroyer. Then, he was ordered as chief of naval operations. He asked me to go with him as flag lieutenant and I turned him down. Both Admiral Wellborn, then Commander Wellborn, who had been asked to go as his flag secretary, and then Captain Lee, who was our chief of staff - Willis A. Lee - got me in a corner and said:

"You're crazy, Smeddy. You can't possibly go to any job

in the Navy where you'll learn as much about the Navy and enhance your career as much as going as aide to the chief of naval operations."

Q: Sound advice.

Adm. S.: Yes. All I could think of was I wanted to be executive officer of a destroyer.

Q: You were blinded by that!

Adm. S.: Because I'd been told that in a normal career you had to get to be executive officer before you could get to be commanding officer, and I wanted to command a destroyer.

Q: Since you mentioned Willis Lee, will you detour for a moment and tell me something about him? A young chap over at the Naval Institute, the second in command of the Proceedings, is about to write a book on Willis Lee. Tell me something about him from your own experience.

Adm. S.: He was one of the most brilliant naval officers I've ever known. He had a mathematical mind that could solve problems in his mind like a computer. He could do mooring board problems in his head. For instance, whenever we would have a change of formation, we on the staff would rush to the maneuvering board to figure the new course to the station in the new formation, Lee would just give it to us and he'd be right within two or three degrees. He'd come right out with the new course. It might be a course as much as 200 or 300 degrees from the course we were on, and this would be the course to the station. We never did understand how he could do all this. He was just magnificent. We'd work it out and take a few minutes to get it down on the mooring board and we'd come out within a few degrees of Lee's instant decision.

He was just like a farmer. He was slow-moving, didn't talk much, everything he said made a great deal of sense, his decisions were always very sound. He just was a magnificent person - always honest, always above-board, nothing devious about him. Everybody loved him. Very thoughtful. Tremendous loyalty down. As a result, we all would do anything in the world for him.

I had the good fortune later to accompany him when he was in command of, or was riding, the battleship Washington, on the way to the Solomon Islands.

Q: Yes, he was.

Adm. S.: And I was in Lansdowne (DD-486) - one of the four accompanying destroyers that went out to the South Pacific as escorts. It was either the Washington or the South Dakota.

Q: It was the Washington.

Adm. S.: Yes, it was the Washington, in 1942.

He had no children, he had a very nice little, sort of mouselike, wife, who was pleasant and sweet. They didn't go out much socially. Just a very quiet, domestic man, but the kind of fellow we all wanted to go to war with if we ever had to go to war.

He had the kind of mind that, later on, Admiral Tip Merrill had. I was his chief of staff in the Solomon Islands. Tip was one of these fellows who thought best under stress, brilliant. He was another person everybody loved, but he was a very gregarious fellow.

I'm getting way ahead of myself.

Q: Yes, we'll come to Tip Merrill later, but I did want to seize this opportunity for you to say something about Lee.

Adm. S.: One of the things that are bound to come out in this book about Ching Lee in this. When Lee got to be Commander, Cruisers, Battle Force, there was Admiral Stark and he had seven members of his staff, and we were soon dubbed Snow White and the Seven Dwarfs. Each one of us was named after one of the dwarfs. I forget now who we all were.

Q: What was your nickname?

Adm. S.: I'm trying to think. I have a hard time remembering the names of all the dwarfs now. There was Sneezy and Dopey, and I forget the others. Al Krick, I remember, was Dopey, and Al Jennings was Sneezy. I can't seem to remember what some of the other dwarfs' names were.

Q: You can't remember Ching Lee's?

Adm. S.: No, I can't, but he was the head dwarf. Admiral Stark was Snow White. He had snow-white hair, you know. The funny part of it was that the characteristics of the dwarfs were very aptly applied to each member of the staff, we all thought. You couldn't necessarily see your own, but you certainly could see everybody else's.

Q: Going back to immediately following Pearl Harbor, when was it apparent that Admiral Stark was not going to remain in Washington?

Adm. S.: Almost right away. Admiral King was called up and they had a lot of consultation between Admiral King and Roosevelt and Knox.

Q: This is where Knox came into the picture?

Adm. S.: Yes. He began to take over. And, of course, there began to develop a lot of bitterness on the part of Admiral Kimmel toward Admiral Stark because he felt that Stark had let him down. Stark actually was giving Kimmel as much information as he had himself, which really wasn't very much.

Stark, I think, was fearful of crying "wolf" too much. It was very easy to sit in Washington and say "Look out for this" and "Look out for that," and "beware of this" and "Beware of that." He felt that if he did that too much it would dull the edge of a real warning.

Q: Was it apparent that some of the blame for Pearl Harbor would rub off on Stark? I mean was it apparent to him?

Adm. S.: Yes, I think so. After all he was the head of the Navy, and the head of the Navy has to be responsible, just like Kimmel was solely responsible in Pearl Harbor, he and Short. Yet I'd been in Kimmel's squadron when he'd been a destroyer squadron commander, years before, and there was never a man in this Navy who worked harder to prepare a navy for war than Kimmel. He put us through the damnedest paces. He put us through things that no other squadron commander had ever done. I was three years in destroyers at that time and he made us do things that we felt were absolutely outrageous.

For instance, as a signal officer - I was a radio officer and signal officer and communications officer in my destroyer - every single night at eight o'clock in port we had to take a blinker drill. Every night in port! We'd be at sea for three weeks and come back to port for ten days, and every night at eight o'clock we were supposed to go back to our ships and take a blinker drill. Some of us beat that. We'd drive our cars down to the dock, just sit there, and I'd read the blinker and my wife would write it down, and I'd turn in the paper the next morning. I was doing the blinker drill. It was perfectly all right. All we had to do was copy the system that every communications officer, radio officer, and signal officer be able to copy everything, read every flag quicker than any signalman he had, sit in on a radio circuit, and every day in port we had to take our typewriters and go over to the tender and sit for two hours and listen to da-dit-da-dit and type and type until we could sit in and act as a qualified radio operator.

Not only that, but every time two or more ships were nested, one officer in the nest had to be a communications officer. That meant we were getting the duty more often than the others. If you had two ships in a nest, one of the communications officers had to be there every other night. So, here you'd be at sea for three weeks and you'd come into port for ten days, and every other night you had to be on board ship, all night. So we tried to get the skippers to nest in threes and fours so we could have one in three or one in four rotations.

Kimmel was a man who really, I think, would have been a great wartime commander and had done a great deal to get his fleet ready with what he had.

Q: That's the picture I got of the man.

Adm. S.: He was just caught in a vise. He was the fall guy on the scene. It just was criminal. And, of course, he was bitter all the rest of his life. I don't blame him, because he had all his life done more than his contemporaries to get the fleet ready, every unit he'd ever had. When we operated at sea under him, we did some of the most dangerous maneuvers you ever saw, but the kind of maneuvers you'd do in wartime. The kind of stuff the Japs were doing, day and night, before they got into war with us. The Japs were far superior in the handling of destroyers at night, and their ships at night, to us because they practiced all the time. They had lots of accidents. In our Navy everybody was scared to death they were going to have an accident. If you had an accident, bang, the skipper was finished.

But old Kimmel he'd put us out there. He was the guy who had us going like this at 30 knots in the middle of the night.

Q: The irony of it!

Adm. S.: Oh, yes. I tell you when you're in a destroyer doing 33 knots in a kind of a rough sea on a black night, without a light on any ship, except you could have a little blinker tube on the fantail of the ship ahead shining down on the wake, and you had to stay 250 or 300 yards behind that ship, you really had your heart in your mouth all the time.

In those days we had three watch officers. We had a captain, an exec, and three ensigns in my destroyer. At one time the captain went to the hospital with a kidney infection, the exec tried to commit suicide, and that left us three ensigns in the ship. We were all classmates, Joe Mallock, George Chrisman, and I. Joe Mallock was senior, so Joe announced that he was now the skipper so he wouldn't stand any more duties and watches. I said:

"Okay, I'm the exec, so I won't stand any more duties or watches."

And the third classmate, George Chrisman, said:

"I'm damned if I'm going to stand them all."

So we all agreed we'd take a day in three. And we were about four or five weeks with just the three of us, but they wouldn't let us go to sea. That upset us some. We could have handled that ship. We'd been handling it for two years together, but they wouldn't let us go to sea, just made us swing around the buoy, in port.

Then we had the "ready duty" coming up, and we were so excited because on any pretext we were going to get underway the day we had the ready duty. If anything came up, and just before the day we had the ready duty they canceled our ready duty and gave it to another destroyer!

Q: That's some story!

When did Admiral Stark get notice that he was going to go to London? He left in February, I believe.

Adm. S.: Yes. Right after Pearl Harbor I started to move to get out of there, and I finally got the admiral to agree. I got my orders to a brand-new destroyer that was building in Kearny, New Jersey. I don't remember when I was detached, but I had first to go down to the fleet sonar school in Key West, and I think it was near the end of January that I went there.

Q: And by that time he knew that he was going to London?

Adm. S.: Oh, yes, he knew because he asked me to go with him. Does that say when I was detached from the CNO?

Q: First, before you tell me about getting ready to go to sea, comment on the fact that you and countless others in the department in Washington who had responsible jobs immediately wanted to leave your desks -

Adm. S.: Everybody wanted to go to sea.

Q: Is this a sensible move?

Adm. S.: No, of course not, and in many cases people were frozen right where they were. One of my classmates was bitter for a long time, Admiral Charlie Buchanan, because he was frozen in the Bureau of Ordnance for a long time after the war started. He finally got out into it and did a beautiful job.

Q: Tell me about your preparations to take command of a destroyer at last. You wanted to be an exec, and you turned out to be a skipper.

Adm. S.: That was probably one of the most interesting things I did in my career, first taking a command.

Q: It was so long-delayed.

Adm. S.: Well, in those days, actually, we didn't get commands at a very early age like they do today.

We went up to Kearny, New Jersey, after I had been to the sonar school in Key West -

Q: Did you learn anything of any significance there?

Adm. S.: We learned how to operate the current sonar, which was a searchlight type sonar, beam and echo, which really wasn't too effective but was the best thing there was at the time.

We went to Kearny and found a place to live in Montclair, New Jersey. A very wealthy man heard there were a couple of naval officers looking for a place to live while they fitted out their ships in nearby Kearny and he offered us his beautiful mansion. I think we paid $100 a month rent.

Whitey Taylor and I - later Vice Admiral Whitey Taylor, E. B. Taylor - and his wife and two children and my wife and three children all moved into this big mansion. The ground floor was our community floor and he had the first floor and we had the second floor, as I remember it. We lived there about six weeks while we were fitting out our two ships, the Duncan and the Lansdowne.

Q: This reflects the spirit of the time, doesn't it?

Adm. S.: Yes.

Q: This generosity.

Adm. S.: That's why I mentioned it. The man had left his house vacant because his daughter had committed suicide and he and his wife couldn't go back to it. Another thing that was interesting about those times was that in the basement of the house was a great storage bin that was filled with canned goods from S. S. Pierce in Boston. There must have been enough canned goods in there to last a family a couple of years. I remember both Whitey and I said to our wives:

"Don't ever touch a bit of this because it isn't ours," and once one of our wives got a can of mushroom soup and we made them go out and buy another can and replace it.

After we left we heard he sold the whole house, lock, stock, and barrel, with everything in it.

Anyway, we put our ships in commission. Whitey Taylor put his <u>Duncan</u> in commission two weeks ahead of mine. Then my ship and the next ship two weeks later, and the next ship two weeks after that. We took the ships and crews up to Casco Bay.

Q: You said, I think off tape, that you went to BuPers and selected crew members. Tell me about that.

Adm. S.: Oh, yes, that was interesting. I said:

"Do I have any choice now in my officers?" and they said: "Well, we'll let you have one officer. You can pick your exec, if he's available."

I said: "There's one young fellow that I'd like to have. I don't know where he is, I'm not sure what rank he is now, but he used to be the quarterback of the Navy football team when I was at the postgraduate school back in '33 and '34. His name is Richard R. Pratt."

So they looked him up and they found that he was some place, and they said: "Yes, he could be made available."

I said I'd like to have him as my exec but they said he wasn't senior enough for that but I could have him as my gunnery officer.

Q: What were his specific qualifications that you wanted?

Adm. S.: I'd seen him play quarterback for the Navy team and he had more guts - he played sixty minutes both ways. He was a little bitty fellow. He was about 5 feet 7 and must have weighed 160 pounds, and they won nine out of ten games, and had one of the great football teams in Naval Academy history. He was just a tremendous gutsy fighter and I thought in time of war that was the kind of fellow I'd like to have with me.

They located him and ordered him as my gunnery officer and I got a fellow named Frank Foley as my exec. We were the three Naval Academy people we had: the rest were all reserves.

Q: They had been trained where?

Adm. S.: They'd come from various sources - not OCS in those days. Some came from the NROTC program. A lot of them had been directly commissioned in the Navy. My chief engineer, for instance, had been an engineer in some power plant and they just gave him a commission as a JG and said he was available as a chief engineer, and I got him as chief engineer.

I had a crew of 282 men, 33 of whom had never been on a ship before, and, as I say, only three of us officers had ever been to sea in a ship.

Q: That was quite a task, then, to shape them into a team?

Adm. S.: Yes, it really was.

They built the ship at Kearny, but we never got an at-sea trial. They towed the ship cold over to the Brooklyn Navy Yard with a couple of tugs and my crew and I went on board. Then we started learning the ship and we had dock trials alongside the dock, ourselves. I was ordered to pick up my ammunition up the Hudson River at a place called Seal Island, I think it was, south of West Point, just under the Bear Mountain Bridge. That doesn't sound quite right. It's an ammunition depot.

Q: Seal Island Depot.

Adm. S.: I don't think that's quite the right name, but I've forgotten now what the name was.

I was delighted because I thought the first time we got that ship underway it would be nice to get it underway in protected waters like the Hudson River, rather than going right out into the submarine-infested Atlantic.

Q: With all the novices on board!

Adm. S.: With a brand-new crew and none of us knowing much of anything about anything, really.

I backed away from the dock. It's a very tiny little horseshoe basin there in New York Harbor, and right across my stern, across that little basin, was the British cruiser Glasgow, which had been torpedoed. She was in this yard for repairs. Well, I gave the order to stop and then one-third ahead. My ship wouldn't stop and wouldn't stop, and I gave two-thirds ahead and got going faster backwards and we rammed the British cruiser with our stern, which bashed my depth-charge racks. Fortunately, we didn't have any depth charges on yet because I was going to pick them up at this ammunition depot.

So I had to go back into the yard and they worked all night to straighten out my racks. It didn't do any harm. I went over and apologized to the captain of the Glasgow.

Q: She was going to be repaired, anyway.

Adm. S.: The captain said:
"Think nothing of it. You ought to see the damage to my bottom. You just put a little scratch in her."

We had an investigation and what they found out was that the enunciators had been hooked up backwards so that when I rang up "Ahead," it rang up "Astern" in the engine room, and when I rang up "One-third astern" - when I rang up "One-third ahead" to stop my sternway, it rang up "One-third astern," and when I got frantic and tried to ring up "Two-thirds ahead" to stop it, it rang up "Two-thirds astern" and banged right into it.

Q: Just in reverse.

Adm. S.: Yes, and it's funny we hadn't caught that in our dock trials because we weren't moving, and also because we were maneuvering with men on telephones. Actually, the very first order I gave I gave to the man who was the telephone talker right beside me. I said: "All back one-third," and we backed one-third all right. I didn't pay any attention to what the man on the telephone was doing. I don't know what he did. He probably did it all right. They got the "Back one-third" on the telephone and didn't pay any attention to the enunciator, apparently, in the engine room, because they didn't discover at that time that things were backwards.

To make a long story short, we left the Navy Yard and decided that we would go up the East River into Long Island Sound, because that was the most protected passage. None of us had ever been up the East River before and, as we got out of the Navy Yard, a thick fog set in. These car ferries were coming down the East River, big long freights. It was a hazardous passage, I tell you.

We got through that all right and then we began to have fun. We had just had a little SC-1 radar installed and the exec and I and the gunnery officer fooled around with this little radar. We had a radarman who had been trained in the use of this radar before he'd been put on the ship. He got about two weeks at the factory. We found that we could pick up things pretty well with it and we were very excited about this thing because the fog held all the way to Casco Bay.

I was ordered to go through the Cape Cod Canal because it was safer. Of course, my ship was completely unprotected. Oh, incidentally, we had run up the Hudson and we had picked up our ammunition, then we came back and went out the East River. When we got up to Narragansett Bay and to the entrance to Cape Cod Canal it was solid fog, but we could see these little pips around and we came up close to one of them. It was a great big merchantman, and I got out on the bridge with a megaphone and said:

"What's the matter?"

"The canal is closed," he said, "on account of the fog."

I asked him when it was going to open and he said:

"I don't know. I've been here three days at anchor."

There were ships all around.

I had orders to get to Casco Bay as quickly as I could, so, not knowing at the time that there was an order that no Navy ship should go through the canal in fog, I felt my way into the canal and we went up it in the fog and got to the railroad bridge, which was closed. I couldn't get under it, you know. So we backed and filled there and blew the whistle. Finally, reluctantly, they opened the railroad bridge and I went on through and came out the other side and went on up to Casco Bay, still in this thick fog.

Q: Were you reported as having gone through the canal?

Adm. S.: Oh, yes, and I got a letter about it later on. In those days they weren't too mad at you for doing it.

Q: Well, it was wartime.

Adm. S.: Yes, it was wartime.

We finally got to the channel into Casco Bay, in this thick fog, still. None of us had even been in Casco Bay before, but we discovered that we could see a line of buoys on our radar screen, so the exec and I decided that we'd try to go in there.

We had asked in New York before we left if there was any information on minefields or any other danger that we would run into on the way to Casco Bay. They said no, none that they knew of. We felt our way up from buoy to buoy. You'd get right on top of a buoy and you could look down and identify it. You could see about to the forecastle in the fog. Then we found there was a net across the entrance and a net tender. We blew the whistle a lot of times and finally, on the net tender, they reluctantly identified us as a U.S. Navy ship and they opened the gate and in we went, still on our radar, and anchored. When the fog lifted a little bit, and I could see the tender with the flag of Admiral Oscar Badger flying, and I got in my boat - this was about five o'clock in the afternoon, and I went over to the flagship. I was taken to the admiral's cabin by the flag lieutenant, where I told Admiral Badger that I am the commanding officer of

the USS Lansdowne reporting for duty according to my orders.
He looked at me and said:

"The Lansdowne? Where did you come from?

I said: New York, Sir."

"When?" he asked.

"Just today," I said. "We just got in."

He said: "Did you just come in?"

I said: "Yes, Sir."

"My God," he said: "What did you do about the minefield?"

I said: "What minefield?"

He said: "We have a minefield off Casco Bay which is all energized. My ships have been held up in the fog two days. They're all out there."

Q: New York didn't know about this?

Adm. S.: No, they didn't know there was a minefield there.

Q: Communications were bad!

Adm. S.: Oh, yes, they were terrible. And I should immediately jump, I suppose, to a little later part of this story when I took the ship several months later out with the battleship Washington, to the Solomon Islands. The Washington went in to Havannah Harbor and I was sent up to Espiritu Santo to get the mail for our group, which was supposed to be in Espiritu. When I arrived off Espiritu, I saw a great, big, inviting, broad entrance and all the ships anchored inside. Espiritu Santo is just a narrow channel, you know. So I flashed my recognition signal and said "Send pilot. Wish to enter port, send pilot," and the signal flashed back and said: "Enter port." I said:

"Will not enter port without pilot. Send pilot." And they said: "We have no pilot."

So I said: "Will not enter port without pilot."

Well, in about half an hour a little boat came from way around south behind a little island and I got a pilot. He said that the entire open entrance is mined.

Q: And they told you to go in?

Adm. S.: Yes. We went down around the little island and came in the back way. I anchored just inside the minefield. About three days later the President Coolidge, a tremendous passenger liner loaded with all the supplies for one Army division, came through the main entrance, hit the minefield, blew up, and sank. That's what happened.

Q: What was it that deterred you from obeying their instructions?

Adm. S.: My instinct, and that thing had happened to me in Casco Bay. I thought, now, this is such an inviting entrance, there are the ships in there, they can't be unprotected.

Anyway, I was furious when I got in and I found from the pilot, sure, that was a minefield. So I went to see the port director. He was a young man who apologized and said:

"Sir, I'm ashamed to say I've only been port director about three days. I've never seen a port or a ship before in my life. I came into the Navy because I'm an expert on the Packard engine. Here I find myself port director on Espiritu Santo and I don't know one part of a ship from another."

Well, to go on with this story, a few days later I was 600 miles north, Guadalcanal. We anchored in Purvis Bay where a classmate of mine, Commander Henry Farrell, was in command of the motor torpedo boats in Purvis Bay, Guadalcanal, Savo Sound. I invited him out to the ship to have supper with us and asked:

"How are you doing, Hank?" And he said:

"Smeddy, we can't keep our engines running. There isn't anybody in my squadron who knows how to run these damned Packard motors."

I said: "Have you got Packard motors in these things? Do you know that the port director down at Espiritu, 600 miles south of here, is an expert from the Packard Motor factory?"

He and I concocted a dispatch, we sent it from my ship to Admiral Ghormley that night and within a week that Packard Motor guy was up there and he got all those motors running.

Q: You were a personnel man even in those days!

Adm. S.: This is just the kind of thing that was happening all over the world. We were getting so many thousands of people in, had so few experienced personnel, and they were trying to put people where they belonged, but some were going askew all over the place. This was just one of the many, many instances I could cite that came to my personal attention during the war, one or two of which I was able to correct.

But, to get back to Casco Bay now -

Q: At this point, tell me about the Lansdowne herself.

Adm. S.: The Lansdowne was a 1,650-tonner, we had 18 officers and 282 men. She was a twin-stacker. She only had five torpedoes. Beautiful little ship. She could do 36 or 38 knots, maybe that's a little fast. Maybe 35 or 36. And we immediately started doing all kinds of stuff, spur-of-the-moment stuff that had to be done. I'm getting a little ahead of myself.

One of the interesting things that stick out in my memory was the time that I put in to Noumea, which was Admiral Ghormley's headquarters - and Admiral Halsey's later - I worked for both Halsey and Ghormley, I got a dispatch from Kelly Turner who was in Noumea at the time to report on board his flagship. I got on board and I had the exec fuel the ship - I went over to the flagship and Admiral Turner said:

"Smedberg, how much ammunition can you carry in your

ship?" And I said:

"I don't know, Sir. We're full now. Our ammunition is all on board for our complement."

"Well," he said, "I want you to take 81-mm howitzer ammunition up to General Vandergrift on Guadalcanal. He's completely out of ammunition and all that we have in the South Pacific is right here in Noumea and it's about 90 or 100 tons worth. Can you carry it?"

I didn't know, so I said: "I've got a 1,650-ton destroyer." I never was a very good mathematician. I didn't know how much it would raise my center of gravity, but I said:

"I guess we can take it, Sir." So we went and anchored near the ammunition ship, and all night long the Marines loaded my ship. We loaded all the compartments, we loaded all the decks all round to the top of the lifelines, we got every bit of it on board and I was ordered to make best speed up to Guadalcanal and deliver it to General Vandergrift at night, during the dark.

Q: It was a great gamble, wasn't it, to put it all on one ship?

Adm. S.: Yes. It was a 900-mile trip. It was a desperate situation. That's the kind of situation we were in all the time in those days. This was in September '42.

So when I got outside the reef, there was quite a swell running, and I found that my ship was almost topheavy. In fact, it would roll and just hang. We didn't know whether it was going over or whether it was coming back. I was scared to death, frankly, the whole way up because it was very frightening. I think my ship must have been pretty close to losing its stability. But I made the best speed I could, 20-25 knots.

On the way up there, coming in to the Solomon Islands, my radar picked up two ships ahead coming toward us in black night and, since the Japs were the only ones who had many ships around there, I was sure they were Japs. But just before we got to them we ran into a heavy thunder squall and sped between the two of them. They were about 2,000 yards apart. My gunnery officer, Dick Pratt, saying to me all the time, "I'm on one of them, Captain, I'm ready to open fire any time you give the word."

I said, "No, don't open fire." We were just a tinder box, you know, with all the ammunition on deck.

I was after midnight when we entered Sealark Channel, which was a tricky bit of navigation. We had been told to make a blinker signal toward the shore at Lunga Point and we'd get a blinker answer. Well, believe it or not, about three o'clock in the morning we got in there, we got the blinker answer, and pretty soon a lot of Higgins boats came out manned by Marines. They got alongside and started throwing this ammunition down into the Higgins boats. Came daylight, the most beautiful day in Savo Sound you ever saw in your life. The water was absolutely like a mirror. There wasn't one ripple. There wasn't a whiff of air. The two young Marine lieutenants who had come out in charge of unloading operations were up on the bridge with me. They both had showers in my shower down below, and they were eating scrambled eggs and bacon and toast and coffee, and were saying: "Oh, Captain, you guys in the Navy really have it good. We saw those sheets on your bed down there on your bunk, and that shower. We haven't had a shower like that for months and months."

Just at that moment my lookout grabbed my shoulder and shouted, "Captain, periscope," pointing out into the Sound.

Coming toward us about 1,500 to 2,000 yards away was a periscope cutting a wake with a V falling out behind it, aimed right at us. I was looking right into the eye of the periscope. We are anchored, unloading. However, the anchor was under foot and the chief bo'sun up there with a sledge. I grabbed the enunciator, rang up "emergency full speed ahead," yelled to "slip the anchor." The anchor and chain are still down there. For some time I expected the Navy Department to make me pay for that anchor and chain!

Anyway we got out just as everybody in the ship yelled "Torpedoes!" We saw the submarine fire and two torpedo wakes heading toward the ship.

Immediately astern of Lansdowne was an ammunition ship, which had come over from Tulagi about seven that morning; the Majaba. He had anchored just astern of us. As we pulled out, we saw these torpedo tracks coming for us. One of them hit the Majaba square amidships and sank her right there. The other torpedo just slid right under where my stern had been and went up on the beach. The torpedo was later recovered and is in the Torpedo Museum in Newport right now, today. I've seen it there.

Q: It was one of the big Jap torpedoes?

Adm. S.: Yes, one of the "Long Lances." Anyway, we were very busy trying to get that submarine. We didn't get him. He got away from us somehow. I don't know how. The main reason was that the water was so shallow that my depth charges, which were set on 100 feet, were going down to about 75 feet and gradually rolling down the sandy bottom until they dropped off the 100 foot curve, when they exploded. We never did get the submarine, but, anyway, when we finally settled down, these two young Marines came and said:

"Captain, for God's sake let us get out of here. You can have your sheets and your wonderful food and your shower, we want our foxholes, we don't want any more of this."

Q: That was a conversion, wasn't it?

Adm. S.: A quick conversion, that's right.

Q: Let's go back to Casco Bay now and hear some more about the training exercises.

Adm. S.: We came a long way, didn't we?

We had to train everything, showing each individual man every little thing he had to do. We had to train the laundrymen how to use the laundry machinery. Few of us knew how to use any of this equipment. It was a brand-new ship. And, of course, we fired a great deal. I'll never forget our first firing. It was a night star shell practice to test our star shells, and our batteries. We were off the Maine coast.

On the bridge, I gave the order to commence firing. We fired one full salvo first to see how many star shells illuminated. We're all looking out to seaward, to watch the spectacular bursts. We see nothing. We figured they were all duds. I was just about to give the order to fire another salvo when everybody on the other side yelled, "Look," and there over the Maine coast, about a mile inland, is a whole string of five star shells, brilliantly lighting the beaches as the flares drifted slowly downward on their parachutes.

This is hard to believe. Again our system had been hooked up backwards, and when our indicators indicated that we were firing on a bearing of 090 we were actually firing on $270°$. We were trying to fire east and were actually firing west. Now you'd think somebody would see that, but in the black of the night; a very black night and there isn't a light on the ship, even the officer in the director didn't see that his guns were pointing in the wrong direction. He couldn't see the land at night. It was 10,000 yards away. Our range was about 12,000 yards. I remember it. So we were illuminating about 1,000 yards inland, over there on the

Maine coast.

Q: It must have frightened the natives, didn't it?

Adm. S.: I never heard one word about it, but for months I was scared to death I was going to get a court-martial for this. We found out the system was hooked up wrong, reading backwards again. We had never found that out. You'd think that would be impossible, but with just a few people who knew anything about the system, you can perhaps understand it. Today, I find it hard to believe it ever happened.

Q: Did you hear tales of this being repeated in other ships?

Adm. S.: Oh, yes, all kinds of different things but never those two specific things. Of course, I reported them right away. I had a classmate who was on duty in the New York Navy Yard, to whom I wrote, telling him about, first of all, my engineroom telegraph being hooked up backwards, and then later on about this other thing that happened.

We trained our crew every day that wasn't foggy. It was rough, nasty weather. It was February and March 1942. We had a young doctor, a very brilliant young doctor, who'd been at the New York Cancer Hospital. He was a surgeon and loved to operate and was apparently very skilled at it. He was woebegone because we never had anybody sick in our ship the whole time he was on board. During this period I complained to him one time. I said:

"You know, I don't know what's the matter with me but my stomach is upset all the time."

A few days later he came up to me and said: "You're not going to believe this, Captain, but I've had a watch on you and I've had a study made. Do you know that you drank 42 cups of coffee on the bridge yesterday?"

That sounds impossible. I was drinking coffee all day long. I was just so nervous and cold. So I quit drinking coffee and drank beef tea for the rest of the war. I never had another cup of coffee in the war. I drank bouillon cubes.

Q: That was sufficient to frighten you?

Adm. S.: Well, it kept my stomach upset all the time. I didn't know what was the matter with me. Nervous stomach, I guess.

But, anyway, we trained our crews. In the middle of this training, I got orders for <u>Lansdowne</u> to proceed immediately at best speed to Cape Hatteras, where a German submarine was sinking U.S. ships. So we raced south on four boilers. My crew was fairly well trained by this time. We'd been training about four weeks, I guess. We went through the Cape Cod Canal again. I went too fast through the canal and got a letter later complaining about my wake going through the canal. When we came out through the canal's southern end, about midnight, and almost came a cropper. My exec,

Frank Foley, who was also the navigator, was down below the bridge in the lighted chart room. As you come out of the south end of the Cape Cod Canal, you're struck by a myriad panorama of lights. Every kind of red light, green light, white lights, flashing light, blinking light, on all sides, because there are a lot of small channels going into Falmouth and other ports, New Bedford and so on. I said:

"Frank, give me a course." He gave me a course to steer. After a short while I said:

"Frank, are you sure that you know where we are?" He said:

"Frankly, Captain, no," so I said: "Emergency full speed astern." We got the ship dead in the water and I said:

"Okay, now let's try to figure out where we are." We took bearings on every light in sight and finally found that we were within a quarter of a mile of about five feet of water. If we'd kept going, we would have been high and dry. We'd mistaken one light - my quartermaster was taking bearings on the lights that he was instructed to take the bearings on from down below, but, it's very easy to get confused in that kind of situation. There were all kinds of lights there. So we were taking bearings on the wrong lights.

We finally got down off Hatteras and as we steamed into the area, coming in about 30 knots, there was an absolutely flat calm. My orders were to proceed to a certain latitude and longitude. Upon arrival we saw the surface littered with chairs and tables and desks and cushions, and mattresses, one floating lifeboat, everything. The SS City of Birmingham had been torpedoed and sunk. We found no survivors. They had been rescued earlier. That's what bothered us. No one had told us. We searched for a long time, finally making a sonar contact on a submarine. We reported it and made a depth-charge attack. We got some oil and bubbles. Eventually we were given credit for probably damaging a German submarine - probably.

After the war, the records showed that the U-boat that had sunk the City of Birmingham had been our target. We had knocked off her periscope and damaged her conning tower, so that she got back to Germany about six weeks later, damaged. We had damaged her.

Then we went back up to Casco Bay and finished our training. After that, I escorted ships between Norfolk and Guantanamo and between Guantanamo and the Panama Canal for several months. On one such escort, in July 1942, we got in to Cristobel with our very slow convoy - and I had my ship, a destroyer, and about six little converted yachts which were called gunboats. Each one had several depth charges, to roll over the stern.

Q: How many ships in the convoy?

Adm. S.: Perhaps 80 or 100, maybe 60 or 80, an awful lot. I may have magnified it in the days since then. It seemed to me that you could see ships every place you looked.

When we arrived in Cristobal, I got ordered immediately, by the Commandant of the Fifteenth Naval District, to go out to a certain latitude and longitude where a German submarine had been sighted by a patrol plane. We went out there at full speed and, sure enough, when we arrived the patrol plane had dropped a couple of bombs and reported that he was sighting an oil slick, oil coming to the surface - we found this oil trail and followed it for about ten miles, steamed over the origin of the rising oil, got a fathometer depth of about 50 feet on a submerged object, in soundings which, as I remember, were 1400 to 1500 fathoms, made another run and dropped depth charges. We got a lot more oil. The moving trail ceased. We stayed around there about two days. The oil kept coming up. We took samples and specimens, and sent them in, and we were given credit for probably destroying a submarine, which after the war we learned was sunk right there. It was U-153.

After doing that for a tedious period, we finally - I think it was in August, end of July or August '42 - rendezvoused with the Washington, took her down to Panama, went through the canal with her. When we arrived in Balboa, Admiral Lee and the skippers of the four destroyers, myself included, and our division commander, who was Commander Tommy Ryan, Commander Thomas J. Ryan, were ordered to report to the Commandant, Fifteenth Naval District, who was then Admiral van Hook. When we reached his office, he got up, closed his door, locked it, and said:

"Gentlemen, I have the most terrible thing to tell you. We have just lost the cruisers Chicago, Vincennes, Quincy, Astoria, and the Australian cruiser Canberra," or something like that.

Q: Coral Sea?

Adm. S.: No, this wasn't the Coral Sea. This was the first Battle of Savo. He said: "This is very highly classified, but since you're on your way out there, I feel I have to tell you about it."

I remember Admiral Lee said:

"God, what did we do to the Japs? How many Jap ships did we sink?"

And Van Hook said: "As far as I can tell, we didn't do anything to the Japs. They suffered no damage, as far as I know."

I tell you that really shook us because we wondered what could the Japs have that we didn't have that could do something like this. The dispatch said it was in a night action. Here, of course, we were, starting out for the Solomon Islands and that was a thoroughly shaking thing, I tell you. We drilled all the way out there, making the best speed we could. We fueled from the Washington all the way, the destroyers, so we went nonstop all the way.

We went directly to Espiritu on that occasion, I think.

Q: From Panama?

Adm. S.: From Panama. We went to Havannah Harbor, which is just south of Espiritu - Havanah, I think it is. That's when I was detached and sent up to Espiritu to get the mail for our group and discovered that I just missed that minefield.

Q: There was not much danger from the enemy on the way out, was there?

Adm. S.: No. We went way south of the Marquesas, way, way into the South Pacific. We didn't even zigzag, going out. We were so far south that we figured the Japs couldn't possibly be down there, and they weren't.

Our first assignment after we got out there, was some convoying. We took the Chicago hither and yon. We were assigned as escort for the carrier Wasp, my division. The Lansdowne, the Duncan, the McCalla, and the Lardner were our four destroyers. "Whitey" Taylor, later Vice Admiral Taylor, was skipper of the Duncan, I had the Lansdowne, a classmate of mine named Bill Cooper, who later was Vice Admiral William J. Cooper, had the McCalla, and another classmate of mine, named Merton Sweetser, from Portland, Maine, had the Lardner. We were assigned as escorts for the Wasp, and on a beautiful day, the 15th of September 1942, we had just completed recovering planes, we were turned into the wind, and the signal went up on the Wasp to resume base course, and we were all turning. I had my binocs on the Wasp so that I could turn with her. We had a circular screen around her. All of a sudden I saw a terrific explosion, then another, then a third. Some airplanes were thrown up off her deck, a huge explosion of flame going up, and we realized that she had been torpedoed. First we thought she'd blown up inside. Shortly after that, we saw a torpedo coming right from her at us in the Lansdowne. It was another one of these South Pacific flat calm days when the water is just like a mirror. Oft times there's not even the whisper of a breeze down there - hot and breathless.

This torpedo was coming right at us. I gave a "left, full rudder," to try and head into it, and my exec jumped to the pelorus, took a bearing on it, and to this day I don't know how he did it, subtracted in his head 180 degrees to get the true bearing of the torpedo, picked up the TBS, gave the heading of the torpedo to the whole task force as it went under us. As it got to about 20 or 30 feet from us, I could see it running several feet under the surface.

Q: Three or four feet.

Adm. S.: Yes, and I was drawing 18 feet. The thing dove just as it got to us, went between my flag staff and my No. 1 stanchion, went down the whole length of the ship, came up and knocked the bow off the O'Brien, the next destroyer over.

When we put that ship in commission I announced that she was going to be known as "the Lucky L," the Lucky Lansdowne. All through the war, she never had a scratch from a plane or a bullet or anything. We called her the Lucky Lansdowne the whole way.

Then we went to pick up the survivors. Admiral Lee Noyes was in command of the task group. The Duncan picked up something like 500. I got 447, of whom 41 were officers, including later Vice Admiral Wallace Beakley and Rear Admiral Jack Greenslade, picked them out of the water. They had on oil-stained shorts. During the time we were picking them up - the submarine that sank the Wasp was still around there - one of the destroyers would get an echo back and we'd all take off from picking up survivors and go and try to find the submarine. It was very hairy because, to pick up the people, you had to stand still in the water, and there's nothing a destroyer skipper likes less than being dead in the water with a submarine around.

Well, anyway, we picked up most of the people, including the Wasp's doctor, Bart Hogan, later surgeon general of the Navy - Captain Dr. Bart Hogan. We picked up Rear Admiral Leigh Noyes. I didn't get him. I think Whitey Taylor got Leigh Noyes, but I know that I had seven officers stretched out on the deck of my cabin. We had 40 severely wounded or badly burned men because the oil was burning around the carrier though a lot of these people were burned on board Wasp. Of the 40, only the four who died that first night, failed to survive, and my young doctor who had had nothing to do for months, with his one corpsman - we picked up three of the Wasp's corpsmen, incidentally - worked all night and the next day, and the next night before we could get back to port with these people. He saved all but those first four who died.

Anyway, the next morning my exec reported to me on the bridge - I'd been on the bridge all night - that four men had died, one was a young lieutenant commander from the Wasp, and would I like to say the burial service. They were all in canvas bags and we were going to slide them over the side. I said yes and asked my exec if he had a prayer book.

"No, Captain," he said, "I thought we'd use yours." I said:

"I don't have a prayer book."

He said: "Well, Sir, I've asked every officer on the ship and nobody has a prayer book."

"Well," I said, "get a Bible. I'll read some passages out of the Bible."

We didn't have a prayer book or a Bible on that ship. That's hard to believe. I said:

"All right. I'll go back and make up a little prayer," and, as I walked aft a stocky young man in a pair of oil-soaked shorts came up to me and said:

"Sir, I am the assistant chaplain of the Wasp, Chaplain Williams. Could I be of any help to you? I understand you're going to have a burial service."

I said yes, so he went back with me and, from memory, he gave the burial service, as they slide into the sea in their weighted bags. In three weeks Chaplain Williams was back in

Washington, D.C., where he was an assistant dean of the Washington Cathedral. He was preaching in the Cathedral the day that my mother happened to be in the congregation, and he was telling this story; of the miracle when the captain found himself with no prayer book, no Bible, and was going back to conduct the service, and he just happened to be there and could help the captain out by conducting the service.

Q: What was his name? Do you remember?

Adm. S.: His name was Williams, Dean M.F. Williams, a most attractive young fellow. My mother went up to him afterwards and identified herself, and he was able to tell her about me and the ship. Everything was so hush-hush in those days that I couldn't write much about where I was, but I had written a letter after the Wasp's loss, which Mother had gotten, saying that we had been in a frightful experience, which I couldn't write about but it was something that I would remember as long as I lived. And here was this fellow preaching the sermon.

Isn't that an amazing thing? But this is the kind of thing that happened time after time throughout the war, which turned me into a complete fatalist. I lost many of my good friends, many of them better naval officers than I, others, in my opinion, perhaps not as good. I never could figure out why He took them instead of me or some others. You learn a lot in those horrible, frightening moments of war.

Q: I suppose your capacity as a fighting ship was really limited when you took all these survivors on board?

Adm. S.: Oh, yes, we had no capacity at all. Then, to make the story even more interesting, and this is history, after we had recovered all the survivors we could find and I got the order from Admiral Noyes, who's on board the Duncan: "Lansdowne, remain with the Wasp. Sink her with your torpedoes. Do not leave her until she has sunk."

Here I am with all these survivors on board, the ship topheavy, very little fuel in my tanks - we'd been out there a long time and were due to fuel from the Wasp either that afternoon or the next morning. I had gotten the tank ready for fueling. I had pumped the ballast water out. You know, we used to pump water in our tanks in those days, for ballast as we used our oil. So I was kind of topheavy and with all these extra folks, 750 people, on board, it was very, very unpleasant.

I got the torpedo officer up. It was the first time we were to fire a torpedo from my ship. We had fired slugs, but we'd never fired a live torpedo. Apparently, there weren't enough torpedoes to let us fire any, in the early days when we were training. So we got about 1,000 yards abeam of the Wasp, read the instructions, which were so secret that nobody was allowed to know about the magnetic exploder device. Only the captain and my torpedo officer knew that we had a magnetic explosive device in the torpedo which, when you fired it under the keel of the ship, would explode and blow the hole in that ship. It didn't have to hit the ship.

I said, "Set it for 15 feet under the keel." We set it, we fired, the torpedo makes a perfect flight down to the middle of the carrier, and nothing happens. So we take the next one and get in to about 800 yards, and we fire right at her broadside. This time, I said, "Set it at keel depth, the Wasp's keel depth," so we'd just hit the keel.

Q: Making contact.

Adm. S.: The second torpedo went right under the middle of the ship and we never heard a sound. Nothing happened. This time I said:

"Can you make that magnetic exploder inoperative? Can you get rid of it? Obviously it isn't working."

He said, yes he knew how to do that, and he and his chief torpedoman did something, and I said: "We'll fire these set at 10 feet." We fired the last three. I only had five torpedoes. They all hit and they blew holes in the side of the ship and the ship began slowly to fill.

In the meantime the day was going on. She was torpedoed at two forty five in the afternoon. It got to be pitch-dark. The Wasp was still blazing. Incidentally, before this period I had picked up the assistant engineer of the Wasp and a considerable number of his engineers. They apparently abandoned ship together so I got that group.

He said:

"Sir, I secured the engineering plant of that ship and there's no fire aft or amidships of the ship. I think we can go back on board. I can get that ship underway and we can get that fire out."

I reported to the task force commander that I had the assistant engineer in my ship and he felt certain he could go back on board, start the engines, and either get the fire out or get the ship going astern, which would keep the fire in the forward part of the ship while they fought it. I requested permission to put him back on board and then take her in tow. The answer came back negative, sink her. But she didn't want to sink.

In the meantime I've got this heavy load of people. We are outlined by this blazing ship. I know the Jap sub is around there watching me. I'm zig-zagging, you know, just to keep the Jap sub from lining me up. Finally, at nine that night she sank. Meantime I'm getting as far south from her as I can and still keep the fire in sight. When I arrived back at Espiritu Santo I had practically no oil left in the ship. If anybody had overtaken me I couldn't have run away. I had insufficient fuel oil. I went back to Espiritu at 15 knots because that was the best way we could get back.

When the war was over and we read the Jap records, we found that a big Jap cruiser-destroyer task force had the burning Wasp in sight from the north and was coming down at full speed. If she'd stayed afloat another hour or two, they would have been down there and had me. They got there just after she sank.

That was a pretty fascinating experience.

Q: A fabulous story. Again, the fatalism.

Adm. S.: Yes, that's right.

Another thing. The night of the Battle of Tassafaronga - I guess it was called the Battle of Cape Esperance, my squadron, which was commanded by Commander Thomas J. Ryan, who was the young officer who won the Medal of Honor for taking a naked woman out of a bath tub in Yokohama in 1923 - after the earthquake.

Q: I've heard that story!

Adm. S.: You remember that story?

Q: Yes.

Adm. S.: Well, he's the fellow, and it happened, it really happened. He was a great character, a wonderful fighting man, too. Tommy Ryan. He's dead now. He died in New Orleans not long ago.

We had been told that we were going to go up with a cruiser task force and stop a Jap Tokyo Express run that was coming down from up around Rabaul.

Q: Down The Slot?

Adm. S.: Yes, down The Slot. So we had a conference in Espiritu of all the skippers. We got the battle plans and started forth. Well, on the way up to Guadalcanal, the task force commander got word that there was mail for our group in Espiritu which we apparently missed while we were there.

Q: The task force commander being Norman Scott?

Adm. S.: Norman Scott. I was ordered to go back in Lansdowne, pick up the mail for the group, and rejoin. While I was doing that, the Battle of Cape Esperance took place during the night. When I came back up with the mail it still was night. I ran into a single ship. We had picked it up on my radar. I got on the TBS and, in trepidation said: "This is 86." My number was 486; we just used our last two digits. The other fellow came back and gave the McCalla's number, which was a ship in my division. It was Bill Cooper, my classmate, and he said: "I have Whitey on board. I've picked up Whitey."

Q: You didn't know the Duncan was gone?

Adm. S.: No, I didn't know that the Duncan was gone. What

had happened after that action was that the ships pulled out, they didn't know the Duncan was gone until finally they discovered she was gone and they sent the McCalla back up to find her. The McCalla got up there. The night I made contact with her was the second night after the action had occurred. McCalla found the Duncan afloat and abandoned; dead in the water.

They sent an officer on board, a very famous young officer - I can't think of his name, but later famous - and he found a lot of dead people on board; nobody living. So they steamed on to find out what survivors they could pick up. They picked up survivors for a distance of ten, fifteen or twenty miles. The ship had been steaming and people had been jumping overboard all the time the ship was steaming, being conned from after control. When they returned to find the Duncan, she had sunk. They never found her again, just their own boat with the one or perhaps two officers and a few men.

Then the McCalla and I rejoined our task group. I remember going alongside the Boise, Mike Moran was her skipper, and sending the mail over on the highline and being right alongside that still-smoking, blackened, what was the forward mount, which had blown up with all in it killed.

That was another case where, somehow, I wasn't supposed to be in that battle; I'd been ordered to go and do something else during the period.

That was the time when a very serious error in maneuvering

really cost us the Duncan. The task force was in a line of ships. They had three or four destroyers in the van and either three or four - I was missing, so I guess there were seven left - in the rear. The cruisers were in the middle. They were patrolling across the line they expected the Japanese to come down. This was at night, no lights. Norman Scott gave "column left" to the head of the column. The destroyers did a column left, he gave another "column left," and the destroyers came back down. Just about as they got abeam of the cruisers, they picked up the Japs on beyond. So when the order to commence fire was given, the Duncan was really in the line of fire between the Japs and our column; i.e., between our column and the Japs.

I was told by the officer who went on board the Duncan before she sank that there were a number of 8-inch holes on her port side, which was the side facing our force. So we think that some of our own shells were going into the Duncan as well as Jap shells. The Duncan got off a salvo of torpedoes before she went down and either hit or damaged a Jap cruiser, I believe. That's what they claimed and I don't know whether it was ever confirmed or not.

I don't believe Norman Scott lost his life in that battle. I believe he lost it later.

Q: He lost it in the Helena.

Adm. S.: Yes, the night of November 30th, in the Battle of

Savo Sound, I guess they call that, or maybe they call it the Battle of Tassafaronga.

Q: It was right off Savo Sound.

Adm. S.: Yes. Incidentally, to go on to this November 30th battle, again my squadron of destroyers was escorting the cruisers. I had been detached, with my division commander on board, incidentally, which was a strange thing, to patrol across the entrance to Tulagi to protect the stores ships and ammunition ships that were anchored in Tulagi at night and supplying the Marines in the daytime. At night they'd anchor in Tulagi and they'd keep a destroyer patrolling across the entrance.

So I was patrolling across that entrance the night of November 30th when the Japs came down The Slot and our cruiser-destroyer force engaged them.

Q: And the task force commander was with you and not in command - ?

Adm. S.: Not the task force commander, just my division commander, Tommy Ryan.

Q: Yes, I see.

Adm. S.: He was my division commander, and he was a very

heavy sleeper, a very sound sleeper. We used to complain to him all the time that we couldn't wake him up to get word to him, and he'd say: "You've got to wake me. You've got to shake me and wake me up."

I sent my junior officer of the deck down a couple of times to tell the commodore to get on the bridge or he was going to miss the damnedest sight he'd ever seen in his life. I was a spectator at this battle between the American battle line and the Japs. Over my TBS I was hearing all the orders, over all my circuits I heard all the orders. I saw the shells going back and forth between the two. I saw torpedoes hitting into our ships, sinking the Northampton, blowing the bow off the Minneapolis; the Portland also lost her bow. I'm patrolling back and forth there and here's this battle going on within ten or fifteen miles of me on this clear beautiful night. You've never seen such a thing in your life, and, do you know, to this day I haven't got Ryan on the bridge yet.

Anyway, when our forces withdrew I was ordered to pick up survivors from the Northampton, the ship that I had commissioned years and years before and lived in for three years. She was a beloved ship to me, the Northampton. She sank. Then we escorted the Portland, with no bow, and the Minneapolis, with no bow, back in to Tulagi, and we covered them all up with trees. We put branches all over their top sides to camouflage them from the Jap planes.

Not long thereafter, when they put a wooden bulkhead for the bow of the Portland, another destroyer and I were to take her to Sydney. We were ordered to take the least-frequented route, so we went through a portion of the sea I imagine few ships had ever been in before. I don't know, but, anyway -

Q: The Great Barrier Reef, down in that area?

Adm. S.: We hadn't gotten down to the reef but we went through a section between the Solomons and Australia that had never been charted.

Q: Oh, it hadn't been charted?

Adm. S.: No. We had charts but most of the stuff on our charts was from old German sailing charts.

During this interminable passage - the <u>Portland</u> could make 6 or 7 knots in smooth weather, but whenever it blew up a little bit she had to turn around and back because the wooden bulkhead would break, and she could back at about 3 knots. So here are these two destroyers, we were just patrolling back and forth and I was up ahead patrolling, it was the middle of the night and I was sleeping in my emergency cabin right up next to the sonar, and I woke up like this. The sonar was going "ping, ping," then I heard "ping bup, ping bup." I woke up, jumped to the operator, and said: "What's that?"

He said: "I don't know what it is, Sir. It doesn't

sound like a submarine, but it sounds like something." And here was this funny mushy echo coming back.

We turned on the fathometer although we were in 2,000 fathoms of water. The first reading we got was 46 fathoms. So I backed the ship and we stopped. We got down to 15 fathoms before the ship went dead in the water. In the meantime, I blinked back to the cruiser with the blinker light to stop, there was an obstruction in the water ahead. We gradually sounded around this pinacle. It was a sea mount, which now is named "Lansdowne" for my ship. We named it. It's on all the charts of the world, Lansdowne Bank or Lansdowne Sea Mount, I forget what they call it now.

Q: Was that a coral formation?

Adm. S.: No. I think it was a great volcano that came up 2,000 fathoms from the bottom of that sea. It was a great tremendous underwater sea mount, volcano.

Anyway, to finish that trip, we had orders to maintain radio silence. By this time, it's getting near Christmas 1942. We began to intercept messages from our various commanders wanting to know if anybody had heard of the Portland or the Lansdowne - I can't think of the other destroyer that was with me. Because of our orders to keep radio silence, we couldn't tell them where we were.

Finally, we were reported lost. First, we were reported overdue, two days and then five days overdue, and then presumed lost.

Q: And you still could not break silence?

Adm. S.: No, we had orders not to. We didn't want anybody to find out where that ship was, you know. So we got to Sydney and came in through the capes on Christmas Eve 1942, and my crew hadn't had a single liberty overnight off that ship, either officer or man, for seven months. As we came in through the capes behind the Portland - she went in first, we brought up the rear - I got on the TBS and told the crew that we were in Sydney, Australia, that I didn't know what we had to do but the entire period would be devoted to relaxation and liberty. The ship would be divided into two sections. Half the ship would be on liberty all the time.

The greatest cheer you ever heard in your life went up throughout the whole ship and, as I hung up the TBS, the signalman handed me a dispatch he'd been getting from the signal station on the headland which said: "Lansdowne fuel and depart immediately." This was from ComSoPac, Admiral Halsey.

Q: Gosh, what a let down.

Adm. S.: I looked at my exec and I said:

"Frank, what does 'immediately' mean to you?" He was a great fellow and, with a twinkle in his eye, he looked at me and said:

"Captain, to me 'immediately' means seven o'clock tomorrow morning."

I said: "You know, Frank, that's exactly what it means to me. I'll take the ship alongside the fuel tender and get her fueled. You go down and divide the officers and the crew into two parts. Just as soon as you get ready you can let one half of the ship go on liberty. Try to pick the light drinkers in the first half. They have to be back at ten o'clock tonight." This was three o'clock in the afternoon. "Then, as they get back, the man who's been assigned as each man's relief can go ashore and he has to be back at 6:30 in the morning. We will sail at seven."

He divided them up. One half went ashore. They all came back. The second group went ashore. Every man was back by 6:30 in the morning. After I got the ship fueled I went ashore and stayed ashore all night. I danced with all the beautiful Australian girls and had a wonderful time with my two groups of officers, the first group and the second group. I was the captain, so I could stay. I came back to the ship at a quarter to seven. As I came on board I imagine I was a little bit exhilarated because I'd been drinking all night, gently, and dancing and so forth, and I said to the officer of the deck:

"Tell the executive officer to take her to sea. Are you ready to get underway?"

He said: "Yes, Sir, all is prepared for getting underway."

I said: "Tell the executive officer to take the ship to sea at seven o'clock. I'm going to turn in."

So he said: "The exec was carried back about half an hour ago. We've been unable to rouse him." So I went into his cabin. He was dead out. I shook him, I pulled him. I pulled his hair. I rolled him out of his bunk onto the floor. He was just dead drunk. He couldn't move. I stayed on the bridge all the next day. He never got out of his bunk all day long. All day I was on the bridge of that ship.

We were ordered to go out and meet a big troopship, the Mount Vernon, and take it in to Noumea. She was coming out of New Zealand and I met her and took her to Noumea.

When we got to Noumea I went to see Admiral Halsey and said:

"Admiral, you almost had a mutiny on your hands recently."

He said: "Is that right? What happened?" I said:

"Sir, the crew of the USS Lansdowne almost mutinied and the mutiny was almost led by her captain." And I told him what had happened. After seven months without a liberty, we arrived on Christmas Eve in Sydney and received his dispatch saying to sail immediately. I said: "We almost mutinied." He said:

"By God, I would have. I wouldn't have obeyed that, Captain. If you ever get an order like that, send a dispatch and say why you can't do it."

"Well," I said, "Sir, you've got four stripes on and I'm a lieutenant commander. I can't do that."

He said: "If you ever get in a fix like that again, the thoughts of your crew come first."

Q: Tell me, when you watched the battle between the Japs and our fleet units, what was your impression? How skilled were the Japs?

Adm. S.: My impression was that all the firing was done from our side. I saw almost no explosions on their side, and I saw a tremendous number of heavy explosions on our side. The skipper of the Minneapolis was Rosendahl, the lighter-than-air fellow. I went over to his ship after we got them all back into Tulagi, to talk to him about what happened during the night, and he showed me a copy of the report he'd just written, telling the number of Jap cruisers they sighted, the number that they saw blow up, et cetera.

I remember thinking it was rather peculiar because I hadn't seen any of the Jap ships explode. History tells us there were no Jap cruisers there. There were something like nine or ten Jap destroyers making that supply run. They dumped all the oil barrels and stuff over the side and then shoved off, but as they came down they sighted us and we sighted them, and they let go all their torpedoes and turned around and beat it. They didn't have one bit of damage, I think. I may be wrong. Maybe we hit one or two.

We lost the Northampton and, of course, the Portland and the Minneapolis were put out of action for a long time.

Q: Part of that was our own gunfire, wasn't it?

Adm. S.: No, not in that action. That was all Jap torpedoes.

Q: The Japs at that period were using illumination of some sort of the skies, were they not?

Adm. S.: That illumination was from flares, but mostly dropped by float planes. The Japs had planes that they used in concert with their surface operations in The Slot there, and the planes were dropping the flares. Excellent flares they were, too. I don't know whether the Japs were using star shells or not, but on this occasion I don't remember seeing many flashes from the Jap battle line. All the projectiles were traveling from our side to the Jap side. It was just like a 4th of July pyrotechnical show. It was just magnificent because those shells found a fiery trail as they flew over.

Q: Did you land on Guadalcanal at all during this experience?

Adm. S.: Oh, yes, I was on Guadalcanal a number of times, but not during the fighting. The area was pretty well secured when I would go ashore. As a matter of fact, a year later when I came back with my destroyer, the Hudson, which we'll get to some other time, we got word that we were going down to Sydney, Australia, for R & R, what they later called an

R & R tour, of ten days.

Q: Rest and relaxation.

Adm. S.: My exec, by that time, was Dick Pratt (later Rear Admiral R.R. Pratt - he was my gunnery officer in my first destroyer. I took him back to the States with me as exec of my second destroyer. We brought her out and a year later he relieved me as skipper of that ship. He came to me one day and said, just before we went to Sydney:

"I met a very attractive Marine captain over there at Guadalcanal, at Henderson Field. He and I cooked up a deal whereby, if I could get a lighter he'd put a jeep on it. We might want to take the jeep down to Sydney with us."

So I said: "Gee, what a wonderful idea." We got a lighter, got the jeep on the lighter, we lifted the jeep onto the stern of my ship, and went down to Sydney. That was our transportation in Sydney.

Sydney had almost no gasoline at all, you know, at that time and, boy, were we really top dogs down there with our jeep and all the gasoline that we needed, in our own tanks. We brought this jeep back and gave it back to that great Marine on Guadalcanal when we got back. I don't think even our task group commander knew about that!

One of the first things that we learned when we went back, Whitey Taylor and I, we went back to the States. He'd gone back when he lost the Duncan and I was detached a little while later and ordered to command another destroyer that was building. This time the ships were building in Boston. Whitey Taylor had the first one in the new division again and I had the second one again. We went out again in the same way, only this time we took the battleship South Dakota out to the South Pacific.

Q: The same procedure?

Adm. S.: The same procedure, yes, but that's way ahead of us. I'll stop now and let you ask me the questions.

Q: Did the Washington figure in these operations?

Adm. S.: The Washington mostly, with one exception, never seemed to make contact. On the Savo patrol that I made with her when we were looking for the Japs coming down The Slot, they didn't show up. On a night that I wasn't with her, she and the South Dakota ran into a Jap force near Savo Island and I think they sank the Hiei, the Jap battleship. I think. One of the bombarding battleships.

Q: Yes. The South Dakota was damaged, was she not?

Adm. S.: I think so. Those battleships were magnificent ships. It's just a shame that they never really got a chance to come to grips very often with the enemy. Years later, in the Korean War, I commanded the Iowa.

Q: I know you did.

Adm. S.: Not really a sister ship, a much more modern ship than the Washington and the South Dakota.

Incidentally, when I took the South Dakota with three other destroyers out to the Solomons in my second ship, the Hudson, I led her out of Bora Bora where we had refueled and she ripped a gash in her bottom on a coral reef that I had apparently gone over safely. That took her out of the war for a while. She had to go up to Pearl and get a new plate put in her bottom.

In that same Hudson, when I was taking her up to Casco Bay and training her crew, I did the same thing for the Hudson I'd done with the Lansdowne, a year earlier. It was in the late winter or spring of 1943, we trained the crew of the Hudson in Casco Bay. One time about halfway through my training I was ordered to go to New York, rendezvous with the brand new battleship Iowa, and escort her up to Casco Bay. On the way down to New York, my chief engineer came up to me and said:

"Are we going to need four boilers for this trip back?" And I said: "I don't think so, Gene" - this was Gene, my chief engineer - "I think we can do 28½ knots on two boilers."

So I didn't tell him to light off all four boilers, and we met the Iowa. Nobody had told me about these battleships, the new ones. The Iowa started working up to speed for a speed run up to Casco Bay. She almost ran me down. Admiral Earl Mills, who was then Chief of the Bureau of Ships, was on board, and Captain John McCrae, both good friends of mine, who was the skipper, kept sending me messages saying: "If you can't keep up with us, fall in astern and we'll escort you."

That irritated me. I got my chief engineer and said: "Get those other two boilers on the line immediately." Unfortunately, with our superheated steam plant, when you put two new boilers on the line you had to drop your speed, you had to slow to get the new boilers hooked up.

Q: You were going to lose her entirely?

Adm. S.: Well, we were able to do it and just be able to stay ahead, but I tell you I was right close on the Iowa, by the time I was able to pick up speed and get out ahead of her again. She was going over 32 knots. When I had her I got her over 33 knots, in the Korean War.

Q: Tell me about Admiral Halsey and his command down there. He was in command when you came there?

Adm. S.: No, Ghormley.

Q: Ghormley was there?

Adm. S.: He was there and he had almost no forces. He had just a handful of them. In fact, every time we went around a promontory or an island, we expected to sight the whole Jap fleet. He had almost nothing. We were running ammunition back and forth and doing all kinds of operations in individual ships, groups and escorting our carriers. We only had one carrier, the Wasp, and then later on we got one other. Escorting the cruisers and our cruisers were getting torpedoed. The Chicago got torpedoed one night. I was with the Chicago when she got torpedoed.

Many was the time torpedoes went either under my bow or under my stern in the night with that luminescence that was in those waters out there. We had torpedoes just pass us astern. One was coming up on our stern, we got over a little bit, and it just ran right up beside us and disappeared ahead of us. I tell you, we had so much luck in that war.

Q: Tell me about the transformation that was apparent when Halsey took command.

Adm. S.: Well, Halsey began to get more ships and more supplies, and he also brought with him a very optimistic attitude. In other words, he exhorted us. He had the ability to make each one of us feel that we were a part of his team and he knew exactly what we were doing all the time. And every now and then he'd send a message to the individual ship, "That was a great job you did" at such and such a time.

He just made you feel that he knew exactly what you were doing. He would come up and come on board ship every now and again - fly up and come out on the ship, say hello to you, and you got the feel that you knew him and he knew you. He developed a great esprit. Of course, his cry was "Kill Japs, kill Japs, kill more Japs."

He just pepped us all up, like a pep talk.

Q: He galvanized you.

Adm. S.: He did.

Q: What there was of the fleet.

Adm. S.: He did. That's right. We had a very small number of ships out there for a long time, just barely holding on, and it was very discouraging. In my first ship we had periods when there was almost no food - the crew wouldn't be paid for a period of three, four, five, six, eight weeks. One time we had no clothing. After the Wasp, we gave all our clothes to the survivors of the Wasp. Many of my crew were barefooted for a long time thereafter. We couldn't get any shoes. I had seven pairs of shoes, including my golf shoes, and those officers who left my cabin had all my shoes on. I had one pair of shoes left. Greenslade went off with my golf shoes, my classmate Jack Greenslade. Do you know Admiral Jack Greenslade?

Q: No, I don't know him.

Adm. S.: He's the curator of the Naval History Museum, the Decatur Museum. Anyway, he's one of the benefactors, one of the strong supporters of it.

At times we had very little food left in the storeroom. I know one time we ran through a school of fish. I dropped a depth charge and we collected 400 or 500 pounds of something that looked like a red snapper. We fed the crew for two days on that. We stunned them all and we went out in the whale boat and picked up whole boatloads of these stunned fish.

Q: This is a part of the story I've never had before, the lack of things. No wonder morale was not good.

Adm. S.: Morale <u>was good</u> but we never knew when we were going to get any help out there, or whether we were going to be expended. We never knew whether they were going to pay more attention to the South Pacific after a while. The big war was in Europe and we were just at the end of a long, long string, out there in the South Pacific. If it hadn't been for Admiral King we never would have gotten anything, but he kept insisting that some things had to be kept coming to the Pacific.

I've got lots and lots of stories about some of the things that happened out there that will gradually come out if we have enough meetings.

Q: Well, let's come back to the States to put the Hudson into commission.

Adm. S.: Yes. I flew back in early '43 from the Lansdowne. My exec, Frank Foley, relieved me in command of the Lansdowne. He'd been a wonderful exec of mine for a year. I flew in an old PBM back to Pearl Harbor.

Q: Was that a hazardous experience?

Adm. S.: Not particularly, but it was an old flying boat and you never knew when she was going to have to put down for something. We had one old gray-haired JG nurse in the boat, and I remember we had long eight- and ten-hour hops, and whenever she had to relieve herself we would all put the can in the middle of the plane and we'd all turn our backs to her and form a ring around her while she sat on the can. It was just one big open hull, you know, no privacy in it whatsoever. But she was a nurse and it didn't bother her any.

I mention her because when we got to Pearl, another commander, Whitey Richards, and I had come all the way from Noumea in this PBM, and we were told we were lucky that one of the PanAm clippers was flying back to the States. So we rushed down there and we were the last two people accepted for the clipper that was going to take off in several hours. We were to be back an hour before takeoff. We came back -

Q: What kind of priority did you have on this trip?

Adm. S.: I had a reasonable priority, but not a very high one. I think it was a priority 2.

We got back, got on the plane, sat down, and in about five minutes, the stewardess came back and said:

"We're awfully sorry, Commander Smedberg and Commander Richards, but you were the last two to board and we're going to have head winds. We have to take two passengers off to lighten the load, so you can't go."

I was furious. I said to her:

"How come that JG nurse is up there? She came all the way from the South Pacific with us. How does she happen to be going when two commanders have to get off?"

And she said: "She has a higher priority than you two gentlemen do."

I later learned that she was being flown back because she had cancer, to a hospital in the States. So we reluctantly left that plane, which flew on to San Francisco, which was fogged in, flew up to Clear Lake, crashed in the mountains and every soul on board was burned and killed.

Admiral Bob English, the Submarine Force Commander and several of his staff, including two classmates of mine were lost in that crash.

The next day I bummed a ride for myself, as the only passenger in a PBY full of mail sacks, with a JG pilot who looked about twenty-three, an ensign co-pilot who looked about twenty, and a young second class mech. The four of us took off from Pearl Harbor, and I lay down on the mail sacks and went to sleep. About midnight I was awakened by the co-pilot, who shook me and said:

"Commander, we need a decision from you. We either have to turn around and go back to Pearl or something because San Francisco is fogged in. We just got word."

"Well," I said, "how about San Diego?"

He said: "We checked with San Diego and that's fogged in also."

I said: "We're due there about eight or nine in the morning, aren't we?"

"Yes, Sir."

"Well," I said, "I've operated out of San Diego for years and the fog generally clears around nine or ten o'clock there."

He said: "We have just about enough gas to get to San Diego."

I said: "All right, let's go to San Diego."

So I sat up between the two of them for the rest of the night. We got beautiful sunlight over the San Diego area, solid fog underneath us, we cruised around with the gas getting lower and lower until suddenly there was a little hole in the clouds and I spotted Pyramid Head Light on San

Clemente Island, which I had operated around for years in destroyers. I said, "Dive down through that hole." We dove down, came out about 100 feet off the water, came down on the water and ran out of gas just as we got inside the harbor.

You talk about fate!

Q: Yes. The design for one's life.

Adm. S.: Then I went back to Washington, and I should say that on my way back I stopped in Noumea and said goodbye to Admiral Halsey where one of my good friends, Captain Bill Ashford, was Halsey's aviation officer. Bill said:

"Smeddy, when you get back to Washington, please go to see Admiral King and tell him that we have exactly seven planes in the South Pacific that can fly today because of a lack a spare parts." Seven shore-based planes, these big land planes. "That's Air Force and everything."

I said: "Come on, Bill, I don't believe that. I've just come down from Espiritu and I've seen the airfield there with what look like hundreds of planes lined up."

"That's right," he said, "but not one of them can fly. We can't get spare parts out of Washington."

Q: They were all going in the other direction?

Adm. S.: I don't know. When I finally got back to Washington

I had dinner with Admiral Stark, who had just come back from London. I heard he'd just gotten back so I called him up and he invited me out to the house for dinner. During dinner I told him that I'd seen Admiral Halsey and that his aviation officer had asked me to give Admiral King the message that there were only seven flyable planes. I said:

"Of course, I'm not going to tell Admiral King that. I wouldn't have guts enough to tell him that. That's ridiculous."

Stark said: "I think you ought to tell him." I said, "I'm going home now, Admiral," so I went home. Next morning about six o'clock I get a call to report to Admiral King immediately.

I get dressed and got over to Admiral King's office; was shown right in. King said:

"Smedberg, I hear you've come back with some cock and bull story about only seven planes being flyable in the South Pacific."

I said: "Yes, Sir, I did."

"Where did you get that information from?" he asked.

I said: "From Captain Bill Ashford, Admiral Halsey's aviation officer, who asked me to give you the message in person. Frankly, I didn't have guts enough to bring you a message like that because I figured Admiral Halsey would have given you all the dope, but I did tell Admiral Stark about it last night."

He said: "I know. Stark called me and told me that.

This I don't believe."

In two days he sent for me again and said:

"Smedberg, you were right, and not a goddam person on my staff ever told me about that condition."

They had planeloads of spare parts being sent out from then on.

But, isn't that unbelievable?

Q: Why wasn't it communicated to him by Halsey?

Adm. S.: Well, it's communicated through the various department head levels, you see. It got back to the supply system. The supply system gets it but it doesn't get up to the boss man, Admiral King.

Q: That was a real crisis.

Adm. S.: I am surprised that Halsey had not sent a message, a personal "eyes only" message to King saying: "I've only got seven planes flyable here," but I'm sure Halsey's staff was assuring him that everything was being done to get the parts out. That's the way staffs work. When you have a big staff and a lot of responsibility, you can't personally know about everything. You have to depend on all the people under you to keep you informed of anything that's bad, and very often they don't know it's bad, or they don't want you to know how bad it is.

Q: And that's why the system is not always effective?

Adm. S.: That's right. The system very often is defective. These instances are just ridiculous. And, incidentally, flying back across the continent this time, the second time, I got fogged in in Corpus Christi, and while I was eating in the BOQ there and waiting for the fog to lift so my plane could go on, I was talking with a swarthy-looking officer who spoke with an accent. I said:

"Where do you come from?" And he said: "I come from Morocco."

"Oh," I said, "you do? What are you doing here?"

"You won't believe this," he said, "but I'm a ship's service officer here at Corpus Christi." This was Corpus Christi, Texas.

Q: Yes.

Adm. S.: He said: "I was brought into the service because I'm one of the few people who can speak all the native dialects of that part of Africa. My father was a missionary there and I was brought up there, and here I am as war bonds officer in Corpus Christi, Texas."

Well, when I got back to Washington I could hardly wait. I told everybody in Washington about that, and, boy, that guy was jerked out of there so fast and sent over to Europe. But that's the way things were working. The fact that he was a specialist got lost somewhere in the shuffle and he was ordered to some place that needed a war bonds officer.

Q: Because it was too vast an effort to discover him?

Adm. S.: Yes.

Q: There wasn't time for the thing to function properly.

Adm. S.: The Navy in 1939 - I've forgotten the figures now - but we only had 8,000 or 9,000 officers. It was a tiny little thing, and suddenly when it expanded, most of the experienced officers were sent to sea immediately, or tried to get to sea, or went to sea, except when they had people who were strong enough to hold them against their will.

I'm sure every military man felt that when war came he should get out and fight, not sit at a desk.

Q: That's what he'd been trained for.

Adm. S.: That's right, and he didn't feel it was fair for his superiors, who couldn't get out because they had responsibilities in Washington or elsewhere, to hold them there. But the very strong ones like Admiral Blandy in the Bureau of Ordnance held every single good officer. They wouldn't let one of them go.

Q: He established a rule, didn't he, and King wouldn't let them go for a year?

Adm. S.: He wouldn't let a lot of them go for a long time, that's right, and that's what you have to do in time of war. Actually, if you had all your experience suddenly go out, then you're in a worse condition than you were before.

Q: Tell me what you learned from Admiral Stark that night at dinner.

Adm. S.: He was mostly interested in hearing about the war in the Pacific, and as I remember it he kept me talking about what it was like out in the Solomon Islands and I, of course, was very anxious to talk about what it was like in the Solomon Islands and how happy I was to get out of there. He didn't tell me much about what was going on in Europe because all of it was classified, highly classified. He was just back for a conference.

Q: Building up to what happened the following year?

Adm. S.: Yes.

I went from Washington up to Boston, where I helped get the crew ready and the ship out of the builders' hands in the Boston Naval Shipyard, put the crew on board, took her up to Casco Bay, trained her all over again, the same kind of thing, called out once or twice.

Q: Was she a new design or was she - ?

Adm. S.: She was brand new. This was a bigger destroyer. The first one was what they called a 1,630-tonner. The Hudson was a 2,100-tonner, and she came out with one of the most marvelous things I'd ever seen. I think they called it an SD radar, and that was the most magnificent thing you've ever seen. It was a great radar, except that in enclosed places like Savo Sound, where the land was all around, we didn't get very good pictures because there was too much echo from the land all around. But it was a beautiful thing.

Q: By this time, you'd acquired a working knowledge of radar?

Adm. S.: Oh, yes. I knew exactly what radar should do and what was the maximum we could get out of our radars.

Whitey Taylor and I also brought back from the South Pacific two convictions. One was that we were going to get ice cream machines in our new destroyers. We went down to the Bureau of Ships and fought like tigers and finally got ice cream machines authorized for every destroyer going out there. And the next thing we got - this was sort of a sub rosa authorization - was authorization to fill up our forward peak tanks with cases of beer. We both went out there with our forward peak tanks filled with cases of beer, which we had the key to, and whenever our crews would get ashore on a lonely island we'd give them two cans of beer apiece and they'd have a great time. That was absolutely against Navy regulations, to carry liquor on board ship.

Q: Yes. But you served it on land?

Adm. S.: Oh, yes, we never served it on the ship, we never allowed that.

Q: While you were in Washington were you called upon in any way to impart the knowledge that you'd gleaned from combat in the South Pacific, the lessons that you might have been able to pass on?

Adm. S.: Not really, because frankly we were rushed right up to the places our ships were building. We got some of our experience into the ships that were building. For instance, we found that in the Hudson class there was no outside ladder going up to the bridge. That had been the defect of the Lansdowne and the Duncan class. The reason that Whitey Taylor had to jump off his bridge was that there was no way to get below and his inside ladder was a roaring inferno of flame. There was no outside access to the bridge or from the bridge. He had to jump overboard, and in that ship the bridge was flush with the side of the ship and he had to go over it.

We came down to the Bureau of Ships. We tried to get the outside ladder installed. They refused to modify the design and put it in. We went back up to Boston and my wonderful classmate, Hugh Webster, who was a naval constructor and who was in charge of the building of these ships, put them in on his own authority without telling the Bureau of Ships anything about it. Every ship he built up there he had outside ladders to the bridge on them. We told him it was a matter of life and death, which was the absolute verity.

When we came down to the Bureau of Ships and talked to these naval constructors who'd never been out in a battle, didn't know what we were talking about, said: "No, we can't delay anything by putting a new design on a ship. It's too much topside weight," and that kind of stuff.

Q: That's the value of coming back from combat.

Adm. S.: That's right.

Q: What about damage control?

Adm. S.: Oh, yes, we were asked lots of questions about everything. We had a lot of influence on the development of things like CIC. Originally, we had no such thing as a CIC, combat information center.

Q: No, but it was beginning to come in?

Adm. S.: That's right, it was coming in and we got a lot of our ideas into the development of the combat information center that came out in later models, later destroyers and cruisers.

But frankly we were so busy really looking into every detail of our ships to make sure they got finished and trying to get our men trained as best we could get them trained -

Q: You knew what you were going to face.

Adm. S.: That's right, and we were far more interested in it this time than we were the first time when we didn't know what we had to face either.

Q: What about the crew as it assembled? Were they - ?

Adm. S.: They were far better trained than the first crew because the Navy had started training batches of men for destroyers. They had all these schools set up, and when you got your crew you had electricians trained, electronics men trained in the stuff that was in your ship. The Navy started, you know, about that time when they bought the equipment for ships they bought always some spares for the schools in which they were going to teach the people who would operate the equipment. In the old days, they'd just buy one equipment for one ship, so you had no place to train them except on the ship. But the Navy gradually got wise, and during the war we began to realize that you had to have equipment on which to train the people before they got to the ship.

Q: What was the complement for your 2,100-tonner?

Adm. S.: I had, as I remember, about 25 officers and maybe 330 men. I'd have to check that. The first one I distinctly remember as 282 men and 18 officers. The second one was something like 22 - I've had as many as 25 to 28 officers on board at one time. You see, we carried a lot of extra junior officers in those ships to train them because there was such a heavy demand for the ships coming on. After a year or so these young kids began to get heads of department on their own and then exec and then skipper. Some of them, after two or three years, became skippers of these ships. They did a wonderful job.

Q: It was quite a task, as you went to the Hudson and began assembling this number of men with different skills, quite a task to meld them into a fighting unit?

Adm. S.: That's right, but I had a wonderful, wonderful man in Dick Pratt, who later became a rear admiral. He had been my gunnery officer in the first ship and had shared everything I had in the Lansdowne. He knew everything that we had to do and he was one of the finest officers I've ever met, ever, anybody, one of the finest men I ever met. Honesty and integrity such as no man you know possesses, so conscientious and loyal. Well, he possesses every qualification that the guy you want to go to war with should have. He was just magnificent.

Q: How much time did you have to effect this fighting unit?

Adm. S.: I would say that we trained about four or five weeks in Casco Bay.

Q: And this was all protected, in Casco?

Adm. S.: Well, it's protected in the bay. Of course, when you got out - and I don't really think the submarines were up there because they didn't like all those destroyers running around. There was no merchant shipping for them to sink and a submarine didn't pick on a destroyer to sink, if it could help it. Destroyers are pretty effective -

Q: And by that time they were less prevalent along the coast, anyway?

Adm. S.: That's right. In the Hudson we went right on out to the South Pacific, again that southern route, stopping in Bora Bora, this time.

Q: You didn't convoy in the Caribbean?

Adm. S.: No, we didn't have any of that.

Q: Which is part of the shakedown.

Adm. S.: That was part of the shakedown, but a deadly part. Except, of course, I did get quite a few chasings of submarines the first time in the Lansdowne and got credit for probably destroying one and actually sinking another.

Q: There were plenty of them down around that area at that time?

Adm. S.: That's right.

Q: So, you went through Panama?

Adm. S.: We went through Panama, through Bora Bora, where we lost the South Dakota when she ripped out part of her bottom on that coral head, and went on back to the same stamping ground, Guadalcanal, Espiritu Santo. One of the first things I did when I got out there was to escort the Marines in to Bougainville for the landing there. My assignment there was particularly interesting because I was the lead destroyer responsible for the navigation and leading-in of all the transports.

We had had a submarine up there for reconnaissance purposes before the landing. She had reported that the charts were very inaccurate, that the shoreline was in places as much as six to seven miles from where it was supposed to be. In other words, on the chart the shoreline was shown sometimes as much as six miles away from where it really was. That was very disquieting. Also, it reported numerous coral heads in the bay that we had to go into, Empress Augusta Bay, going into Bougainville.

The night that we headed in to Bougainville, my *Hudson* was the lead destroyer with the transports in column following behind me. We were all darkened, of course, except for a little blinker light, a little tube on the stern. I had a war correspondent assigned me who stood up on the bridge with me and got more and more nervous and made me more and more nervous. My exec, Dick Pratt, who was also the navigator, was down below, two decks below on this type of destroyer, sang up to me in this agonized voice:

"Captain, can't you sight anything yet? We're already two miles on dry land on my chart."

Then we'd see the glowing light of this big volcano up there in Bougainville, way up there in the clouds, just a little thing up there. My sounding gear began picking up coral heads and we changed course as necessary, everybody in column behind me following, to avoid the coral heads. This correspondent kept saying:

"Captain, supposing we get hung up on one of these coral heads, what would happen when the Japs found us next morning?" That's the kind of thing he kept saying to me. "Boy," he said, "I'd much rather be ashore than out on one of these ships."

Q: That leads me to ask what value were these correspondents on board ship?

Adm. S.: They weren't any value to us, I'll tell you, but I'm sure they wrote lurid and interesting things for the people back home to read. This fellow could hardly wait to get off the ship when it was all over. We got in and we went in toward the beach, then we turned hard left and paralleled the beach. The transports all anchored and the destroyers went out and patrolled to seaward again; to protect them from seaward.

Early the next morning a mess of Bettys came over and bombed our formation. We got underway, went out, and fortunately the Japs were a very untrained bunch because I don't think I saw a bomb land closer than 500 yards to any ship in the formation. Nobody was hit, including one ship that had run aground on one of the coral heads - one of the transports.

Q: Does this indicate the fact that the Japs' trained pilots were beginning to diminish?

Adm. S.: Oh, yes.

Q: And they had to put in second-stringers?

Adm. S.: Yes, I'm sure of that. In fact, one Jap pilot who was shot down, his log, which was picked up later, showed that he had come right out of training, been put in a plane and flown down the island chain, and was down on this mission, all in about a week. He didn't know anything about anything, except how to fly that plane.

Q: One more question about the correspondents. You said that they would send lurid stories back to the States, was this not one way of publicizing the herioc actions of the Navy, in spite of Admiral King?

Adm. S.: Yes, I think it was, and I suspect that it was Forrestal perhaps who was pricking Admiral King to release some of these things. I suspect that. Of course, I don't know what stories were released back in the States because we never got to read the newspapers. We never saw them. Maybe their dispatches weren't published. I don't have any idea. In the early days, I don't know that they were. They were heavily censored in many cases.

Q: Yes. In that area, did you have any contact or were you the recipient of any information supplied by the coast watchers?

Adm. S.: Yes, we were on many occasions, although frankly they didn't supply it to us directly. They would supply it to, say, Kelly Turner or Admiral Wilkinson, who was on Guadalcanal, and they would tell us that a certain force would be coming down at a certain time so that our force could go up to meet them.

On one occasion after the initial landing at Empress Augusta Bay, we went on back down and I was ordered to be a part of the escort - in fact, I was in command of the escort - of the first LST resupply echelon for the Marines on Bougainville in Empress Augusta Bay. During the course of our going up, it turned out that the convoy commander was a man two classes ahead of me at the Naval Academy, whom we both assumed was the commander, he was designated the commander but we found out later that he had been passed over a couple of times and I was way senior to him. We didn't know that at the time. Anyway, I was the escort commander. Before we went up there, I'd gone over my charts with this other man - he was class of '24 but I can't think of his name now - we had gone over the route we expected to take. He told me where he was going, and of course he was the convoy commander, as far as I was concerned. I went over to a survey ship we had in the area, surveying around there because on all of our charts they had little dotted circles saying, for instance, "Victoria Shoals, P.D." That meant "position doubtful" but somebody had reported it in that area once in the last fifty years, or something like that. Quite often the shorelines were dotted which meant that they were there someplace but we weren't sure just where they were.

Q: They came originally from British sources?

Adm. S.: From German. We may have gotten them through the British, but the Germans originally, the old German sailing-ship captains did many of them.

I talked to the skipper of the survey ship to ask if he had been able to locate Victoria Shoals shown on my chart with a P.D. on it, a dotted line.

"No," he said, "we've searched the whole area and we can't find them."

Fine, I said, because it was fairly close to where we were going.

We got underway one morning about four o'clock and by the time we're headed up around the Russell Islands, north of the Solomon Islands, I'm out on the starboard wing, starboard side of the convoy, nearest the islands, and it's beautiful, about eight o'clock in the morning. I go down to my cabin and just as I get firmly seated on the throne, the whole ship jumps up and down and shakes and shudders. I thought we'd been torpedoed. I rush up to the bridge and I say to the officer of the deck, "Did we get torpedoed? Where did the torpedo hit?"

He was speechless. I looked over and we were right on top of this huge coral head that looks only 12 or 14 feet under the water, or 15, and my propellers are drawing $18\frac{1}{2}$

feet. We're bumping along the top of this coral head. When we finally slide off into deep water the ship was jumping - literally shaking all over. We could hardly talk in that ship for days because she was going up and down all the time, vibrating and with our bent props and shafts. We couldn't go very fast, but we had to proceed on up to Empress Augusta Bay.

We finally got relieved and I was sent in to one of the floating dry docks down in Havannah Harbor, Efate, where I got new propellors. I made a long report of my grounding, turned it in to Admiral Wilkinson, and he read it and said, "Very interesting," tore it up and threw it in the waste basket. I thought this was the end of my career. I'd grounded my ship.

Q: You started to say something about coast watchers.

Adm. S.: That's right. The coast watches used to report, as you well know, anything coming down The Slot. We individual ships never had individual contact with the coast watchers, but we were told where to go at what time, just the way, later on when I was back in combat intelligence, when I would know a position of a Japanese submarine I would never tell one of our escort ships near there about it, but I would tell them to patrol in the area of such and such, and they would go there and generally get the Jap sub.

You know that magnificent exploit by USS *England*, in

which she knocked off those six Jap subs in a line. We in combat intelligence in Washington know exactly where those subs were.

Q: Marvelous intelligence.

Adm. S.: It was. We could never have won the war without it, never. We wouldn't have had a prayer. The Japs would have surprised us at Midway, they would have captured the Hawaiian Islands next, and we couldn't have done a thing about it, in my opinion.

One of the most interesting experiences I had later when I was chief of staff of Task Force 39 riding the cruiser Montpelier was when I had Morison, the great historian –

Q: Sam Morison?

Adm. S.: Sam Morison, as my roommate for about ten days when we were patrolling south of Rabaul. I found him one of the most fascinating people I'd ever met in my life. Of course, I've read not all, because I can't read as fast as he can write apparently, but I've read many of his works and find them all fascinating. He had my upper bunk for quite a few days in the Montpelier, and I often think why wasn't I gentleman enough to let him have the lower bunk! He was a lot older than I was. I don't know, I can't imagine why I didn't give him the lower bunk. Probably because I was on call all night long and had to get in and out of the bunk in a hurry.

Interview No. 3 with Vice Admiral William R. Smedberg III
U.S. Navy (Retired)

Place: The Nimitz Library, Annapolis, Maryland

Date: 9 June 1976

Subject: Biography

By: John T. Mason, Jr.


Q: When we broke off last time, you were in the South Pacific with the Hudson and you were involved in the Bougainville activities, landing Marines and that sort of thing. Now, if you will take up your story from that point?

Adm. S.: That's a big jump.

Q: You were escorting and involved in operations in The Slot down in that part of the world.

Adm. S.: That's right, and one day - I guess probably it was in December or early January of 1944, as I steamed into Purvis Bay, the signal was flying for the commanding officer to report on board the flagship of the Senior Officer Present Afloat, who was Admiral Tip Merrill in the Montpelier.

After we had gone alongside the tanker, I got in my gig and went over to call on the admiral, whom I had met just once.

Q: But whose reputation you knew!

Adm. S.: Oh, I knew his reputation, yes. He headed that wonderful Augusta Bay action several months before and he stood very high in the estimate of all of us as one of the top fighting commanders in the South Pacific.

I was met by Bill Brown, who was his chief of staff, the same Bill Brown who later was skipper of the Missouri when she went on a mud flat in Norfolk. He took me into the admiral's cabin and the admiral said: "Sit down, Commander Smedberg, and have a cup of coffee." He went on:

"I looked up your record and you've been pretty lucky. You've had command of two destroyers out here, the Lansdowne and the Hudson, haven't you?"

I said, "Yes, Sir."

"You're enjoying it?" he said, and I said:

"Yes, I am, very much."

"Well," he said, "how would you like to come over here as my chief of staff?"

I said: "Frankly, Admiral, since you've asked me, I wouldn't like it because I've had so much staff duty. I've already had more staff duty than I think most officers have in a lifetime."

"Yes," he said, "I appreciate that, but you've been in command now of two ships and here's a dispatch that I've prepared to send back to Washington. I'd like you to read it."

The dispatch said that he requested that I be the relief

of Captain Brown, that I had told him that my executive officer was qualified to command the Hudson, and that I was willing to accept the assignment. I read it and smiled, and he was grinning at me. He said:

"Is there anything in there that is not all right?"

I said: "Well, Sir, I really would enjoy working for you but I don't want to be on a staff again. I love being in command of my ship and I'd like very much to tell you that I'd rather stay where I am."

"I thought you'd say that," he said, "but I'm going to send this, anyway. It is true that your executive officer is qualified to command your ship, isn't it?"

I said: "Yes, he certainly is. He was my gunnery officer in the Lansdowne and my executive officer in the Hudson, Lieutenant Commander R. R. Pratt (later Rear Admiral Pratt). He's eminently and thoroughly qualified to command the ship."

So he said: "Well, I'm going to send this."

I really didn't know what else I could say. I'd said all I could. Within forty-eight hours I got orders detaching me and to report on board the flagship, the Montpelier, as relief of Captain Brown, chief of staff to CTF 39.

Q: That's one of the penalties an effective officer has to pay, isn't it!

Adm. S.: I don't know about that but I know that Bill Brown and I had only about two days together, as I remember it, before he was detached and came back to the States. I think he was going to get command of a ship, and he told me, just the last thing:

"You'll find that working for Admiral Merrill is a perfectly delightful experience, but there's one thing I want to tell you about it. You go ashore to the club every night you're in port. He loves everybody. He loves people and he'll have a drink with anybody who wants to drink with him. He'll never leave the club until he has to, when there isn't anybody left there."

Q: He was very gregarious.

Adm. S.: Very gregarious, yes. And Brown said:

"One of your problems is to get him to go back to the ship because he's having such a good time he doesn't want to go back to the ship."

I found that was true. He had a perfectly wonderful time. I never had but two drinks. It was a rule I established early in my life because, frankly, when I have more than two drinks I felt a little tiddly and I don't like to feel that way -

Q: You lost your effectiveness?

Adm. S.: Yes - so I had a rule. He used to call me a killjoy and a wet blanket. He and I would end up being the only people left in the Round Bay Club or the Ironbottom Bay Club or one of the clubs up The Slot, and he'd say:

"My God. Smeddy, you're the biggest wet blanket I've ever been shipmates with. Okay. We might as well go back to the ship if you won't have another drink."

But he was the most marvelous fellow to work for you can imagine.

Q: And his drinking at night didn't affect his activity in the day?

Adm. S.: Oh, no, he never got tight. He just got more and more convivial. I never saw him what you might call "under the influence." He just seemed to get happier and more talkative and he enjoyed life more the more he drank.

Q: It was his way of relaxing, I suppose.

Adm. S.: Yes, it was his way of relaxing.

I found very soon that he expected his chief of staff to do a lot of things that the rest of the squadron didn't realize the chief of staff was doing. For instance, when we would come back from a run up The Slot and we'd get within maybe an hour of Purvis Bay, which was our base, he'd say:

"Okay, Smeddy, I'm going in and take a nap. Take the ships in and let me know if anything unusual happens."

I think about the first time I had that responsibility

of taking the ships in, assigning the berths, and so forth, the Cleveland, which was commanded by Captain Shepherd, had a hard time getting alongside the tanker after we got in. The first thing we always did when we came back from a run was top off with fuel oil because Tip Merrill always had his ships ready to go. At the drop of a hat, we were ready to go. The Cleveland had a terrible time getting alongside the tanker. I stood up there on our flag bridge and watched them. When they finally got alongside the tanker, I saw the gig leave the Cleveland and it came over. Captain Shepherd came on board. I greeted him at the head of the gangway and he said he wanted to see the admiral immediately. I said:

"Well, Sir, the admiral is resting right now and he'd rather not be disturbed."

He said: "Well, I want to see him right now. It's very important that I see him."

So I went in and roused Admiral Merrill; he came out into his main cabin, and Captain Shepherd said:

"Sir, I want to apologize for that perfectly terrible landing," and then he went on and on with a lot of excuses. Tip just listened to him and nodded. Finally, Shepherd left and he said to me:

"What did he do that was so bad?"

"Well," I said, "Sir, I wouldn't have mentioned it, but he made a perfectly lousy landing alongside the tanker. It was just inexcusable."

"What the hell did he come over and tell me about it for?"

I said: "I don't have any idea. I think he thought you were standing up on the bridge watching."

Q: I'm sure he must have!

Adm. S.: I wouldn't have mentioned it.

Q: No, for fear it might get into his fitness report?

Adm. S.: Sure, everybody has problems from time to time. He just had a combination of wind and tide that made it difficult for him to get alongside. But he was so afraid he'd made a bad impression on the admiral that he completely ensured that it would get into his fitness report at some time, which I believe it later did.

Q: Just as a footnote, what about Captain Brown? He must have been an effective officer?

Adm. S.: Very. He was a very fine officer. I only know from hearsay that when he ran aground in the Missouri I think the only thing he said at the time was that his officers had let him down. He had his full navigating staff on the bridge and they just got that Wolftrap Buoy, or whatever it's called, on the starboard bow and you've got to keep it on the port bow always, and nobody noticed it and they just plowed up on a mud bank.

I know, years later, when I was ordered to command the Iowa the chief of naval operations called me into his office and said:

"Now, Smeddy, you go out there and get the Iowa and put her back in commission, but under no circumstances are you to run that ship aground. We don't want another Missouri. No matter what orders you get, if you don't think there's sufficient water for you to carry out the orders, don't do it, don't carry them out, and I'll back you in any decision you make." Which later on I had occasion to remember.

Q: It was useful, was it?

Adm. S.: Very useful to me, yes. On one occasion I didn't quite have the moral courage to do what he told me and I got away with it. On the other occasion I did have the courage and got in a little trouble but it worked out all right. I don't know whether you want me to mention those occasions now or later?

Q: You might as well, since you are talking about them, yes.

Adm. S.: When I was told that I was to put the battleship Iowa in commission, it was after I'd been head of a department at the Naval Academy in June, 1951. I'd had orders to command the cruiser Columbus, which was the flagship of the Sixth Fleet. I was absolutely delighted with the orders. I had sent my express shipment over to the Med already, when I got a phone call from the detail officer in BuPers, who was then Frank T. Watkins, later a vice admiral. He said:

"Smeddy, I've got some startling news for you."

I said: "What's that?"

"Well," he said, "your orders to command the Columbus have just been canceled.

That was a terrible blow to me and I said: "Oh, my gosh, what have I done?"

"You haven't done anything," he said, "but they've decided that you're going to command the battleship Iowa."

Q: This was for the Korean War?

Adm. S.: Yes, it was during the Korean War. I was absolutely stunned.

Q: She'd been in mothballs, hadn't she?

Adm. S.: Yes, and I hadn't been in a battleship since the New Mexico in 1927, and I said:

"Where in the world is the Iowa?

He said: "I'm not sure where she is. She's in mothballs someplace."

They finally located her at Hunter's Point and I was

sent out there to get the ship in commission as soon as possible. They took the enlisted group that had been trained in various schools for either the Bremerton or the Pittsburgh, which were new cruisers working up, and they took the officer group who were all trained for either the Bremerton or the Pittsburgh - I forget now which it was - and changed all their orders and ordered them to the Iowa. They reported about the same time I did at Hunter's Point, San Francisco.

Within a very short time, I think it was less than three weeks, we had that ship manned and operating.

Q: She must have been maintained fairly well?

Adm. S.: Yes. She had been mothballed. We just opened her up and started operating with her. The first orders I got were to take her and work her up to, as I remember, about 20 knots in San Francisco Bay. They were a little afraid she might break down so they didn't want her to go out into the open. Everyone was trying to get her in commission quickly. Those were the orders from Washington. They wanted her to run around inside the bay to see if there was going to be a machinery breakdown where she could anchor if anything happened.

I didn't want to do it because San Francisco is a very tricky bay. It's full of mud flats. They've got a lot of currents in there that are hard to figure. The current rushes in and out under the Golden Gate Bridge and around

Alcatraz. My instinct told me not to do it, but when you have someone senior to you tell you that that's what they expect you to do, I agreed to do it. So my navigator and I worked out a course around the bay and around past Alcatraz, close to the Golden Gate, and then back around. We ran around two or three times, and several times the current caught us and once I was sure we were going to hit the shore off Alcatraz. We were just being set right on. There wasn't anything I could do. We didn't strike. We didn't hit. We didn't scrape, by, I'm sure, a few feet!

The next day I was calling on Admiral Nimitz, who was living in his home in Berkeley which overlooked the bay, and he said:

"Smedberg, I saw you taking the <u>Iowa</u> round that bay yesterday, and I've never seen such a foolhardy stunt in my life. Why did you do it?"

Well, I said: "I had orders to do it, Admiral. He said: "You shouldn't do it. You should have said you wouldn't do it. We've had many battleships go aground in San Francisco Bay through the years. The currents are tricky, the mud flats shift in there. You were very lucky you didn't go aground. You should have refused to do it."

I said: "Admiral Nimitz, you're a five-star admiral. I'm a young captain. Who am I going to refuse to?"

He said:

"Smedberg, you've got to think about the safety of that ship. You shouldn't have done it."

Later on, when I was having our _Iowa_ "shakedown", I was ordered to proceed to San Diego and ordered to anchor in a berth inside the harbor. Looking over the charts and because I had operated out of San Diego in destroyers, I knew there was a 36-foot spot off Sparrow's Point in the channel on the way in. I was drawing 38 feet. So I sent a dispatch back to the man from whom I had received the dispatch, Admiral Tommy Sprague. He was the SOPA there. I think he was at the time Commander, Naval Air, Pacific, or whatever they called him in those days. I told him there was insufficient water for my ship and I requested an anchorage in Coronado Roads. I got a curt message back saying, "Carry out my order."

I had had a bad time with Admiral Sprague before, when he was chief of the Bureau of Navigation, and I had been the aide to Secretary Forrestal in 1946-47. Sprague had recommended and Admiral Nimitz had agreed that we would not ask the Congress for a pay raise for the Navy. I knew that the reason for that decision, which Sprague had convinced Admiral Nimitz was sound, was that the aviators were afraid they would lose their flight pay if we went for a pay raise. So when Mr. Forrestal asked me what I thought of it I said I thought it was the worst thing that could happen to the Navy. We needed a pay raise desperately. We hadn't had one for many, many years. Forrestal overrode Admiral Nimitz and Sprague. We went for a pay raise and we got it for the Navy.

Sprague came over to me and shook his fist under my nose. I was then a brand-new young captain in the Secretary's office. He said:

"Smedberg, if it's the last thing I do, I'm going to get you, in this Navy."

Well, when the chief of naval personnel, then the chief of the Bureau of Navigation, shakes his fist under your nose and says that to you, you can imagine how I felt!

Q: A pretty powerful man.

Adm. S.: And out there in the Pacific here I am with the same man and I'm not carrying out his orders. I anchored in Coronado Roads.

Q: You thought of this, that he was going to get you?

Adm. S.: The minute I anchored, up goes the signal, "Commanding Officer report to the SOPA." I went the long around through the channel in my boat, reported to him, and he was furious. He said:

"Again you're refusing to obey orders."

"Sir," I said, "there isn't sufficient water to bring my ship in and I have orders from the chief of naval operations not to hazard my ship."

"Oh, hell," he said, "my carriers go in and out of there all the time. They draw a hell of a lot more water than you do."

"No," I said, "they don't, Sir. They draw about 34 feet and I'm drawing 38 feet and there's a 36-foot spot in that channel."

That ended it, anyway, as far as I was concerned and I went back and I stayed at anchor in Coronado Roads in between my exercises. Whenever I anchored at night, I anchored out there. I knew that I was on safe ground and in safe water, because the chief of naval operations had said that he would back me up.

Q: But you didn't have to appeal to him?

Adm. S.: No, I didn't have to say anything to him but I was awfully nervous whenever I was in company with Admiral Sprague, or within 1,000 miles of him, from then on, always.

Q: Well, let's go back to Admiral Merrill.

Adm. S.: We ought to get back to Tip Merrill, a wonderful man to operate with. I was never in any action with him and he was detached not long after I got there and was relieved by Admiral Bob Hayler, who became CTF-39 and who was an entirely different sort of man. He was very quiet, very studious, very thoughtful, rarely took a drink. He would go to the club occasionally. I think he would perhaps have a drink sometimes. I suspect that he had an ulcer. I don't know, but he was not really physically very well. Once or twice during our time together he'd be in his bed for several days and I wouldn't let anybody know about it. We'd be cruising and I would run the outfit and he would insist that I shouldn't have any other captain take command of the outfit. I kept him informed, but he was pretty ill.

Q: Rather remarkable that he'd get a command like that under the circumstances?

Adm. S.: Yes, but I think whatever his infirmity was was known only to him.

Q: That was a pretty hot spot, wasn't it?

Adm. S.: Yes, it was. We were preparing for the Leyte invasion and we were to head the pre-invasion bombardment before the landing, our cruiser force and attached destroyers. We were preparing the plans for it in the staff.

Q: You were under Kinkaid then, were you?

Adm. S.: I can't tell you at the moment whose orders we were operating under. I can't remember right now. I do not think we were under Kinkaid. That bombardment force, I can't tell you who it was. My memory has slipped on that.

Several days before we were due to sail from Ulithi

where there was a tremendous fleet assembled, I was standing on the open bridge about five or six o'clock in the morning when an ensign came running up and handed me a dispatch. It said:

"From CominCh to CTF-39,

Commander Smedberg hereby detached. Report CominCh

Washington D.C. immediately. Priority One."

I looked at the dispatch and said:

"Where did you get this? Whose idea of a joke is this?" The young officer said:

"Sir, I just broke it." It had been in cypher. So I said:

"Go down and get the communication officer."

I still thought it was a hoax. I'd never seen a dispatch from CominCh detaching an officer, specially an admiral's chief of staff. So I got the communication officer up, who was Fred Ruhlman. He came up, rubbing his eyes, and said he didn't know anything about it. He went down to investigate and found it had come in, as a priority.

When the admiral got up, about seven o'clock, I went down and had breakfast with him in the cabin, which we always did in the morning, and I said:

"Admiral, here's something that just came in. I don't understand it, but here it is."

He read the dispatch, read it twice, and finally said:

"Well, I'm certainly not going to detach you before this operation."

I said: "No, Sir, I wouldn't think you would, but read it again." It said "From CominCh to CTF-39 (Hayler), Commander Smedberg hereby detached."

Q: You were already detached!

Adm. S.: He said: "I've never read a dispatch like this in my life. This is the most discourteous thing I've ever heard of, to detach an admiral's chief of staff."

Well, to make a long story short, in one hour I was in a boat on the way to a PBM and headed back for Pearl Harbor.

Q: He didn't attempt to communicate back to Washington?

Adm. S.: No. He read it, he studied it, and he said: "Well, as I read this thing, I don't have any authority. You're already detached. You don't belong to me any more."

Q: What a tremendous handicap to him, though, facing this operation.

Adm. S.: It was a terrible thing. He got one of my classmates, Commander W. L. Anderson, over to be his chief of staff within the next day or two, after I left. I later found that out. I don't remember where he got Andy. But it was an awful thing, really, for Admiral King to do, but it was the kind of thing that he occasionally did.

By a series of amazing coincidences, and due to my priority One orders, I was in Washington in about two days, hitchhiking, riding on top of all kinds of freight, and planes, and so forth. When I got back to Washington I reported to George Russell, who was the flag secretary to Admiral King, with this dispatch, and George said:

"What are you doing here? I thought you were out in the Pacific."

I said: "I was out there two days ago, or two and a half days ago, but here's this dispatch you sent."

He looked at it and said: "I've never seen this before." He was King's flag secretary. He knew everything that was going on, he thought. He said, "The old man must have written it himself."

He took me in to see Admiral King. King looked at me and said:

"Where have you been? What took you so long to get here?"

I'd known Admiral King casually through the years because I was aide to Admiral Stark and he relieved Admiral Stark, you know. I was in tremendous awe of him, scared of him, to be honest with you, like most of us younger officers were. Anyway, I said:

"Sir, two and a half days ago I was in Ulithi Atoll. I think I've made remarkable progress in getting here."

He said: "Do you know why you're here?"

"No, Sir."

"You're here because I want you to go down and relieve Captain Henri Smith-Hutton."

He said: "He's the head of the combat intelligence division on my staff."

I said, "Admiral, I've never had any intelligence duty in my life." I was absolutely flabbergasted. King said:

"That's exactly why I sent for you. You've had command of two destroyers out there in the Pacific in the war, you've been chief of staff of a task force. You know what kind of intelligence you need out there. I want you to go down and see that that intelligence gets out to the fleet. These professional intelligence officers are so afraid of jeopardizing their sources that half the intelligence they get they don't put out where it should go. I want you to see that the intelligence that's needed is gotten to the people who need it and nobody else is to see it."

Q: He did have a point, did he not?

Adm. S.: So he said to Admiral Russell, then Captain Russell:

"Take Smeddy down and have him relieve Smith-Hutton right away."

Captain Smith-Hutton was four classes senior to me, I think. I was a commander, he was in the class of '22 and I was in the class of '26. I was in a daze. In the first place, I hadn't had much sleep for about two days and nights. We went down the main Navy corridor where I was introduced to Smith-Hutton. He very pleasantly said:

"What are you doing back in Washington?" and I said:

"Sir, I just received orders to come back here," and George Russell said: "He's just been told by Admiral King to relieve you."

Smith-Hutton was astounded. He said: "Why, Smedberg, I don't seem to remember you in intelligence. What kind of intelligence experience have you had?"

I said, "Absolutely none." He said, "My God."

I think I did get several days in which to relieve him because I was like a babe in the woods. I had no idea what he did, and, of course, his assignment was the most top-secret - ULTRA One - that we had in the Navy.

Q: Yes, I remember it.

Adm. S.: We knew everything there was to know about everything.

Q: He, in turn, had been rushed back from the Gripsholm!

Adm. S.: Probably. Of course, he was a Japanese-language student.

Q: Yes, and he was coming back on the Gripsholm and had to be yanked off in Rio and sent by plane up to King.

Adm. S.: Well, this whole thing was very hard for me to

understand. I felt that Admiral King had gone off half-cocked because I didn't know, really, anything about intelligence. I knew the necessity of getting the intelligence to the operating forces, and I had a wonderful bunch of people under me. The people who headed the several sections under me were all senior to me, with one exception. Bill Sebald was a Naval Reserve commander, head of my Japanese section, later ambassador to Japan.

Q: An able man.

Adm. S.: Extremely able, of the class of '22. And Rear Admiral Ray Thurber, who had been chief of staff to Admiral Ghormley out in the South Pacific when I had my first destroyer, was one of the section heads who came under me. Stanley Jupp, a commodore, headed another one, and Jack Phillipps, of the class of '18, headed another. Commander Kenny Knowles was the only one I was normally senior to. Mind you, I was a commander. I made captain soon after getting there, but it was very, very difficult. I remember Ray Thurber saying to me:

"If you think you're going to write my fitness report, you're not."

I said: "I can assure you, Sir, I have no desire to write anybody's fitness report."

Q: What a difficult spot to be plunged into!

Adm. S.: It was a terrible spot.

Q: Was there any further communication with King?

Adm. S.: He would send for me and tell me what he wanted. I hadn't been there, well, it seems to me now, more than just a few weeks, at the time of the Battle of Leyte Gulf, when I was summoned by Admiral Edwards, who was King's number two, and he said:

"Smedberg, Admiral King has just sent word that you are to brief the "combined chiefs of staff" on what's happening out there in the Battle for Leyte Gulf, in one hour."

Q: Of course, you knew the picture?

Adm. S.: Well, yes. We had been living with the picture. In fact, I'd been sleeping in my office there for the past two or three nights. I hadn't been home. I went back to my office, got Bill Sebald and all the heads of my other groups and we went over everything that we knew that had gone on in the battle, including what we had been reading from the Japanese, which, of course, I'm under oath never to speak about.

I went over to the meeting, across Constitution Avenue in that little gem of a building where the "combined chiefs" met, and I made this presentation with charts. I was telling about the Japanese force that was coming down from the north that Admiral Halsey had gone up after. About that time, I'm not sure that we really knew where Admiral Halsey was.

Q: Other people didn't know, either.

Adm. S.: No, I know it, and I was told to find out. I can't remember whether I'd found out or not, but I think I did know that Admiral Halsey had gone north after what we later called the decoy force coming down from the north. I said to this group - the combined chiefs of staff - I was briefing that, in this Jap force were included two old battleships, the Ise and the Hyuga. Admiral King interrupted me and said:

"Gentlemen, Captain Smedberg (I think I'd just been promoted) has only been here a short time and he's made a mistake. Ise and Hyuga are two of the newest Japanese battleships."

I'd been out in the Pacific a long time and I knew every ship in the Japanese fleet because we had been kept informed. I knew the Japanese fleet almost as well as I knew our own. I knew that the Ise and Hyuga were not new battleships, but I debated for a few seconds about whether to let that information pass or to correct Admiral King. I finally decided that since I was briefing the top military and naval leaders of the U.S. and Great Britain, the combined chiefs, I ought to correct it. So I said:

"I beg your pardon, Admiral King, but Ise and Hyuga

are old battleships, about the New Mexico, Idaho class. They have been converted so they have flight decks in the after part of the ship. They're not carriers. They can fly planes off but they can't get them back."

King fixed me with a steely gaze and said: "Proceed, Captain Smedberg."

I went through the rest of my briefing and went back to my office. About two hours later I was sent for by Admiral Edwards, who took me in to Admiral King. King said:

"Smedberg, if you ever correct me again in the presence of my peers, I'll crucify you, but you'd better be damned sure you're right. I found out you were correct in this instance. That's all. You be damned sure you're correct the next time you ever do a thing like that."

Of course, I left shaking like an aspen leaf, but King never held it against me. The fitness reports he gave me were among the best I've had in my career.

Q: Did Edwards try to help you in this difficult spot?

Adm. S.: Oh, yes, Admiral Edwards, I think, was one of the most wonderful officers we ever had in the Navy. Under him was Vice Admiral "Savvy" Cooke. When I first reported to that staff I was wearing khaki, which we wore in the Pacific. Everybody else on the staff was in the new "King grey." The third day I was there, Savvy Cooke, who was chief of staff, said:

"Smeddy, have you noticed how the old man's been looking at you for the last two days at the morning briefing?"

I said: "No, Sir, not anything in particular."

"Well," he said, "I thought he was going to blow up this morning. I know he'll blow up tomorrow if you appear in khakis again. Get yourself a grey uniform and don't show up in khakis any more."

I was burned up because I didn't like the grey uniform and I have to admit that when one young ensign reported to my ship in the Pacific with a uniform of grey, I said: "Never wear that on my ship," and he never wore it. I didn't let him wear it.

Q: Chickens come home to roost!

Adm. S.: The next day I had a suit of greys and I reported from then on in greys.

Q: And what about your staff? Did they heave to and help you in this?

Adm. S.: Oh, my staff was magnificent. In the first place, it was the first experience I'd ever had with WAVES. I found seventy-five WAVES working for me in the Pacific Section, Sebald's group. What I would call my flag lieutenant, except a captain didn't have a flag lieutenant, but my administrative assistant, was a perfectly magnificent lieutenant WAVE who had been a private secretary with, I think, International Harvester in Chicago before the war. She was efficient, mature, and she did everything before I could even ask her to do things. I remember one day when the first WAVE came bursting into my office, crying and saying that some other girl had said something to her and she wanted something done about it, I was aghast because I didn't know what to do with a crying female. This lieutenant administrative assistant of mine came in and took her out and said:

"I'm sorry, Sir. This won't happen again," and I never again had any problem with a crying girl coming into my office!

My girls stood watches throughout the twenty-four hours. A third of them would come in at midnight and stand watch till eight in the morning, and the ones going off would have to go home in Washington at midnight, stand on corners and get buses, and go to lonely places.

Q: It was somewhat safer in those days.

Adm. S.: So I was, I think, the mainspring behind getting a dormitory for those girls so they could sleep in the building.

Q: Over by the Reflecting Pool?

Adm. S.: No, it was in the Main Navy Building. We then had a place for them to sleep at night, so they didn't have to go home in the middle of the night. They were a wonderful group and I was tremendously impressed with what the WAVES did for our war effort, particularly in our intelligence setting.

Q: How long did it take you personally to get on top of the situation?

Adm. S.: I wouldn't say that I ever got on top of it, but I got so that I felt I was managing. I never learned all there was to learn about it. I was constantly being amazed by the progress we were making in getting more and more information. In about June 1944 I was sent for by Admiral King, who said:

"Smedberg, now this is very, very secret, what I'm going to say to you. I want you and your staff to get to work and in the next two or three days, I want you to tell me when you think the Japanese will surrender, if the most awful thing you can imagine happens to them in, say, the next two or three months."

I said, "Aye, aye, Sir," went back to my staff and got Bill Sebald and said:

"Bill, I don't know what this means but what is the most awful thing you could think of that might happen to the Japanese in the next two or three months?"

He said: "Another earthquake like they had in Yokohama in '23." And he and I decided, because we knew that the allies were considering the possibility of something like this, that we were planning on sinking a line of ships loaded with explosives in the Japanese fault line, along that fault line, and detonating them in hopes of creating a tremendous earthquake. That was the only thing we could think of.

But Bill and his staff went to work and he predicted, as I remember it, that in August 1945 the Japs would surrender if that kind of thing happened. To me that was the most amazing prediction because that's what happened, of course.

This was June of '45 that Admiral King put the question to me. Of course, I realize now that King then knew about the atom bomb, but none of us knew about it. We didn't have even an inkling. But I think that Bill Sebald with his knowledge of the Japanese, of course, he had a Japanese wife, you know - he had a lovely girl whose mother was Japanese and whose father was an Englishman - really understood Japanese thinking. I think Bill Sebald was one of the most thorough, conscientious, intelligent people I knew. I was a tremendous admirer of his. I always have been.

Q: Do you see him in Florida?

Adm. S.: No, I haven't seen him.

Q: He lives there.

Adm. S.: He does? I didn't know that. I'd like to see him because I'm a tremendous admirer of his. At no time did Bill ever make me feel that he really felt he ought to be senior to me although he had graduated from the Naval Academy four years ahead of me. He had been out of the Navy and had come back as commander, U.S.N.R.

Q: An interesting commentary on the fact that you were the top intelligence man on King's staff and he was not able to impart this information to you and was rather elliptical in what he said about the atomic bomb!

Adm. S.: That's right. This thing was held so closely that he couldn't tell us. I was not his top intelligence man.

When you say "the top intelligence man," I was the head of the Combat Intelligence Division that produced this ultra intelligence and kept track of all the Japanese fleet units, where they were, and so forth. I was also a member of the board that awarded credit to our submarines for Japanese ships sunk. No submarine skipper was given credit until we had okayed it on our board. Of course, we had access to the Japanese messages so we knew whether ships were sunk or not, and we were the ones who would cut the 14,000-ton freighter down to a 1,400-ton trawler. The skippers used to get mad as hell about it, but we knew what had been sunk. Many of the great 20,000-ton liners claimed by the submarine skippers with a quick glance through their periscope turned out to be 2,000- or 3,000-ton freighters, you know.

Q: Yes. The same thing pertained to aviators?

Adm. S.: Yes, the same thing pertained to aviators and aviation claims and to the surface-ship claims.

Q: There was a board for that?

Adm. S.: Yes. I wasn't on that board, but I knew that the extravagant claims made by our surface ships of numbers of planes shot down were ridiculous. As a matter of fact, I remember in one action when I was in the Hudson, when we were attacked while we were protecting the transports in the entrance to Augusta Bay, right after the Marine landing. I think it perhaps was the first re-supply echelon, or maybe it was shortly after the first landing, we had a tremendously heavy air attack made on us. We all got underway and stood out, except for one transport which hit a coral head and got stuck on it. She was just sitting there and they didn't bomb her, but she was stuck on this coral head. It was a big attack but the flak we threw up discouraged the Japs so that I don't think any bomb landed within half a mile of any ship, but there were a few planes shot down.

Of course, after the action each one of us claimed to have shot down planes we were shooting at. I know that there were several destroyers in my division all shooting at one particular plane that was hit and went down. I claimed it, the Wadsworth claimed it, somebody else claimed it, so the reports that went in were at least three or four to one. Maybe one plane would go down and four of us would claim to have shot down a plane, so that's four planes shot down. So when I got back to Washington I was always saying we had to cut the number down to a third or a quarter, for what actually happened. Our people were keeping track of the size and numbers of Japanese aircraft and so forth and they knew that the attrition was nothing like what was being reported by our forces.

Q: What control did this have over the communiques that came out daily in the newspapers? They were somewhat extravagant.

Adm. S.: They were very extravagant and, of course, we made no effort to correct those because we didn't want to let the Japanese know that we had a better idea of what the truth was. In fact, we were happy to have the Japanese think we thought they were suffering these great losses, as long as our own intelligence wasn't deluded. We in intelligence knew.

In this period I had a terrible thing happen to me. I had one or two occasions when I had briefed the Secretary of the Navy, James Forrestal. One day I was sent for by Admiral King. I arrived in the office to find Admiral King very red-faced. It was obvious that he was angry. He was standing there talking to Mr. Forrestal and he said:

"Smedberg, Mr. Forrestal wants you to brief the press and radio and news media at least once a week on our operations." He looked at me and I said:

"Admiral, I can't do that. I'm the last person in this headquarters who should do that."

And Admiral King said: "That's exactly what I told the Secretary," and Forrestal said:

"Admiral King, I've told you that I want Captain Smedberg to brief the press." Then he said something to this effect: "The Japs haven't been able to sink our fleet, but if you had your way, you would sink the United States Navy. You refuse to permit publicity about our Navy. Pretty soon this whole country is going to think this war's being won by the Air Force and that the Navy has nothing to do because you won't permit anything to be written about the Navy. I want Captain Smedberg once a week at least, and before every impending operation, to give the press the background of the operation coming up."

King dismissed me and sent for me later, after the Secretary had left. He said:

"Smedberg, you know and I know that you're the last person in the world who should do this. I have my orders. You're to do it, but God help you if you ever tell them a damned thing about what we're going to do."

Q: He certainly trusted you, didn't he?

Adm. S.: So I had at least a weekly meeting, sometimes two or three times a week, with the press and the radio, the news magazines, and so forth, the commentators. I asked them not to use my name; to refer to me as a naval spokesman. I was "the high naval spokesman." Not one of them ever violated any confidence or trust. Before each landing, I would give them all the background of the country in which we were going to land. Not one of them ever violated it.

Q: You'd give them the background, but not tell them that there was a pending operation?

Adm. S.: Yes. I would say there is an operation coming up. I wouldn't give them the date, but this is the type of terrain we're going to encounter and so forth and so on. This was for their background. As soon as the operation landed, they had this stuff all ready to release.

Q: Did the group vary from week to week?

Adm. S.: Oh, yes. I had all the big commentators, Baukhage and all these people were quite often in the group. I had great admiration and respect for them because not one of them ever violated a confidence. But I had a perfectly terrible thing happen one time.

It was in the middle of MacArthur's attempt to recapture the Philippines, when we were trying to retake Corregidor.

I had a scheduled press conference at eleven o'clock in the morning. About ten that morning, Bill Sebald came in to me with a dispatch that they had just broken from the Japanese commander on Corregidor to his commander in chief in Japan saying he had just surrendered. I said to Sebald:

"I've got to go to my press conference." This was about fifteen or twenty minutes before my press conference. "You take this up and show it to Admiral King immediately."

I went to my press conference and the first question I got was "What luck are we having on Corregidor? Have we persuaded the Japanese to surrender yet?" I said, "Yes, we have," and the moment I said that I realized that there had been no word from MacArthur or any American source telling me that. The only way I knew it was from this intercepted Japanese message. This was eleven o'clock in the morning.

At four o'clock that afternoon, when the evening papers hit the street, they had great headlines "Corregidor Recaptured by Americans." Half an hour before that had come a message from MacArthur saying, "I have captured Corregidor." That was the work of the good Lord, you know. It was the one real bust that I made, and it just came out involuntarily. I could have been crucified for it.

Q: It's inevitable, however, that a man working under tensions -

Adm. S.: That's right, and Admiral King knew it and I knew

it. Forrestal wouldn't accept it. And actually, you know, from that job I was picked by Forrestal to be his naval aide.

Q: Well, Forrestal giving this order to King indicates the fact that Forrestal, as SecNav, had really taken over -

Adm. S.: Public relations. That's right.

Q: He had asserted his civilian authority?

Adm. S.: That's right and he was quite correct. I heard Admiral King say to Forrestal one time:

"Mr. Secretary, what the Navy does will speak for itself. We don't have to blow our own horn," and Forrestal replied in words to this effect: "Admiral, you're going to sink your Navy if you don't let the people of this country know what you're doing, because the Air Force is telling everybody what they're doing, and they don't hear anything about what the Navy is doing. We're going to start telling them what the Navy's doing.

Q: We learned that lesson with Midway, did we not?

Adm. S.: Yes.

Q: The Air Force really won that victory, according to the

press.

Adm. S.: That's right.

Q: And this is when that whole agitation began. I wonder how the president felt about this?

Adm. S.: I can't say. At that time I was not privy to what I later became privy to. When I was the naval aide to Forrestal I did learn a lot more.

Q: Yes, you would, naturally.

Adm. S.: But at that time, when I was on King's staff, I knew nothing about the political situation or what the president was saying or thinking.

Q: King's attitude was dictated not only by the war situation itself, but he was a carryover from the "silent Navy" days, wasn't he?

Adm. S.: That's right, and I remember him saying one time when there was a question about whether or not we should go for a pay raise: "When we have won this war, a grateful nation will see to it that the services get a pay raise." And I remember someone - I don't remember who it was but it was somebody like Dick Edwards - said wryly:

"Admiral, since when has a grateful nation ever appreciated what the services have done once the war is over?"

And King said: "Well, I'm not going to take time from the war effort to go to Congress and plead for more money for the services."

Q: His attitude, in a sense, seems to indicate that he didn't really appreciate the power of the press?

Adm. S.: No, he did not. Admiral King did not appreciate the power of the press, or perhaps he was afraid that the press would go overboard. There has been a lot written in stories, but we always had several plans working, and a good "cover plan" is designed to make the enemy and the people of the United States think something other than what we are planning to do to the enemy. We had some magnificently elaborate cover plans that went down to the tiniest detail. You plan something somewhere and it comes out in the paper and you plan something else, and it all looks like there are leaks, you know, so the enemy gets this and thinks what we want him to think.

Well, King was really afraid that the press would dig out the truth about where we were going next and things like that. And I can understand Admiral King's reluctance to take the press into confidence because he honestly didn't trust the press. I became converted. I had felt pretty much the way Admiral King did about the press until after this experience I had with them for six or eight months and found how faithfully they carried out their promises to me, I had great admiration for them and respect for the press.

Q: Tom Buell was telling me the other day that he, through his investigations and talking with people, had learned that King did have friends among the newspaper tribe with whom he did meet.

Adm. S.: I'm sure he did.

Q: And in a most relaxed way and he talked frankly. But it was only a small coterie.

Adm. S.: That's right.

Q: On the other hand, Hanson Baldwin told me that he learned a great deal about naval activities through Admiral Horne, who was something of a spokesman for the Navy. Can you comment on that?

Adm. S.: I knew Admiral Horne pretty well in the old days when he was the Vice Chief of Naval Operations. But no, I never served close enough to him to be able to comment. All I can say is that Admiral Horne was very much respected by us younger officers. I really don't feel competent to comment any more on Admiral Horne.

I remember on one occasion Admiral Horne pinned my fifth Legion of Merit on me. At the end of the war I was given the Legion of Merit for my work in combat intelligence and when Horne pinned this one on me he said:

"My God, five Legions of Merit. Good Lord, we're going to have to think of something better than this the next time!" I never forgot that, because I think I was the only one who had that many.

Q: An incredible collection!

Adm. S.: I was awfully lucky. I got a couple of them for a couple of German submarines that my ship was lucky enough to either damage or sink in the early part of the war.

Q: You, in effect, with these press conferences became the spokesman for the Navy?

Adm. S.: I was called "the high naval spokesman" or "a high naval spokesman." Never once did they ever mention my name. It was part of my request to please never identify me.

I smile now when I read about Kissinger and his "high official" with the Kissinger party. You know that he himself gave these background briefings, but he can disclaim it.

Q: The Navy did have a public relations section?

Adm. S.: Oh, surely.

Q: But they didn't do anything of that sort?

Adm. S.: What they did I don't know.

Q: I think they confined themselves to awards of the Navy Es.

Adm. S.: That's right. Forrestal used to, on occasion, borrow me. I remember one time he borrowed me and we flew in his plane out to Denver where we had a dinner with a lot of the wealthy people of the area, influential people, at a country club out in the woods some place, or a hunting lodge. And about ten or eleven o'clock at night I gave them a briefing and told much more than I was really supposed to tell because the Secretary of the Navy insisted that I give them a factual picture of what was going on. Of course, I didn't divulge any of the ultra business, but I did tell more than I would normally tell because the Secretary of the Navy said I should.

We got in the plane after this was over and flew back to Washington, got to Washington about a quarter to eight, went right to the office, and went to work. That was typical of Forrestal. We'd leave the office at five, six, or seven o'clock at night, get in a plane, fly where he was going to make a speech or do something, go on all day, then sleep in the plane coming back, and go to work in the office the next day. He was a fiend for work.

Q: At this stage in the game, was he fairly briefed on the activities of the Navy. Did King reveal everything to him?

Adm. S.: Well, of course, he was reading all the dispatches. One thing that used to bother me very much was the fact that the most closely held dispatches Forrestal would put the gist of them in his diaries. He had a confidential secretary, Kate Foley, and he would dictate to her. I knew he was taking material from the dispatches that was top secret for his diary entries. As a result, years later, when I heard that the Forrestal diaries were to be published, I wrote back to Washington right away to the chief of naval intelligence, or the director of naval intelligence, and told him what I was worried about, because I knew that Forrestal had in his diaries information that came right from ultra dispatches, and, for God's sake, to get them out of there. So the whole diaries were gone over and all that material was removed.

Q: Forrestal, apparently, didn't have the same attitude toward classification that the Navy did?

Adm. S.: No, he didn't. He felt that we were unduly cautious.

Q: This in itself must have irked Admiral King?

Adm. S.: It did. Admiral King and Forrestal were at cross-points a great deal. They crossed swords. Both were good for the Navy. Forrestal did some things that should have been done over King's objections, and I think Admiral King occasionally prevented Forrestal from doing damage.

Q: I've heard from other sources, from George Dyer, for instance, about King's absolute insistence that the various bits of intelligence be limited.

Adm. S.: That's right. As an example of that, when I first came to this Combat Intelligence Division, on King's staff, Admiral "Frog" Lowe, who was at that time on the staff - I think he had the title Commander Tenth Fleet, which was submarines, came to me and said:

"Now, Smedberg, I know that there is intelligence coming into this headquarters that I'm not getting about submarines. Isn't that correct?" And I said, "Yes." "Well," he said, "I want every bit of it." And I said:

"Sir, my orders from Admiral King are that any submarine in the Atlantic you are to know about. If I know of a Japanese submarine coming from the Pacific into the Atlantic, you will know about it quite a long time before it gets into the Atlantic. But my orders are that you are not to know anything about the submarine picture in the Pacific, nor is the Pacific submarine commander of ours to know anything about the Atlantic enemy submarine activity."

Well, he was furious with me about that and I said:

"Sir, I can understand your position. If you get Admiral King to change his order, I can do it, but I can't do it otherwise." He never got Admiral King to change his order and, as a result, if I knew the Japs were sending, as they did occasionally, or the Germans, who would sometimes send a submarine around into the Pacific waters, and the Japanese into the Atlantic waters - the proper, cognizant authorities were notified by me.

Q: This was the type of service that you were engaged in?

Adm. S.: Various things I did, yes. But that was the kind of thing that made it very difficult for me. All these people were very much senior to me.

Admiral King had a fleet staff. Seniors were F1, F2, F3, F4. We were known as F and I was F-20 on the staff and one of the few officers who had personal orders to Admiral King's flagship. It used to irritate the other members of the staff because I got sea pay because I was ordered to the Dauntless. In other words, King had a few of us who, if he moved into the Dauntless and had to go to sea, would go with him. So we drew sea pay. The rest of the members of the staff, who weren't attached to the Dauntless also, didn't get sea pay, and that used to burn them up.

I was F-20, my boss was F-2; Rear Admiral Tommy Inglis, who was additionally chief of naval intelligence, and later Rear Admiral Leo Thebaud. After the war was over and the fleet staff broke up, I became an assistant chief of naval intelligence under, I think, first Tommy Inglis and then Leo Thebaud. Of course, all the pressures were off by that time.

Q: Yes.

Adm. S.: The war was over and I don't remember very much about that part because it was so sort of routine.

Q: Admiral, how did Admiral King control or attempt to control intelligence that was shared by the Army when it had to do with some combined operation?

Adm. S.: I can't answer that.

Q: Naval information that the Army had -- how did he control it?

Adm. S.: I can only answer it this way. One of the jobs I had as head of the Combat Intelligence Division was to brief Admiral Sir James Somerville. He was a four-star

British admiral here in Washington, the liaison with King, and he and I got to be very good friends. I was very fond of him, but King said to me:

"Now, Smedberg, you're not to tell him a damned thing. You tell him all he wants to know but you're not to tell him anything about our future operations."

So Somerville would look at me with a twinkle in his eye. He used to come to my office and he'd say:

"Smeddy, you're not telling me everything that's coming off, are you?"

I'd say: "No, to be perfectly honest with you, Admiral, I'm not."

He said: "Yes, I understand. You're under some kind of restriction. Is that right?"

I said: "Yes, Sir."

He knew that Admiral King had told me I couldn't let him in. King would never tell anybody about what was going to happen, and I think he was absolutely right because the more people you tell the more chances there are of leaks. But it was very difficult at times.

As soon as the Russians came into the war with us, toward the end of the war -

Q: Into the Pacific war, you mean?

Adm. S.: Into the Pacific war, right. I was told that a Russian naval captain, intelligence, would report to me daily, and he and I could exchange information of mutual value. What I was to learn from him was the location of all mines and defenses in the harbors around Tokyo, Yokohama and so forth. Then Admiral King told me, of course, under no circumstances was I to tell him anything that would be of any value to him whatsoever about our forces. This Russian came over and he was very cooperative, anxious to be cooperative. He gave us a tremendous amount of information about the defenses of the Japanese islands, which they had gotten from very highly placed people, their people, in Japan. I would tell him a few things that were sort of common knowledge. I mean I had some things I could tell him that sounded like we were telling him something but we weren't telling him anything that he couldn't have dug out some other way.

Q: But you weren't fooling him, really?

Adm. S.: I don't know whether we were fooling him or not, but he continued to supply me with information up to the very end. Of course, we were only in this situation about ten days. I forget how long it was but just a short time. The Russians just got into the war long enough to get what they wanted out of it, which was a hell of a lot.

Q: How did Admiral King think that it was possible to get things from other people in terms of intelligence and not exchange anything, and not give them anything? It doesn't work this way on a practical basis.

Adm. S.: I think Admiral King hoped that our side would be intelligent enough to appear to be giving something and that we would get as much as we could in exchange for what really wasn't secret. And, at times, I could tell him things that wouldn't affect our forces in any way, shape, or form, but that he perhaps couldn't learn otherwise. It was just that I could never tell anyone what we were <u>going</u> to do.

Q: Did Admiral King in any way attempt to check on what you told people?

Adm. S.: No. King was quite amazing. Once he had confidence in someone, he let him go ahead and do his job. He'd give you hell occasionally but rarely in front of other people. He called me into the office every now and then to tell me in no uncertain terms that he didn't like something.

Q: On the contrary, did he ever engage in praise?

Adm. S.: No. Very rarely.

Q: Duty is duty!

Adm. S.: Very rarely. He felt that's what we were supposed to be doing. I've seen him once or twice smile when he told me something that he thought was all right. I remember I put on a briefing one time and when I left the room he said:

"Well, done, Captain Smedberg." That was about the highest accolade that I ever heard King give - to me, anyway.

Admiral King, you know, was held in such awe by all of us. One of the things I ran was the war room, in which we kept on the walls all the charts of all our fleets and all our ships and all our positions and everything. And it was visited by all of the admirals and senior captains and occasionally commanders who were in the operations part of the business. I had a regular group of watch officers in there. John B. Connaughton was one of my watch officers. You've probably heard of John B. Connaughton?

Q: Yes.

Adm. S.: And I had a standing order that whenever Admiral King stepped into that room I was to be notified and I'd be there immediately because King always wanted to ask me questions. Well, King would come in there, I would get there within a minute.

Q: Was it next door to your office?

Adm. S.: I was right close, yes. There might be six, or seven or eight admirals and senior captains in there. Within three or four minutes there wouldn't be a soul in the room but King and me. Everybody else would just ease out. I don't know why, but Admiral King had that ability to make everyone else want to be someplace else, quick!

Q: Did you overcome your sense of awe in his presence?

Adm. S.: Never. I respected him very much, but I was afraid of him, too. Really.

Q: Was this true of Edwards and people like that?

Adm. S.: I think they respected him and I think they realized that he was an individual who would not and could not be crossed. Both Savvy Cooke and Edwards, who worked closely with him as his chief of staff, and deputy, I think understood the old man so well that they got along with him.

Q: When he went to these conferences, planning conferences, with the British and with the president and so forth, did you go?

Adm. S.: No, I was not privy to any of that. Mind you, I was not in any operational part of his staff. I was pure intelligence-gathering and I made presentations on the intelligence side of the picture. One of King's basic tenets was, you do not have to know anything except that which pertains to your job. So he didn't believe in the intelligence people being in on operations or the operational people being in on the intelligence picture, except for getting that intelligence they needed to plan their operations.

Q: That was the basis of his summons of you from the Pacific?

Adm. S.: Yes, that's right, and to this day I just can't believe that it happened. It was so odd.

Q: And no explanation ever came forth?

Adm. S.: No, and even his staff didn't know he'd sent for me. They were flabbergasted when I arrived. Maybe Savvy Cooke knew it, maybe Dick Edwards knew it. I don't know. I never found out, but his own flag secretary didn't know it, George Russell. He didn't know I'd been sent for.

Q: What relationship did you have with ONI in that time? What use did you make of ONI?

Adm. S.: My boss, who was Admiral Inglis, who was F-2 - I was F-20 - I had the division under F-2, one of the divisions, was also chief of naval intelligence, so I got a flow of intelligence through ONI sources in addition to my own ultra sources. So I had all the intelligence flowing in to me from ONI, but none of our stuff went to ONI.

I was on Admiral King's personal staff as combat intelligence division officer and later ordered to ONI as assistant chief of naval intelligence.

Q: This was after the war had ended?

Adm. S.: Yes, when the war had ended. Then I went as aide to Mr. Forrestal. I relieved Whitey Taylor as his naval aide, and on the occasion of Forrestal's and my trip around the world in July of 1947, we flew from Washington to San Francisco and then were going out to Bikini to see the first atom bomb burst, you know.

Q: Yes.

Adm. S.: With the fleet out there, and then we continued on around the world in the same plane. The trip lasted about thirty days. When we got to San Francisco to refuel we were about to take off when Forrestal was called to the telephone in the operations office and he cleared the room. It was the President of the United States, Truman, on the telephone. Forrestal came back to the plane visibly disturbed. They had a little forward compartment for him in that plane and he went up there. After we got airborne he sent for me and said:

"Sit down, Smeddy, I want to tell you what happened. That was the President of the United States and he told me in no uncertain terms that if I wouldn't go along with a single department of defense (you know, Forrestal didn't believe in that) he would transfer naval aviation to the Air Force and he would transfer the Marine Corps to the Army."

Q: Sounds like blackmail!

Adm. S.: It was blackmail, and Forrestal said:

"I recognized that I had no alternative. I had to say I would go along with a single defense department."

During that trip, Forrestal would quite often say:

"It isn't the current idea that I object to. I wouldn't object to a secretary of defense with a staff of 100 people who could advise him, provided he would stick to making decisions that couldn't be resolved between the services. But I know that any good man who is secretary of defense is going to have to have more knowledge than 100 people can provide. He's going to build up a staff that will be as big or bigger than any of the staffs today in the Army and Navy. I know that before long he will be operating the armed forces. This current idea is not for him to be an operator, it's merely for him to make decisions that can't be made between the Army and Navy. Then there'll be the third service, the Air Force. It won't work. There'll be a tremendous, top-heavy defense destablishment sitting on top of the services, and it won't work. It will never work in war time."

Q: He had prescience, didn't he?

Adm. S.: Oh, he was a man who had tremendous imagination and could foresee what was going to happen. He had a greater ability to look into the future than any man I've ever met in my life. And he worked harder for the United States with less thought of his own person and personal interests than anybody I've ever met. He was a tough fellow to work for but I sure admired him.

Q: You stayed on with King until King gave up his job to Nimitz, did you?

Adm. S.: To be perfectly frank, I can't really remember. I went with Forrestal and Nimitz relieved King, but I think when I first went with Forrestal, King was still in the saddle. Then Nimitz relieved him while I was still with Forrestal, because Nimitz was the CNO when I had this flap that I mentioned earlier about the pay raise for the services. We went all out to get a pay raise and got it. Nimitz agreed with the chief of naval personnel not to push for it, and he was a little bit irritated with me, also, although he patted me on the back for it later.

Q: Well, he was quite a different man!

Adm. S.: Oh, yes.

Q: Admiral, was there anything that pertains to the dropping of the atomic bomb on Japan that might be useful to an historian?

Adm. S.: I can only say that up to perhaps within two or three days of the dropping of the bomb we in my branch of intelligence had no inkling, but perhaps within two or three days we were told that a great catastrophe would be brought about in Japan. I remember thinking to myself that it would be another of those terrible fire bombings.

Q: To be used on Tokyo?

Adm. S.: Yes. But not one of us even had a suspicion or had heard of any atomic bomb up to the time it went off.

Q: You knew nothing about the Manhattan Project?

Adm. S.: Nothing whatsoever. I think it was probably the best-kept secret of the whole war.

Q: Did you get involved in any way in an intelligence way with any plans for what happens after the war is over?

Adm. S.: Yes. I was involved to this extent. I can't give you the time frame but I would guess it would be within four or five months of the end of the war. I was a member of an intelligence committee that was sent to England. There was Major General Corderman of the Army, Brigadier General Carter Clark of the Army - these were either brigadier or major general types. Carter Clark was the head of intelligence in the Army. A man from the FBI, a man from OSS, Rear Admiral Wenger, who was one of our top communications experts, and I. It was a small group. I think perhaps not over twelve of us who went over and discussed with British intelligence: their top group. We were billeted in a vacant house on Grosvenor Square, surrounded by guards, for about six weeks, and we worked out the top-secret intelligence agreement, which as far as I know, still operates today, and it included the most unmentionable of all intelligence. In other words, we had agreements on the swapping of intelligence. We learned at that time that the one thing they wouldn't share with us was their commercial intelligence. They have the most magnificent network of intelligence concerning trade and commerce with every nation in the world, which they apparently give to their own merchants to give them advantages in the commercial markets. That was something that was completely outside the scope of our agreements.

Q: But it was discussed within the group?

Adm. S.: Not really. As we got to know each other better, we began to compare little bits of information that we picked up and we finally put together a pretty good story of what they actually did. For instance, they were reading all the commercial cables of all the countries and they knew whenever General Motors was going to reduce the price of its cars, say, in South America. They would let their automotive people there know, so that they could undersell our people just before our new price got out. That kind of thing. I mean it was a very, very clever nationwide system. I probably shouldn't even be talking about this on this tape, but after all, it is history.

Q: I rather suspect that it's broken down in these days. There's no evidence that it's working effectively, at least.

Adm. S.: That's right. I think the British are pretty close to being on their uppers - or their downers, unfortunately.

Q: What sort of an exchange was there? Was there a free exchange of intelligence when you were operating the war room?

Adm. S.: We had a very good exchange of intelligence with the British. They gave us much valuable information and we gave them information. Again, it was only on a need-to-know basis, and by that I mean I wasn't allowed to give them anything that they didn't need for their own operational purposes. I couldn't give them a broad picture. I had to give them only those things that they absolutely needed to know in the area in which they were operating.

Q: So you were under restraints?

Adm. S.: Yes. If there were no British ships operating in the area, I didn't give them any intelligence on the area.

Q: Of course, when their units went out to the Pacific to operate with our units then they got -

Adm. S.: Oh, then they got the picture. We'd tell them all about the Japanese fleet, what the units were, where they were, how they operated, their bases, and what they were doing. We'd give them all that. And we were the people, of course, who were providing the information that made some ships look so successful, like the little DE England that sank those six Japanese submarines. We knew where they were. All she had to do was go and sink them. It's phenomenal what she did.

Q: This is looking way ahead, but when Admiral Smedberg was head of the Naval Academy, Admiral King died. You were going to tell me about that?

Adm. S.: We had his official state funeral at the Naval Academy. There'd been a religious ceremony in Washington and the cortege came down to the Naval Academy, where we buried him. I had invited all members of the King family to come and use the superintendent's house as their headquarters and to meet after the funeral.

Q: Why was he not buried in Arlington?

Adm. S.: He wanted to be buried at the Naval Academy.

Q: I see.

Adm. S.: The King family accepted our invitation. I had said to my aide, who is now Admiral Ike Kidd, SacLant and CincLANTFleet, he was my flag lieutenant:

"Don't serve any liquor to these people because I'm broke." We had just had June Week and the superintendent's funds had been completely exhausted. I had hoped during the summer to be able to build up enough money to meet the heavy expenses of the entertaining that we had to do during the football season in the fall, when everybody from Washington came down to see us. So I said to Ike Kidd:

"Now, don't serve them any liquor." So Kidd came to me as soon as the people started arriving. The first man to come into the house was Admiral King's older brother, who looks more like Admiral King than anybody you ever saw.

He may have been one or two inches taller than Admiral King, straight as an arrow, a fine-looking man, and he looked exactly like Admiral King. He came up the stairs and Ike Kidd had a mess attendant there with trays of ginger ale, iced tea, and orange juice, and he said:

"What would you like, Sir? Would you like an orange juice, or iced tea?"

He said: "I want a double Scotch and I want it quick."

So Ike Kidd came to me -

Q: He was like his brother in other ways!

Adm. S.: Ike Kidd said: "What do I do?" Well, I said:

"Get him a double Scotch and soda but don't tell anybody else." That didn't last. They drank over a case of my liquor before they left. The whole family arrived, including little Joe, the lieutenant commander son, and all the daughters and their husbands. We had a perfectly wonderful time with all of them. They all sat around and drank my liquor. Everybody thinks it's government liquor, but that wasn't, because the government funds had long ago run out to pay for it. It was my war bonds that I had to sell when I was superintendent of the Naval Academy that was paying for all this. We left the Naval Academy dead broke, having cashed in everything we saved up during the war.

Q: Tell me. Why is it that nothing at the Naval Academy

has been named after Admiral King? He is not generally honored and acknowledged throughout the Navy, whereas other naval heroes have buildings named after them and what have you.

Adm. S.: That's a good question. I hadn't realized that. As I've walked around here lately, I've seen several buildings that have names to them that I didn't know about before - Halsey, for instance, Leahy Hall, for instance, I saw. I went in there to find out what it was, and I found out that it was now the old administration, the registrar's office, which used to be in the superintendent's office. I hadn't known that there wasn't a King Hall or something like that. I can't answer that question. I think there's no question but that something should be named for Admiral King here. If it isn't, there must be some jealousies along the way. I don't know.

Q: Well, Admiral, in May of 1946 you became aide to the Secretary of the Navy, Forrestal, whom you knew and whom you admired. Tell me about that exciting period. I know it was just as busy as was the one with King.

Adm. S.: Yes. Actually, it was even busier. This is the time my wife referred to as being worse than sea duty because the secretary was a full-time, seven-day-a-week worker. While we didn't work on Sundays regularly, we oftentimes did. We'd go early in the morning and we'd leave late at night. I was on call all the time. For instance, it was nothing for the secretary to call me up at home, say, at 7:30, after I'd just finished dinner, and say:

"Come out here immediately, Smeddy, somebody's just dropped out and I want you to fill in at my dinner."

Q: You mean at Prospect Street, where he lived?

Adm. S.: Yes, and I'd have to go out there and sit through a dinner, replacing somebody who had dropped out at the last minute, having just had dinner at home myself.

I remember the first Christmas that I was with Forrestal, he called me on the 23rd of December and said:

"Smeddy, get the plane ready tomorrow. You and I are going to fly down to Palm Beach." I said:

"Oh Christmas Eve?"

He said: "Yes, we'll go down there and we'll spend about a week or ten days down there, getting some relaxation. Bring your golf clubs."

Well, I knew he was going down for relaxation. I knew it wasn't on official business, so I said:

"Mr. Secretary, if this isn't official business, I'd like to be excused because I've been away from my family on Christmas Eve for a long time during the war, and we're all looking forward to spending Christmas Eve together."

He looked at me and he said: "Okay, Smeddy. I'll

send the plane back and you come down there on the day after Christmas," which I did.

Q: Does this indicate the fact that he wasn't very compassionate?

Adm. S.: He was not the least bit. My private life didn't concern him in the slightest, really. He had no private life of his own. He didn't get along with his wife very well.

I hesitate to say some of these things because it sounds sort of like gossip and it's not really history.

Q: No, it isn't. It's a part of Forrestal's story.

Adm. S.: That's right, Forrestal's story. It's not history, but he had problems with his wife and I was involved in them. The very first thing that happened to me when I went as his aide, I hadn't been there two days, when I got a call from her and she said:

"Captain Smedberg, I want you to come out to the house immediately."

I said: "All right. Is there some emergency? I'll be right out." I got out there and she said:

"I'm going to have a ladies' luncheon next week for the sub-cabinet wives, and I want you to run it."

I said: "Mrs. Forrestal, I've never run a ladies'

luncheon in my life. I don't know anything about running a luncheon. That's not what my job is."

She said: "Well, I want you to run it." I said something noncommital and went back to the office, went in to see Forrestal and said:

"Mr. Secretary, I want to tell you about this call I just had," and I told him about going out there. I said: "If this is what being your aide is like, I don't want to have any part of it. I'm a naval officer and I'm not going to run ladies' luncheons."

He said: "I don't blame you. Don't worry, I'll take care of that. You'll never hear about that again."

She and I were enemies from that point on. It was very difficult. We had a lot of very difficult problems.

Q: She had her lapses, I understand. I know about them. Did he have an Army man also?

Adm. S.: Who? Forrestal?

Q: Yes.

Adm. S.: No.

Q: He did later on?

Adm. S.: When he was Secretary of Defense, but I was only

with him when he was Secretary of the Navy.

He had a very small staff. He had Marx Leva, who was his lawyer type. Well, he had a very small staff and we all got along very well together.

Q: But part of your difficulty on his staff, part of the long working hours, was due to his own personal habits?

Adm. S.: That's right.

Q: His predeliction for being there unusual hours.

Adm. S.: His hobby was work. He was happiest when he was working, and he had no relaxation. I felt certain that he'd kill himself because he had no relaxation, he had no outlet, he had no way of releasing the tensions that he had.

Q: You just went to Florida right after Christmas and played golf every day?

Adm. S.: That's right. To give you an example of how little home life he had, I think his wife was in New York for Christmas. His two sons flew in the plane with him.

Q: Michael?

Adm. S.: He flew Mike, as I remember it, and Peter, and he

dropped one of them some place and the other some place with friends, when he flew south. He dropped them on the way down because I didn't go down with him that Christmas Eve. I went down two days later. But his family was all scattered, you see, that Christmas. They didn't get together for Christmas. They had no family relaxation. I thought young Mike was a very fine young man. I've been surprised he hasn't been high up in a political situation today because he was a brilliant youngster.

Q: You were talking about his inability to relax and the fact that his hobby and his life was work.

Adm. S.: That's right. He was one of the first people who recognized the insidious influence of certain Communist forces at work in our government, and I think he and perhaps Averill Harriman were the two people who realized that the Communists were beginning to work into high positions in our government, in places. I don't know who they suspected, but I know that Forrestal did a great deal to alert our administration to the fact that Communists were trying to work into high places in our government.

Q: It was in that time, too, that he concerned himself about the Communist threat to the Italian government and provided his own funds to - Do you recall anything about that?

Adm. S.: No. I was on the fringes of some of those things but I don't know enough to comment intelligently on them.

Q: What was his relationship with President Truman?

Adm. S.: I think they had a friendly understanding. They weren't basically friends because they were such different characters. A rather humorous incident was the time that Forrestal told me that it was his turn to have the president to a poker party. You know, Mr. Truman played poker at different places. Forrestal personally did not like to play poker. It was a waste of time, as far as he was concerned, but it was a passion with the president. He played two or three times a week. So he said:

"Now, Smeddy, I'm going to have a stag dinner for the president at Prospect Street and I want you to get Mrs. Forrestal up to New York. I've arranged for her to go to New York. You go out to the house and see that she gets there. You set everything up with the secret service and everything because they have to station people so that no one could ever see the president playing poker or drinking. That's tabu."

So I went all over the grounds with the secret service, learned what blinds had to be drawn, where secret service men would be stationed on the grounds. The afternoon came of the day that we were to play poker. I was to be there and sort of take care of everything and see that everything went smoothly. I think there were eight invitees, including the chief justice of the United States, Les Biffle, Averell Harriman, Senator Magnuson, and Clark Clifford, of course, was the naval aide and he ran the party. Clark never took a drink. He drank milk, I think.

I went up to the house from Main Navy and told Mrs. Forrestal I was there with a car to take her to the train for New York. She said she wasn't going.

Q: Did she know the President was coming?

Adm. S.: Yes. She said:

"If Jim thinks that I'm not going to be here to greet the President in my own house, he's crazy."

I reported this back to the Secretary and he said: "You get her on the train. If you can't get her on the two o'clock, get her on the three o'clock. If you can't get her on the three o'clock, get her on the four o'clock. Get her out of that house."

I went back there. Mrs. Forrestal was upstairs and she wouldn't come down. I kept changing the tickets for the different trains. Finally I phoned the Secretary: "I can't do anything about this." So he came home early from the office, went upstairs. I was downstairs. Pretty soon the President arrived. The other guests arrived first and then the President. The Secretary came downstairs. About two minutes after the President arrived, downstairs came Mrs.

Forrestal. She said:

"Jim wanted me to go to New York but I wasn't going to let you come into my house without greeting you."

Forrestal took her gently by the elbow after a few minutes and took her upstairs and said: "Now, Josie, this is a stag party," and we didn't hear from her again that night.

We had the stag dinner and after dinner we arranged the poker table. Clark Clifford, the President's naval aide, was supervising the putting out of the chips and so forth. I was taking care of the stewards and seeing that they had the liquor out for everybody. They'd been playing for maybe five minutes when Forrestal called me in and said:

"Mr. President, would you mind if Captain Smedberg took my hand for a little while because I have some calls I have to make upstairs?" The President said, "No, sit down," so I sat down on the President's right. I had a tremendous stack of money in front of me. They were playing table stakes.

Q: You boss was a banker, after all!

Adm. S.: I said to Clark Clifford: "What was the stake?" and he said: "Everybody got $500." I'd played poker all my life in Navy groups and we generally played table stakes. We would give ourselves $100 in chips and at the end we'd divide by twenty, so you got $5 worth of cash, you know. I didn't know what they were dividing by. I played for a while until Forrestal came down, thanked me, and I got up and went into the library, started reading a book and, after about twenty minutes, Forrestal said: "Smeddy, come in here."

I came in, took his place - Forrestal went upstairs. I figure he took a nap, he never showed up again until the president got ready to leave. So we finished the poker party and the last hand - I don't know that this is historic, you can cut this out - was one that the president himself dealt. He dealt wild games. He loved wild games. He rarely got out of a hand and he always lost, as far as I could determine, because he stayed until the last card was dealt every hand. His favorite game at this time and it's the only time I've ever seen this game played the way he played it, was seven card, high, low. Before he dealt the last card, we had two cards down, four up, and he was going to deal the last one down. I'm sitting on his right. Everybody was in the pot for the seventh card. Aces were either high or low. I had an ace, three, four, six showing, with two aces in the hole. What a hand for high-low. If I match any of my cards I've got an unbeatable aces full house, perhaps four aces. If I don't, I have an excellent chance for a great low.

The President dealt the last card down, looked at his card and, in disgust, threw in his hand; a rarity for him.

After the heavy betting, which I was constantly raising, the President announced that each one, in turn, had to announce whether he was out for high, low, or both; if he didn't win what he announced, he couldn't win anything.

I'm sitting at his right, with the last call and it looks as though I have the low hand sewed up. Everyone else announced for high. When it came to me, and before I could announce for the high hand that I was sure I had, having caught another three on the last card, the President said, "You can fold your hand if you announce for low, since everyone else has gone for high. You automatically win low and don't have to show your hand." That was a strange poker! I did, and split the largest pot of the evening with the President's aide, as I recall. But, when the banker, Clark Clifford called out the winnings and losses, I discovered, to my horror, that we had been playing for "gold"; that the original stake was actually $500.00, not $50 or perhaps $25 that I had assumed. There were several hundred dollars worth of chips on the table at the end of that last hand!

Q: The pot!

Adm. S.: That's right. Clark Clifford counted out the money. The president had lost $700 or $800 and he was about to write a check and Clark said:

"No checks, Mr. President. No, indeed. I'll take care of this and you can take care of me tomorrow."

And I got maybe $200 or $300 in bills and change and all, which I put in my pockets. The next morning in the office, I went to Forrestal and I said:

"Do you want to see how well we did last night, Mr. Secretary?"

"Yes."

So I emptied all my pockets and put all this money on his desk.

"My God," he said, "what's that?"

I said: "That's our winnings from last night." He said: "Gee, you must have been pretty good." He put it all in his pocket and I never heard another word about it!

Q: That's the kind of boss to have!

Adm. S.: Oh, well, there's not much history to that but it's confirmation of the fact that Harry Truman just loved to play poker.

Q: He certainly did.

Adm. S.: And he drank continuously during the poker game. He never got tight. He just got exhilarated and told horrible stories.

Q: Did you go with the secretary down to the little White House ever?

Adm. S.: No. Frankly, I managed to get across to the secretary the idea that I didn't like going to places just for the hell of it. If I had an opportunity to be home with my family when he was away, I welcomed it. If there was anything I could help him officially on, I expected to go and I did go. Whenever he went on any kind of official trip, I was always there. I went with him out to China, for instance, and on this trip around the world we visited General Marshall in Peking.

Q: That was in 1947 you said?

Adm. S.: Yes. We went up to Nanking and met Chou Tse and Chou en lai and Mao tse tung, most of the incipient Chinese leaders, the ones who were just coming up.

Q: Agrarian reformers they were!

Adm. S.: Yes. We were at a big dinner party with all of them. We saw General Chiang-kai-chek in Peking or Nanking, then we went down to Shanghai and had cocktails with Madame Chiang kai chek. That was the time she asked the secretary what he liked to drink and he said he liked martinis. She asked me and I said I'd like a martini, too. She clapped her hands and a servant came in with a great big tray, put it on the chow bench in front of her. She reached for the gin and poured two jiggers of gin, then she reached for the

Italian vermouth, as Forrestal said: "I like mine very dry." She poured three jiggers of sweet vermouth into the two jiggers of gin and fixed it for both of us. Forrestal said later:

"I always thought she was a cosmopolite and knew everything, but, she didn't know anything about making martinis!"

Q: Your original purpose was to go to Bikini to the tests.

Adm. S.: To Bikini but we worked in a lot of other things. We were going from Bikini to Guam. We were going from Guam to Tokyo, where he was to meet with General MacArthur, and General MacArthur was having a big dinner party for him.

When we got to Guam, there was a big hurricane-type storm moving over Japan, so the morning we were to take off I got up at four - we were going to take off at six - I checked the weather and the weather was bad over Japan. But if we delayed four or five hours we could get into Japan behind the storm. Just by instinct I said: "What's the weather like in Manila?" Now, we were going to Tokyo and then we were going down to Manila. In every place there was a tremendous function given for the Secretary of the Navy. They told me Manila was clear. The storm had gone through Manila a couple of days before.

So when I awakened Forrestal about five o'clock I said:

"Mr. Secretary, you don't have to get up now, but I just want to tell you that the plans have changed. We're going to be delayed getting to Tokyo. I've prepared a dispatch notifying Commander, Naval Forces, Japan, to tell General MacArthur we would not be able to make his dinner, unless it were delayed three or four hours." I think the dinner was at eight and maybe we could get there by nine.

He said: "All right, we won't go to Japan now. We'll go later. Let's go to Manila. How's the weather in Manila?"

"Well," I said, "it's good in Manila but we can't do that because they're not expecting us until a week later."

"We'll go to Manila," he said.

So from that part on, everything got screwed up. We went to Manila, and everybody there was upset because they weren't prepared for it. We didn't show up in Tokyo and they were all upset because we had been scheduled to go there. When we finally got to Tokyo, MacArthur wouldn't have anything to do with Forrestal. He finally agreed to see him but he wouldn't entertain him, and I sat in the anteroom while Forrestal went in with MacArthur. He was in there about twenty minutes or half an hour. When we got out and got in a car to go back to the Imperial Hotel, where we were staying, I said:

"What did you and the general talk about?" He said: "I didn't talk at all. I spent the entire time sitting in a chair watching MacArthur stride up and down, soliloquizing, trying to decide what religion he was going to permit the Japanese to pursue. He sounded like he was God." And that's about all I ever got out of Forrestal about that interview.

Then when we got to the Philippines, of course, I was a skunk because I was responsible for changing the schedule, and everything was screwed up in the Philippines.

Q: Were you flying a Constellation or what?

Adm. S.: We were flying in a C-54, as I remember it, a very comfortable, slow plane. It took us eight, ten, twelve, fifteen hours to go any place.

We flew on from Manila. We were going to meet with a lot of officials in Bangkok. We had to stop for dinner in Okinawa. We landed there and Forrestal and I had dinner with the island commander. The crew ate down in the flight area. We got in the plane and about an hour over the South China Sea, all the crew came down with ptomaine poisoning. They were deathly sick. The copilot was so sick he had to take to his bunk and I couldn't get him out of it for twenty-four hours, even though I threatened him with court-martial. The navigator was in his bunk and I couldn't get him out of it. He was deathly ill. The pilot was equally sick, but he stayed at the controls the whole time, going both ends. I got into the copilot's seat, helping with the navigation across Indo China. I find the Mekong River. It's a beautiful moonlight night. We're due to land at six o'clock the next morning at Bangkok, which we do.

All the official people are down at the airport and we

have a great party in one of the hangars. We were supposed to take off about 8:30 in order to get across the gulf before the monsoon set in. We were scheduled to stay with the governor-general of Calcutta in India. We were so slow getting through this formal breakfast in Bangkok that it was about two hours later than we'd expected before we got off for India. So we got caught in the damnedest storm I've ever been in in my life. The plane was thrown and buffeted and dropped several thousand feet and up in the air.

Q: With the pilot still recovering?

Adm. S.: The pilot still recovering from this ptomaine poisoning, and his copilot barely able to sit in the other seat.

Nothing was functioning. There were no beacons. This was right after the war and we had no radio beacons, no nothing. We were lost. Finally, we got down under the storm, broke out of the clouds at about 200 feet and saw this big, muddy delta area. We went back and forth till we picked out the biggest branch flowing through the delta. We followed it up. I was acting as navigator by this time, sitting in the navigator's seat, or right beside it. We had the chief radioman actually handling the chart. The storm was so violent that we were flying between 50 and 150 feet over the river, just over the trees. The river was winding and if we could see the next bend we'd fly round the bend. We had the flaps down to keep us from going too fast.

We couldn't get in communication with anybody. We were so low that our trailing antenna wasn't working. We finally decided that we were not on the right river because we couldn't find Calcutta. Well, it turned out the radioman was using the wrong scale and we hadn't flown far enough. So we turned and we went 50 miles to the right of the river, fifty miles this way, no sign of habitation. Nothing but terrific jungle under us, this forest. Meantime, we're getting low on gas and the storm is going on to beat hell above us.

We get back to the river. I discovered this mistake the radioman had made in the use of the scale.

Q: You must have been over what is now Bangladesh?

Adm. S.: Finally, we sight Calcutta and we're so happy. We located the airport but all we get is the red light flashing from the tower. The pilot said:

"I can't land with the red light flashing. That means you cannot land."

"Well," I said, "My, God, we've got to land anyway. We've got to get down. We don't have much gas."

So they flashed a message at us that said to proceed to another airport, which was about 25 or 30 miles away, giving us the bearing to it. We finally climbed back into the clouds again to trail our antenna so that we can communicate with them and were told that the official party had gone to the other airport. That's why we couldn't land.

We get to the other airport and it's covered with cows, cattle strolling on the runway. We zoomed them a couple of times to scare them off, and finally landed. Then the official party meets us and we're taken in to Calcutta.

This is the way the trip went. This was right after the war that we were doing this. Many of these airports had been run either by Americans or British. They'd all pulled out and none of the communications facilities were working, none of the beacons were working. It was chaotic at most of those fields. For instance, when we got in to Manila, to go back a little bit earlier, one plane had a couple of ice boxes filled with meats and all. Well, they didn't plug in the current that night and every bit of food we had in that plane, all of our frozen stuff, perished, died. We lost the whole thing because they didn't have facilities there to take care of it.

From Calcutta we flew nonstop to Cairo; then to Rome. We spent a night in Rome, where Forrestal conferred with the ambassador. We took off, went over the Alps. We had breakfast in Rome, lost one engine over the Alps and the plane started losing altitude, and we just barely got over the last peak. We had a very heavily laden plane. I should have mentioned that, when we were on Okinawa, we discovered that there was a great field, acres and acres of cases of liquor, all surplus, you know, and they were going to be sold by the War Surplus Administration. I remember each of us picked up four or five cases at $12 a case of Old Forester, Old Grandad, Scotch, a dollar a bottle. So we must have had thirty or forty cases of liquor put in the plane.

Q: You began to regret it over the Alps!

Adm. S.: Oh, yes. Over the Alps we reached the point where we were almost ready to throw everything out of the plane, but we finally got over the rim and down into Berlin. We got into Tempelhof airdrome where they replaced the engine while the Secretary was having lunch with General Lucius Clay.

We took off and flew to Stockholm, where the Swedish Secretary of Defense was having a large, official dinner for the Secretary of the Navy of the United States.

Secretary Forrestal was exhausted by this time, and had a cold. We were all tired, having been constantly on the go for several days and nights; the long flights each night having afforded little real rest. As we approached Stockholm Forrestal said, "Smeddy, I'm not going to that dinner tonight!" My response was that he had to go because it was in his honor. He had made up his mind, saying, "I am not going. You send a message saying that you want a Navy doctor to meet the plane immediately upon our arrival. He will certify that I am too sick to go to the dinner." We had Admiral Kent Hewitt in his flagship in Stockholm.

So, that's what happened. We radioed ahead that the Secretary was not feeling well. The doctor met the plane, I gave him "the word", and he examined Forrestal and announced that he had to go directly to the hotel and to bed. When I left him in the Grand Hotel, to go to the dinner in his place, he looked at me with a twinkle in his eye and said, "Arrange a golf game for the morning!"

I was flabbergasted. You can imagine my feelings, with that directive, as I sat on the Secretary of Defense's right, with Prince Bertil on my other side. The American Minister - we didn't have an ambassador in Sweden at that time - Mr. Ravndahl, sat across the table from me. As I struggled with the impossible task of getting a golf game for a man too sick to attend an official dinner in his honor, in my mind. I managed to tell our host that I really didn't think the Secretary was as sick as he appeared, but that he had been completely exhausted and felt that he just couldn't make that dinner. The Swedes were pretty upset about it!

I have the clipping today that is all about the Swedish-American boy who comes home, as aide to the Secretary of the Navy, and one little squib about the Secretary of the Navy who arrived and went to bed, sick. All the rest is about the Swedish-American Captain Smedberg, who came with him.

Anyway, just before the dinner was over, Prince Bertil said to me:

"Captain, do you like to play golf?"

I said: "Yes, I love to play golf."

"Okay," he said, "we'll go out to my favorite golf course and we'll play tomorrow." He said, "Mr. Ravndahl is a scratch player." I said:

"I know that for a golf game I can get the secretary on his feet tomorrow. He loves to play golf and that would be the best thing that he could do."

So we set up this golf game. For three days we played golf there. The prince and I were partners against Ravndahl and Forrestal, and every day the match was decided on the eighteenth hole. Perfectly wonderful matches. The prince was a scratch golfer, as was Ravndahl. Forrestal and I played about the same, about 12, 13, 14 handicaps. After three days we continued on our trip, spending a week in London and finally flying back to Washington.

I haven't thought about this trip for a long time. Prince Bertil would take us to all his favorite eating places. The minute he walked in to any restaurant, he was surrounded.

Q: He was a bachelor, wasn't he?

Adm. S.: Yes, indeed, and one of the most attractive men you've ever met, a huge man. He spoke English far better than I speak English. He was educated at Oxford. His enunciation and diction were perfect, grammar faultless. At every restaurant, all the little waitresses would surround him and we'd have all his favorite dishes. I remember his favorite dessert was a big chunk of ice hollowed out and in the bottom were strawberries, and then a mousse, and then wild strawberries, and then another mousse on top of that. The most delicious thing you ever put in your mouth!

Some years later, when I was on duty in Washington, Prince Bertil came to the United States, as a guest of the President. I found I was invited to the White House to dinner. Claudia and I were invited. When we went down the line, Prince Bertil greeted me with:

"Ah, my old golfing partner."


Q: Admiral, tell me, in addition to the visit to the Bikini tests, what were the purposes of this round-the-world trip? Were there any objectives other than just to meet people?

Adm. S.: Well, Forrestal looked at every naval installation that we could find on our trip. In other words, every place we went we tried to find what navy there was. He inspected everything in Guam, for instance. Just before we got to Sweden, he said to me:

"By the way, why are we going to Sweden?"

He'd approved the itinerary, which I made up originally, but as he generally did, he left it up to his planners and if it looked all right to him he'd approve it. I said:

"For two reasons, Sir. One is that Admiral Hewitt is in here with a couple of ships of his squadron." He had one cruiser and two destroyers. "The other is that my great-grandfather came from Stockholm and I've never been to Sweden, so I thought it would be good if you and I got back here and looked at it."

Q: And I suppose also, incidentally, the underground defense fortifications. Did you view them?

Adm. S.: Yes. We saw all kinds of things.

Q: They're rather unique, aren't they?

Adm. S.: Yes. They were then; probably still are. Every place we went we saw something. Actually, the thing that impressed us most was the chaotic state of everything right after the war, when everyone was interested in getting home and nobody cared about turning over anything in proper fashion. Everybody just dropped the bricks and wanted to go home. That's why we had trouble getting our plane taken care of. We were lucky in getting that engine replacement in Berlin. We discovered a gasoline leak in an outboard wing tank of our plane about the time we had been in that monsoon, days earlier in India, and a steady stream of gas was pouring out of that thing between the two flames from the two prop engines.

Q: You were in mortal danger!

Adm. S.: Yes. Frankly, I was nervous about it all the time.

About once an hour the mechanic on the plane would come and flash his light out to see if the stream was getting any bigger. No, it was about the same. We had to go all the way through India, we had to go through Egypt, we had to go through Rome, we had to go all the way to Stockholm, Sweden before we were able to get that wing opened up and the rupture in the tank repaired. So we went quite a few thousand miles with that hazard all the time. I never did tell the secretary about it.

Q: It was very rigorous otherwise, too, wasn't it?

Adm. S.: Oh, yes.

Q: Was he apprehensive at all during the trip?

Adm. S.: No, he was never apprehensive. In fact, during the time we were really lost over the Indian jungles, I went back every now and then to tell him that we weren't quite sure where we were, and after we'd come out of the storm he said:

"That was a pretty bad time, wasn't it?" and I said: "Yes, it was. Our pilot has been magnificent the entire time but we're lucky to be where we are." And he said:

"Yes, I figured that." He read continuously. One of the things we took on every plane for a short hop or a long hop was a shelf of books. The minute we'd get on a plane, he'd open one of these books and read until we got where we were going.

Q: What were his particular interests?

Adm. S.: At one time we had <u>The Decline and Fall of the Roman Empire</u>. I mean that was one of the things he read from cover to cover. He read very fast. I imagine he had a sort of speed-reading technique. He got the gist but didn't take a long time reading. He read everything he could get his hands on about dialectical materialism. He was tremendously interested in everything that made a Communist tick, how they operated. I think he was a great realist. If he were alive today, for instance, he'd have recognized detente for what it is - or what it isn't.

Q: He wouldn't be idealistic?

Adm. S.: Not in the slightest. No, he would have recognized that it's just the Soviets way of stalling for more time and a more advantageous position from which to carry out their eventual goal to have the world answerable to them. There's no question. They haven't abandoned their goals in one slight degree.

Q: It must have been awfully stimulating to be with him?

Smedberg #3 - 348

Adm. S.: It was. He was a tremendous student. He was always learning, always studying, and always reading, always asking questions of people in high places about why the government was doing that or why they had this policy and that policy.

Q: What were some of the other things you got involved with while you were with him?

Adm. S.: There were several things that were significant. At one time, and I don't know whether you've run across this or not, but you must have in your briefings with the naval aviators.

On one occasion, the naval aviators got together with most of the senior admirals in the SecNav's office. There were in that room only two of us who were not naval aviators, myself and I'm not sure who the other was. It could have been Admiral Denfeld. Today I'm not sure. But the gist of the thing, the reason they got together, was to discuss with the Secretary of the Navy the possibility of naval aviation going in a body and joining the Air Force. There were several who got up and spoke in favor of it, and there were several others, including Forrest Sherman, who were vigorously against it, opposed to it.

I remember the argument that those who were opposed to it used, which I felt was very telling, was that while aviation might promise everything if naval aviation would go over to the Air Force, it wouldn't be very long before the promises were forgotten and the services that the naval aviation segment would be able to render to the Navy would dissipate and would soon be like the Royal Air Arm to the Navy. They weren't too effective, you know, at one point.

Q: Yes, the RAF took over.

Adm. S.: Yes, and that to me was a meeting that should have been written up in great detail and I'll bet there's no record of it any place.

Q: It was just a verbal thing?

Adm. S.: Yes. As far as I know, nobody took anything down in writing. All the people there were agreed that they wouldn't discuss it outside that room with anyone. The decision was made that they would pursue the subject no further. Naval aviation would stay as a part of the Navy.

Q: We've seen the effectiveness of the carrier in World War II. What was to be the disposition of the carrier if such a thing had happened, and all the naval aviators went to the Army?

Adm. S.: That was one of the fuzzy areas. The proponents of the idea thought that the Air Force would assign groups to the Navy carriers, or the carriers could be part of the Air Force assigned to the Navy. There was rather fuzzy thinking about that area. They all recognized that the Navy couldn't operate without the carriers, without close fleet support from carriers, but they felt that they could look out for the Navy's interests from the Air Force.

The more realistic of them, like Forrest Sherman, said we won't be worrying too much about the Navy after we've been in the Air Force a few years. We'll be fighting for our position in the Air Force, which is absolutely correct. They would be.

Q: Interservice rivalry would continue?

Adm. S.: That's right.

Q: This leads into the whole controversy over unification and so forth, the revolt of the admirals. Do you have recollections of that?

Adm. S.: I have recollections but they're confused, really, now by all that I've read since, and since I was not involved in any of that. At one time I was asked if I'd be part of the group that was working out some of the arguments supporting the admirals' revolt, and I said, no, I didn't want to be a part of it. I had rather a hard time getting out of it, as a matter of fact. I didn't want to be part of it.

Q: Was it not Radford who was masterminding that?

Adm. S.: He was one of the leaders, that's right, and I suspect that he was one of the strong proponents of joining the Air Force, the movement to take naval aviation out of the Navy and put it in the Air Force, and from that position they would look out for the Navy; carrying out their responsibilities with and to the Navy, from the Air Force. But they felt that they could more easily advance themselves and have a bigger share of the responsibility of the Air Force than they could in the Navy.

Of course, later on, the naval aviators became the responsible people in the Navy. They were running the Navy. Now, in 1977, we have a situation, as I view it, where the naval aviators are being pushed aside. The nuclear submariners are running the Navy. Admiral Holloway is a nuclear submariner, Harold Shear is a nuclear submariner, the chief of naval personnel is a nuclear submariner. Most of the people in responsible positions are nuclear submariners today.

Q: I suppose, then, it's related to the philosophy that is paramount at the moment in terms of national defense?

Adm. S.: That, and it's only natural that when someone who is in a specialty gets into a position of responsibility he wants to take as his associates those he knows best and in whom he has the most confidence. They're bound to be the people with whom he's served most closely because he has seen how they react, he knows how they feel about everything, and he's going to call them around when he gets in a top position. So it's more or less natural.

Q: But hasn't there been also a lessening of the antagonism between the black-shoe and brown-shoe navies?

Adm. S.: Oh, yes. There's no question about it.

Q: That's been dissipated.

Adm. S.: Right, and frankly I've always been a black-shoe man who has valued the naval aviator tremendously because I've been so many times in situations in war where, without our air support, we knew we'd be sunk. As I told the secretary at the time that we were talking about going for more pay for the service: "It's ridiculous for the aviators to think they might lose their flight pay. We think they earn it, and when we see the weather in which they fly and the night flights that they make and the carrier landings in rough weather, we take off our hats to them and we don't begrudge them that extra pay one iota."

I've said that to congressmen who used to say to me in the old says: "Well, Admiral, do you think the aviators earn their flight pay?" They earn every cent of it.

Q: Just as the submariners do.

Adm. S.: Yes, that's right.

Q: That brings up the question of congressional relations when you were with Forrestal, as his aide. He was called upon, I'm sure, on many occasions to testify and you went with him, didn't you?

Adm. S.: Yes, I always went with him.

Q: Tell me about some of those occasions.

Adm. S.: I sat quietly by. He was always backed up by people like the chief of naval operations. I went along as his aide and carried his briefcase and had his indexed folders so that I could find the answer to any question, whenever he was asked a question. He had prepared himself well. He generally knew the answer, but I was always thumbing through my index and finding the topic. I always had it ready to let him look at it or to correct him or furnish any information he wanted.

Q: Did he have a rehearsal before he left?

Adm. S.: Yes, but generally the rehearsal - and I would be present - was with the expert in whatever it was that he was going to discuss. If it was a new plane he was going up and talk about, he'd have the chief of the Bureau of Aeronautics with him.

Q: Oh, I see. It wasn't a JAG rehearsal?

Adm. S.: No. He had a magnificent memory. He was very quick on his feet. He didn't waste any time in useless verbiage. There was one thing I was going to mention but it's slipped my mind.

Q: In that area?

Adm. S.: Yes.

Q: What sort of an impact did he make on a congressional committee?

Adm. S.: I think he was very impressive. He was so sincere and obviously businesslike. Never was there any indication of any personal motives in anything he ever asked for.

One of the things I was going to mention is sort of indicative of Forrestal. He was called one time by - he had made the decision that as a result of budgetary cuts we had to close the Charleston Navy Yard. When I say "the Charleston Navy Yard," I mean the Navy yard at Charleston, South Carolina, not the Boston Navy Yard.

Q: That was inviolate, wasn't it?

Adm. S.: And, as he always did, he notified the principal senators and congressmen involved the night before he was going to make the announcement. He notified Mendel Rivers and he notified Senator Maybank and I think Senator Johnson was the other one. Maybank's office was on the phone - the senator was out at the time, but he got back on the phone within a couple of hours and told Forrestal that he should do nothing further until they came down to see him, and the whole South Carolina delegation arrived in Forrestal's office. I only heard parts of the conversation, but I heard parts like, "Mr. Secretary, I can't tell you how many millions of dollars this will cost the Navy, if you try to do that, in your next appropriation."

The result was we couldn't do it. Forrestal couldn't do it, even though he was convinced it was in the best interests.

Q: Was this his first attempt at closing a base?

Adm. S.: No, no. He'd had other difficulties. Remember when he tried to close the rope walk first in Boston, at Chelsea, in the Boston Naval Shipyard? We had plenty of difficulties.

Q: Was he able or did he make an attempt to anticipate the

kind of questions that might be asked by the committee?

Adm. S.: Yes.

Q: Did he through the committee staff get some idea of what was going to be asked?

Adm. S.: He did, and on occasion we would plant questions with the committee staff that he would like to have asked of himself.

Q: That's a perfectly legitimate kind of cooperation.

Adm. S.: I think it's legitimate, and frankly it's one that I used when I was chief of naval personnel. For instance, in the days of McNamara, when he was going for a pay bill for the services in about 1962, we personnel chiefs of the services were all called before him. He told us that he was going to support a 1.1-billion-dollar increase for pay purposes and that he wanted no one to disagree with that position and that every one of us would have to submit, for his clearance, our statements that we intended to make to the various committees that we went before in support of this bill.

Well, he had appointed, nine months before, a special study committee to study the pay of the military. It had two Marine Corps generals, two Army generals, two Navy admirals, and two Air Force generals, this committee. Vice Admiral Tex Settle, for instance, was one of our Navy members. General Bolte was one of the Army members, I remember. Tex Settle worked in BuPers - all of these were retired officers, recalled for this purpose - Tex Settle would report to me every day or every few days on the progress they were making and the difficulties they were having. So at the end of seven, eight, or nine months, he reported to me that they had arrived at the figure, as I remember it, of about 2.2 billion dollars or 2.3 billion dollars as what was necessary to bring the military into some sort of comparability with civilian industry.

Later on he reported to me that the committee had waited on the Secretary of Defense, given him the report, he had looked at it, thrown it back at them, and said, "Take it out and bring it back with a final figure of 1.1 billion."

Q: Study it down to that!

Adm. S.: That's right. He announced that that was all he was going to approve, so that's what they had to come up with.

He submitted his bill to the Congress for 1.1 billion which, he said, would produce comparability with civilian industry. Right away that was nothing but a lie because the study had proven that it would be 2.3 billion, I think or 2.2  So we submitted our statements. They were all cleared by him. We went up and read our statements before the Congress, the ones he had approved. Then, of course, we were asked all kinds of questions. Some of the questions asked me were, for instance:

"Admiral, do you feel that this 1.1-billion-dollar increase will, in fact, bring service pay up to comparability with civilians, with civilian industry?"

I said: "No, I do not."

"Admiral, by how much do you think it falls short?"

I said: "It's about one-half the amount necessary, in my opinion."

When I got through that days' testimony, I got back to my desk and I had a message there to see the Secretary of Defense immediately. I got over there and I got the damnedest bawling-out I've ever had in my life. I stood there and waited till he got all through and he said:

"What have you got to say for yourself?"

"Two things, Mr. Secretary," I said. "In the first place, when I'm asked a question I give a truthful answer."

He said: "What do you mean 'truthful'? You stated this was only 50 percent enough."

I said: "That's correct, Sir. You know that's true. Your own study committee studied for nine months and told you we needed twice the amount you approved, but you told them to go back and reduce it."

He said: "Get out of here," and I got out of there.

I expected to be fired any day but he never fired me.
That's the kind of thing, you know.

Q: Truths and untruths!

Adm. S.: That's right.

Q: And they're in conflict.

Adm. S.: Yes, and I don't honestly think that when you're asked a question you should equivocate.

Q: Well, it's almost like being under oath when you're testifying before a committee and they're trying to ascertain the truth of things so they can appropriate the proper funds.

Adm. S.: Not only that, but I'm working for a lot of people who I know are ready to give their lives for this country. The great majority of people who are career officers in the Army, Navy, and Air Force are very loyal, patriotic people, and they deserve to be supported. Unfortunately, today, there are too many people who are a little too worried about what will happen to them if they don't say what the administration wants them to say. It's a sad thing, and it's getting to be more and more that way. Either you give the right answers or you're going to get out, going to be dropped.

Q: Do you want to talk about the secretary and the Navy budget? How did he get involved in that? What were his strictures?

Adm. S.: He was very much involved, but I was not. In other words, I never sat in on the budget discussions. There was such a large group of people and I had so much else to do that I purposely never sat in on them. I didn't want to get involved in it.

Q: Did he have any favorite aspects of naval life that he was particularly interested in? Was he interested in more ships or was he interested in more planes? What was he interested in?

Adm. S.: He was interested in a balanced navy. He was interested in keeping the fleet modern. He was not interested in things that did not add to or enhance the fighting efficiency of the fleet and the Navy. He felt that we had too big a shore establishment, as many secretaries have felt. But, of course, you know that the shore establishment is often forced on us by the politicians because every shore establishment has a lot of people being fed by the funds that go to maintain an establishment, and they all vote in that district.

I was born and brought up in the Army. My father, and we with him, had to serve in some of the damnedest Army posts you ever saw, which no longer served any useful function except to feed the people in the area with the salaries of the military assigned there. I can't tell you how many Army posts around the country we had for many, many years and perhaps still do have that have no real function any more. I'm not speaking from knowledge today because I don't know what the situation is.

Q: It's inevitable that they would be outmoded in certain areas.

Adm. S.: Yes.

Q: As a result of changes in emphasis.

Adm. S.: That's right.

Q: Did you get involved in any way with reservists and that sort of thing when you were with the secretary?

Adm. S.: One of the strongest feelings the secretary had about the Navy was about his naval reserves. He had been a reservist himself, you know. He did all he could to strengthen our ties with the Naval Reserve and to make the Naval Reserve stronger. He had many, many friends in the Naval Reserve. He was a strong supporter of a strong Naval Reserve and he defended the requirements for it before the

Congress continuously.

Q: And, of course, that was highly political, wasn't it?

Adm. S.: Yes, it's political but at the same time it is the reserves that you really have to fight a war with because the regular establishment is just a small cadre that can hold things together until you can get the citizenry involved in the thing. It's the reserves who together with the cadre of regulars hold things together until all the rest of the citizens can be brought in.

Q: In that time we had no great adversary on the horizon. I mean Russia was looming off in the distance as a potential, but in a Navy sense she wasn't much of a rival -

Adm. S.: You're talking about right after World War II?

Q: Yes, when you were his aide. So, you got involved in reductions, did you not?

Adm. S.: We got involved in tremendous reductions. I went from being aide to the Secretary of the Navy to commander of a destroyer squadron in the Pacific Fleet. It was at a time when we had very little money for fuel oil for steaming, very little money for spare parts, a situation not unlike what we have in the Navy today, only worse then, but not as bad as it's going to be in a few more years, maybe. In the Pacific Fleet, for instance, and the same was true in the Atlantic, we had three types of destroyer squadrons. We had my type of squadron, which was fully operational, I had eight ships in two divisions. We carried out all the exercises, gunnery, engineering, and all other exercises.

Q: With an adequate complement?

Adm. S.: With just enough people to do it. But it was tough when you had to operate three weeks at sea. You were exhausted when you came in because it was at least a watch in three and in some areas watch and watch. That's tough.

Then we had semi-operational squadrons which could steam one or two days at sea, maybe, a week. Then we had the other type squadron which by pooling the ratings in various ships could get one ship underway maybe, one day a week. They stayed alongside the dock most of the time. That's the way we were operating following the great demoralization that was called demobilization after World War II.

Q: How did the Secretary react to demobilization and the cutting-down of his forces.

Adm. S.: Well, he recognized that it was inevitable. That was one thing about the Secretary. He never kicked against the pricks. In other words, if he knew something had to be and was inevitable, he didn't waste his energies trying to stop it. All he tried to do was to keep a viable navy going, and we all felt that there wouldn't be an immediate call for our navy's services right away, or for some years to come. But those of us who were regulars in the service did our best to try to keep what we had ready with diminishing supplies. The aviators didn't have enough money for fuel to fly the number of hours they should have to keep them from making mistakes and having accidents.

We didn't have enough money. For instance, we had a top speed limit of, I think, 12 knots, except when we were actually engaged in operations. We'd have to get underway at five or six in the morning in order to get to our operating areas at 12 knots. Then after we completed our firing for the day or whatever it was, we had to return to port at 12 knots to anchor or "nest" so that we wouldn't burn fuel at night. Then we had to get away at six o'clock the next morning and we mightn't get in till ten, eleven, or twelve o'clock at night, and then get underway at four or five or six in the morning because we're saving that amount of fuel that we wouldn't be steaming at sea.

Q: Reminds me of the 55-mile limit on the highways!

Adm. S.: It's much worse than that, I'll tell you. A very short-sighted policy. Very tough on officers and men!

Q: How did your office function vis a vis the CNO when Nimitz was there?

Adm. S.: They had a very good working relationship. I think Mr. Forrestal was impressed with Admiral Nimitz' capabilities and sincerity, and Admiral Nimitz recognized in Mr. Forrestal a real leader, one who had control, and exercised the control of the Navy. Forrestal left no doubt in anybody's mind that he was the Secretary of the Navy.

We'd had a series, you know, of weak secretaries before Forrestal. Knox being perhaps the first one who started taking charge.

Q: And he only after Pearl Harbor?

Adm. S.: Yes, that's right. Up to that time, the secretary was, frankly, more of a figurehead than anything else. For instance, we had a secretary like Claude A. Swanson who practically never did anything, being sick or indisposed much of the time. His chief clerk signed his name on almost everything.

Q: But he was a former senator.

Adm. S.: Yes, but he was ill much of the time he was secretary.

Forrestal was the first real, positive Secretary of the

Navy that we had, and he took charge.

Q: And he had immediate and ready access to the president, did he?

Adm. S.: It's hard for me to say. Yes, I feel that he did, as immediate as anybody had.

Q: Did you go on any other journeys, other than the one around the world?

Adm. S.: That was the only long one. We made inspection trips and trips for him to make speeches regularly all over the place. For instance, it was nothing for him to be at the office at eight o'clock in the morning, fly to Chicago, for a luncheon speech such as one to the Teamsters Union in Chicago - that was one he had one time - then we'd fly back to the office in the afternoon, work until seven o'clock that night, then be back in the office the next morning.

He went out and inspected fleet units, but not as much after the war was over as he did during the war. He was on the go a lot during the war.

Q: Did he have a great knowledge of the fleet?

Adm. S.: Yes, he did, he had a very good knowledge of the fleet.

Q: Did he know anything about ordnance?

Adm. S.: Yes, I think he did. By that I mean he listened carefully when technical matters were being explained to him and I think he took it in. Also, he could spot a weakness in a man and when he did he remembered it. For instance, on this trip around the world that we made, one of our stops was in Japan. We had an admiral in command there who has just recently died, who insisted that we see some of the back country of Japan. Now, mind you, this was - well, the war was over in August '45, and this was July '46 that we made this trip - I might have said '47 earlier, but it was in July '46 that the atom bomb went off.

Q: You mean the Bikini bomb?

Adm. S.: Yes. So on that trip when we were in Japan it wasn't too long after the war in Japan had been ended. But this Commander, Naval Forces, Japan, wanted to take the Secretary through some of the back Japanese country to see it on the way back to the airport. He was arguing with me in the Imperial Hotel. I said, "No, Admiral, I'm sorry but we have to get back to the airport because we've got a very tight schedule. Everything depends on our making our schedule and we haven't got the time for possible delays."

He said: "I have taken care of everything. I've made out a schedule and I've given you plenty of time between here and the airport to see the back country I want you to see."

I said: "Nothing doing, Admiral."

"Well," he said, "I'll take it up with the Secretary," and while we're still arguing the Secretary comes in and says:

"What's all the argument about? You fellows don't seem to be able to agree on something." And the admiral said:

"No, I want to show you something of the back country and your aide says I can't to it. He says you haven't got time."

And the Secretary said: "What's the matter, Smeddy?"

I said: "Mr. Secretary, we have a very tight schedule set up. We haven't got time for this. If anything should go wrong, the whole schedule would be upset for the next twenty-four or forty-eight hours."

"Oh," the admiral said, "I assure you I'll get you to the airport on time."

The Secretary said: "Okay, Smeddy, let's go then."

We get in our car and we have a jeep full of Marines ahead of us and a jeep full of Marines with rifles behind us. We start off and are soon on a back road, and the first thing you know the road ends on a dike. It stops. A dike between two ricefields. We have to push the car way back to get off the dike. We find there isn't one single soul in our party who's ever spoken a word of Japanese in his life. We're lost in the back country, and we're lost back there where there are nothing but Japanese farmers and peasants.

Q: Some of whom don't know the war's over!

Adm. S.: No. They're friendly enough, but when we ask where the airport is, they don't know what we're talking about. We make motions about flying and planes coming in. Finally one of them gets the word and he points in a general direction, and we got there, but we were quite late getting back, something like an hour or two hours late getting to the airport.

The admiral in the meantime was awfully upset and kept apologizing to the Secretary. I didn't say a word.

We got on the plane and we took off. The Secretary came over and sat down beside me and said:

"Well, you haven't said it yet."

"What?"

"I told you so."

I said: "No, Sir, I was determined I wasn't going to say that, but I sure thought something like that might happen."

He said: "Will you make a little note to see that that admiral never gets another job in the United States Navy," and he never did, he never got another responsible job, a vice admiral.

Q: This question is predicated on what a couple of former

CNOs have told me, a point they made, that the secretaries - not Forrestal but more recent ones - have had a tendency sometimes to interfere in the promotion of admirals and have spoken in favor of the promotion of someone whom they met for half an hour out in Podunk and thought he was a great person. Did Forrestal attempt this sort of thing?

Adm. S.: Not really. Forrestal was generally pretty willing to let the chips fall where they might. He believed in the selection system. I can give you numerous instances of other secretaries where there have been even orders that certain men must be taken off or put on.

Q: Perhaps when we come to the Bureau of Personnel you might talk in general terms about some of these, as a matter of record.

Adm. S.: Yes, and as a matter of fact there'll be probably another session before we get to that, I'm afraid.

Q: This is an example of experiences you had?

Adm. S.: Of things that happened when I was Chief of the Bureau of Naval Personnel, for instance. This is way out of order chronologically, but we had a selection board to select reserve captains for continuation on active duty. Those who weren't selected were dropped.

Q: That's a plucking board?

Adm. S.: A plucking board, in effect. And we had the same thing in this particular year I'm talking about, when I was chief of personnel, for reserve officers because after the war and for some years we had a great surplus of reserve officers in high-ranking positions and we had to get rid of some of them. So we had this board to select certain reserve officers to be continued as captains. One reserve officer was dropped who was a very prominent individual and on the staff of Carl Vinson, who was the very powerful chairman of the committee, as you well remember.

Q: Indeed.

Adm. S.: I have to be a little careful here because some of these individuals are still living.

The chairman of the committee called me up and said:

"Admiral, I understand that so and so was not continued in the recent selection board."

"Well, Mr. Chairman," I said, "I'm not really in a position to discuss it. I don't have in my memory who was and who was not continued, but it was all the result of the selection board."

He said: "I know that, but one individual who was not continued I want continued."

"Sir," I said, "I don't have the authority to do that."

So he said:

"All right. I'll take it up with the Secretary of the Navy."

I called the Secretary of the Navy immediately and told him that he was going to get a call. He called me back in a little while and said that he had told this individual in the Congress that he would take care of the matter. He asked me: "Do I have the authority to change that list?"

I said: "In the case of this noncontinuation board, you do, Sir. In the case of a regular selection board, it has to go to the President."

"Well," he said, "I want you to move the name of that individual from the noncontinued list and put him on the continued list."

I said: "I can't do that, Sir. It's not ethical."
So he said: "I'm telling you to do it.

I said: "All right, Sir, if you'll put that in writing, I'll do it," and, believe it or not, he did put it in writing and I did do it.

Three days later I got a call from Margaret Chase Smith, the lady senator who kept her eyes on the armed forces, a member of the Armed Forces Committee. I'd known her for thirty years. She said:

"Admiral Smedberg, did you by any chance change the name of one individual from the noncontinued list to the continued list? That individual is boasting up here in the Congress now that he is now on the continued list, when we all had heard that he wasn't."

And I said: "Mrs. Smith, you know that I don't have the authority to do that."

"Who does?" she asked, and I said: "The Secretary of the Navy."

"Thank you."

I got the Secretary of the Navy on the phone quick, before she could get him, and I said:

"All hell has broken loose, Mr. Secretary. I warned you we shouldn't do this and now you're going to get asked this question."

He said: "What shall we do?" I said:

"We'll admit that we made a bad mistake and we're going to correct it and put it right back where it was in the beginning."

He called me back in two hours and said:

"Phew, I had a hard time. You're right. Put him right back where he was before," which I did and I tore up the letter that he had given me, the orders he'd given me, to change it.

Then I got a call from the lady senator, who asked me to come up and see her. I went up on The Hill. She said:

"You know, Admiral, I've known you for many years. We depend on you military people to prevent things political like this from happening."

I said: "I know you do, and we fight awfully hard to carry out that faith and trust you have in us, but sometimes we can't."

She said: "Well, I expect you to do it in the future."

Q: Maggie could be pretty firm!

Adm. S.: She sure could. I'm a great admirer of hers.

Q: What about Forrestal and the NROTC and the units? Was he an advocate of that program?

Adm. S.: He was, he believed in it. He believed in it very strongly.

Q: Did you get involved in it as his aide, inspection trips to the units, or anything like that?

Adm. S.: Yes, we inspected units. In fact, we inspected quite a number of them, so many that I couldn't even remember any particular unit. But I know that through the years the emphasis on NROTC has gone up and down like a sine curve.

Q: Related to the popularity of the military or nonpopularity?

Adm. S.: That's right. When I get to talking about some of the problems I had as Chief of Naval Personnel, I can talk a little bit more about that.

For instance, at one time we had an Under Secretary who

was charged with personnel and he was determined that we were going to cut out the universities whose graduates didn't stay in the Navy very long, Harvard, Yale, Princeton, for instance.

Q: The Ivy League.

Adm. S.: Ivy League groups. Take the NROTC units away from those universities and give them to others, some of what are sometimes called "cow colleges", whose graduates stayed in for careers in greater percentage. I used to have long arguments with him. I'd say:

"Look, one of the greatest things about this NROTC is the fact that we get the graduates of universities like Harvard, Yale, Princeton, Stanford, and so forth, for the few years they have to serve. They go out into civilian life carrying with them an appreciation of the necessity for a navy, in most cases a love of the Navy, and a great fondness for the Navy. They become responsible leaders in our society and they are tremendously valuable to the Navy because of that experience. They're just as valuable to us in many cases in civilian life, more valuable, than they would be in the Navy."

I had the most awful time trying to sell this idea to this individual, who was the Under Secretary. His name was Red Fay.

Q: Oh, yes, he was a friend of Kennedy?

Adm. S.: Yes, Kennedy put him in this job. He was an awfully nice fellow but very naive. He didn't know anything about government at all and he was stubborn and determined, by God, that he was going to get the NROTC units out of Harvard, Yale, and Princeton. I told him that the university that had the poorest retention rate of all the NROTCs was Stanford University, his university.

"Oh," he said, "you can't take them off."

We didn't take any of them off.

Q: This came to pass, anyway, with Vietnam, didn't it? They closed their own units.

Adm. S.: Yes. Now they want them back again.

Q: But they may not get some of them.

Adm. S.: Frankly, the infusion of those youngsters from our universities throughout the country was one of the healthiest things about the Navy, and I think the other services, too, but I only have knowledge of the Navy. The smart youngsters who came in from our civilian universities as reserve officers did a great deal for the Navy and took a lot back into civilian life that helped the Navy, in later years.

Q: In 1946 and '47 we were beginning to develop a very small interest, I suppose it was at the time, in missiles and that sort of thing. Did Forrestal show any interest in this?

Adm. S.: Yes, he was very much interested. The very first time that we had an opportunity to see a missile shoot was at White Sands, New Mexico - no, Fort Bliss, Texas. We were invited by the Army to come out and watch a missile shoot at White Sands, Texas, and Secretary of War Patterson invited Forrestal to fly down with him in his plane. Forrestal thanked him very much and said no, thank you very much, but he would fly down in his own plane.

I'll tell you at this point that Forrestal didn't really trust any aviators except naval aviators. He thoroughly trusted naval aviation, but he didn't think other aviators were as good as naval aviators, and there were many times when he refused to fly with the other services because he wanted to fly with naval aviators.

To make a long story short, we said we would meet them at eight o'clock in the morning at White Sands, Texas, near Fort Bliss. We flew down overnight. I had timed our ETA for a quarter past seven to make sure that we'd be there in time. We circled this desert area and we finally found a little landing strip. I'm up there between the pilot and the copilot, and we see a few shacks down there but nothing else. We don't see a sign of a human being. Well, we think it's funny but we land. We open the door and one sentry walks out of the building and comes over. I called down:

"Are you expecting the Secretary of the Navy here this morning?" And he said: "No, I never heard of it." I asked: "Is this White Sands?"

"Yes." I get out of the plane and Forrestal stands behind me and says:

"Smeddy, I thought you said they were expecting us this morning."

Q: No red carpet out!

Adm. S.: Of all the horrible feelings for me! I'm the aide and I've delivered him to a place where there isn't anybody. They have a telephone in one of these shacks where the sentry is so I call up Fort Bliss and I find out that the landing field to which we were to be diverted is 30 or 40 miles away, that they had sent a message about five o'clock the afternoon before. Well, what happened in the Army communications system, in those days after the war, was that they closed up at five o'clock at night and they didn't open till eight o'clock in the morning. Any message that was in the system at five o'clock, or one minute to five, didn't get transmitted until eight o'clock the next morning.

Mind you, this is only a little time after Pearl Harbor. We won the war, and the war's over, now we're right back to the old Army Communication system again. So the message that they had sent to the Secretary of the Navy from Washington - I guess they sent it from Texas and it went up to Washington - was never delivered to us. We never got it, and all the officials were waiting over at Fort Bliss.

Q: Forty miles away!

Adm. S.: Yes. We waited and they all came in their cars. We could see them coming across the country in a great cloud of dust. We got in and went back with them. That was some day, I'm telling you. That was the first missile shoot we ever saw and it was a small rocket firing.

But he was interested and he did keep up with the thing and he believed in the future potential of missiles. Of course, that was in the early days of missilery.

Q: Oh, I know, the infancy.

Adm. S.: Yes, that's right.

Interview #4 with Vice Admiral William R. Smedberg III
Place: The U.S. Naval Institute, Annapolis, Maryland
Date: 23 September 1977
Subject: Biography
By: John T. Mason, Jr.

Q: All right, Sir, let's begin your engrossing story this morning as you concluded your round-the-world trip with Secretary Forrestal. Will you take it from there?

Adm. S.: With these long periods between our interviews, it's pretty hard to take it from several months ago.

Q: Yes, practically a year! Anyway, you had completed your round-the-world trip with Forrestal and came back. You were with him for only a year from March '46 to June '47.

Adm. S.: That's right.

Q: So this year must have elapsed in this time.

Adm. S.: That's right. I was detached not long after that trip and went out to command a destroyer squadron.

Q: This obviously was something you sought.

Adm. S.: Oh, yes.

Q: All right. Will you take the story there?

Adm. S.: Yes. My being ordered as aide to Forrestal was quite a shock to me at the time. I didn't want to go. I'd been on King's staff, you know, and had hoped to get to sea from there. In those days, we felt that getting to sea was the most important thing a naval officer could do. I don't know how they feel about it today, there are so few sea jobs.

Q: It was also very helpful to be aide to the secretary of the Navy, wasn't it?

Adm. S.: Oh, very. That's correct. That did no harm to my career, and I learned probably more in that period than I could ever have learned about the Navy in any other capacity at the time.

Do you want me to go on and tell about the destroyer squadron?

Q: Yes, and the Pacific Fleet.

Adm. S.: It was a particularly interesting period because the Navy was demobilizing. We called it demoralizing. It was a period of great demoralization in the Navy. Everyone was trying to get out of the Navy. Funds were being severely reduced for operations and, as a result, in the destroyer business we had three types of squadrons. We had one squadron that was fully operational. Our personnel were cut to the lowest number that we could perform with, so that during our three weeks' operating period out of our home port we could do all of the gunnery exercises, torpedo exercises, and tactics that we wanted to do, but we were exhausted when we came back to port. Then we had the second type squadron which could maybe take two days at sea by combining people. And we had a third type squadron which could only get one ship under way a week by taking all the people from all the ships in the squadron. That squadron stayed tied up to the dock practically all the time.

Q: Were you able to count on ships in the first category remaining in that category, with so many men leaving at different times?

Adm. S.: We had a tremendous personnel turnover but we kept training them, we kept operating. It was a very trying, very hectic period, and I've been trying to find ever since then the letter that I wrote the night I was detached from that squadron to the Commander, Destroyers, Pacific, setting forth all of the things that were wrong in the administration of the destroyer force in those days. I wrote him a four- or five-page letter, which I finished about three o'clock in the morning, and sent it out by hand in a boat the next morning. I had been detached and was about to start for the East Coast, when I got a call from the admiral, who was then Admiral Savvy Forrestel, saying please would I come on board and talk to him. I think his chief of staff then was Lorenzo Sabin, later Vice Admiral Sabin, a great naval officer.

Forrestel was tremendously impressed with the charges that I made, which were, in effect, that we had too many operations and too little support from everyone else. For instance, we would come in from sea about four or five o'clock Friday afternoon, needing fuel for the division or the squadron, and we'd find the fuel depot was closed. We would have to get under way at six o'clock Monday morning and we had to get fuel before we got under way.

Q: It was closed for the weekend?

Adm. S.: Yes, and we spent hours trying to get the fuel depot opened or a tanker alongside to get our fuel. Then our operations orders would come on board for the next week, probably Saturday morning, or sometimes not until Sunday, and we would have to read the operations orders on the way out to the operating area at five or six o'clock Monday morning. It was a chaotic period.

Q: May I ask at this point why all of that chaos developed? This had been anticipated, there had been planning, I understand, immediately the war was ended as to what would be done with the reduction of forces, and why all this chaos?

Adm. S.: Because the planning never did foresee what really was happening. What was happening was that the country had lost interest in its forces. Our money was being severely restricted. We were not permitted to steam as much as we should steam or the aviators fly as much as they should fly for proper proficiency. The same thing is happening today, right now. We're being restricted again, and the same problems. They're going to get worse before they get better in the Navy today. This is 1977.

I remember that in order to try to build up the morale in my squadron, I initiated a very active athletic program - which resulted in - and I required my officers and men to go to all the athletic events. In other words, we had athletics every afternoon when we were in port. We generally had three weeks operating at sea, two weeks in port.

Q: This was in San Diego?

Adm. S.: In San Diego. During the in-port periods we had tremendous athletic programs, and the captain and the exec and the officers who didn't have the duty, and the wives and families were encouraged to go to the ball games and whatever else was scheduled in the afternoon. Then we'd break up and go home. Well, the thing, after being grumbled at a lot, finally took hold. My flagship, I remember, won the battle fleet athletic trophy. My division stood first in the fleet in athletics, and the second division of my squadron stood second. My flagship won the battle efficiency pennant. That was the Keyes. The Hollister, commanded by later Admiral Corky Ward, stood either first or second in battle efficiency, I forget which. The Keyes and the Hollister stood first and second.

I mention this because the ships' spirit that we built up through the athletic program, I think, resulted in finer performance in everything that we did. All of our gunnery practices, torpedo practices, we won engineering Es, we won everything.

Q: That's the history of emphasis on sports in the Navy, isn't it?

Adm. S.: That's right. Now, today, I don't think there's any such thing as real sports. The ships are too busy. They haven't been able to get together and do the things that we used to have to do to engender ship's spirit.

I remember that in our athletic grouping in the Pacific Fleet, we had eighty-three ships. Two of my ships stood first and second in battle efficiency in the Destroyer Force 08; also first and second in athletics in the Pacific Fleet. We had in that grouping two anti-aircraft cruisers, four destroyer tenders, besides seventy-seven destroyer type ships; lots of ships that were bigger than our little destroyers. I mention this to show that it does pay off when you insist on all hands getting interested and involved in something that you're doing as a ship; as a team.

Q: What sports did you concentrate on?

Adm. S.: We had a rifle team in every ship, we had a pistol team in every ship, we had a golf team in every ship. We tried to have tennis, but in those days tennis didn't take very well. Mind you, we had officer pistol teams, we had enlisted pistol teams. We had officer rifles teams, and enlisted. We had officer golf teams and enlisted golf teams. We had baseball, we had basketball.

Q: Wrestling?

Adm. S.: No, we didn't have wrestling because - I forget why we didn't have wrestling. Of course, baseball was big, basketball was big. I remember the exec of the Keyes who was a young man named Roger Spreen, later Admiral Spreen, was the pitcher on the baseball team, the star of the basketball team, he shot on the pistol team, played on the golf team. He did about everything. His captain sometimes wondered where his executive officer was, but was a good enough sport to realize that he was doing everything in the interest of the ship.

Q: You spoke of morale or the lack of morale and the steps you took to prevent that. At the root of the lack of morale, was there a feeling that perhaps they'd lost faith in the Navy as a career?

Adm. S.: I don't think so. Between wars, the people who stay in the Navy are those who really believe that the Navy is necessary for the security of the country. I doubt if any officer or enlisted man would come out and say that, but the only reason that many of them stay in the service in periods when the whole country is apathetic about the armed forces is the basic gut feeling that there has to be a navy and there have to be some people who are going to hold it together until the crisis comes, and there always have been enough people to keep that cadre together.

Q: That's a pretty intangible thing to cling to, isn't it?

Adm. S.: That's right, very. Many's the time I've been among those who said, "Why in the world are we staying in this Navy?"

Q: Well, this program of sports gave an immediacy to the situation, competition.

Adm. S.: That's right. I remember one of the exciting things that happened when I had that squadron was that one of my divisions, the one of which I was a part, went up to Bremerton and we had installed a brand new underwater search sonar. We used to have a single-beam searchlight sonar, and we got this new sonar which gave us a picture of what was below us, something that was almost as good then as I believe it is today. And the first exercise when we came out of the shipyard that we had with this marvelous new sonar, we got all of the enemy subs, something that we'd almost never been able to do before. The submarines in those exercises used to have to run from out at sea through an area and they generally got home free without our finding them, but we picked them all up and it was quite a feat.

Then the submariners all wanted to come on board our ship and find out how the hell we did it. And I started the procedure of having some of my destroyer officers go down in the submarines for these exercises, and we'd take some of the submarine officers on board our ships, because we in the destroyers wanted to find out what the submariners did to evade our attacks and the submariners wanted to find out what we were doing to counter what they were trying to do. I think it was very beneficial to both of us, both the subs and the destroyers.

Q: This leads to a question about training schools along the coast. Were they cut down in number, too?

Adm. S.: They were continued. We kept our good training schools. We had our sonar schools and our radar schools. Of course, we didn't have as many people going to them because we didn't have as much money available for those schools. But the Navy has been good in peacetime in keeping those schools going. Without them of course, we would be in dire straits.

Q: Yes.

Adm. S.: Even today our schools, I understand are excellent. Of course, I'm some distance from the Navy, but having a rear admiral son and a commander son on active duty and my daughter married to a just recently retired aviator captain - I still know something about what is going on in the Navy.

Q: You talk about the marvelous new sonar that the ships were equipped with at that point. Was there an upsurge in the field of ordnance because of World War II experience? Was there much coming on stream at this point?

Adm. S.: Yes, there was a lot coming on stream, which benefited us. Our radars were better and our sonars were better. I think our gunnery was better as a result of the experience in the war, our torpedoes were better. We didn't have as many duds.

Q: What about CIC?

Adm. S.: We all had CICs and we learned to use them. We started to learn to use them better than we had before. I was trying to think of some of the other highlights of that year in San Diego, operating with that squadron, but nothing particular comes to mind, except it was a very hard-working year that was pretty rewarding because we got such good results. Had I been in one of the squadrons that was in Status 2 or Status 3, I'm not sure I could have got very much interest going. I was just lucky -

Q: You mean you personally?

Adm. S.: I personally - I was lucky that I was a squadron commander of an active squadron. Some of my contemporaries were squadron commanders of squadrons that really did very little. We used to envy them at times because they were on the golf course at Coronado a good part of the time while we were out operating.

Q: That would get kind of boring, though, day after day!

Adm. S.: Well, it got pretty boring going out to sea at five o'clock every morning, too!

Q: Did you get much farther afield? Did you get into the Western Pacific?

Adm. S.: Oh, no, no. We just operated around San Diego the whole time I had the squadron, except for the shipyard overhaul in Bremerton.

Q: What was this Destroyer Division 3?

Adm. S.: That was the immediate division of my Destroyer

Squadron 3. In other words, Destroyer Squadron 3 had two divisions in it. My immediate division, the one I had with me and rode in was DesRon 3, as I remember it. If you asked me offhand what was the number of my destroyer division, I'm not sure I would have come up with it. I know it was DesRon 3, which had two divisions in it. DesDiv 31 and DesDiv 32.

Q: That's right.

Adm. S.: Is that right?

Q: Yes. Well, this was a kind of an interlude between Washington and Annapolis, wasn't it?

Adm. S.: That's right. I was ordered from that squadron to the Naval Academy.

Q: Was this something you sought also?

Adm. S.: No. Really, I had hoped - I had been slated to go to the Bureau of Personnel and I thought I was going as the captain detailer. My very good friend, later Vice Admiral Charlie Wellborn, was in BuPers at the time and had asked me if I would like to go there and I told him I would. But Admiral Holloway -

Q: Senior?

Adm. S.: Yes, the senior Admiral Holloway now - had determined that he was going to bring up the standard at the Naval Academy, which for some period of time had received officers who weren't particularly desired other places. In other words, almost everyone had the pick of the officers except the Naval Academy. They got the best of those who weren't especially asked for by someone up in Washington.

Q: That was a poor policy, was it not?

Adm. S.: Very poor.

Q: The training of young men.

Adm. S.: Very poor, and Holloway was determined he was going to improve that situation. When he was told he was going as superintendent he said:

"Okay, I'll go if you let me pick my heads of department," and then he began picking his heads of department and he picked a fine group.

I wasn't very happy about it, frankly, when I got word that Admiral Holloway had preempted my going to BuPers and I was to go to the Naval Academy because my view of duty at the Naval Academy at that time was the prevailing view, that it was distinctly not career-enhancing.

Q: Yes, it was a backwater.

Adm. S.: Yes, very few people who went to the Naval Academy got selected, up to that time. Very few heads of department were being selected. I further protested when I heard that I was to go as head of the Department of Electrical Engineering. I wrote a letter to Admiral Holloway and said that I did extremely well in languages and history and English and government, but I had a terrible time getting through the Department of Electrical Engineering, which I didn't really like, and I couldn't understand how in the world he had picked me to be the head of the Department of Electrical Engineering.

He pointed out that most of my time would be spent in adjudicating the disputes between the physicists, the chemists, the electrical engineers, and the electronics people, all of whom wanted more of the midshipmen's time each semester. And that was true. I did spend most of my time trying to keep a balance between the four disciplines. The chemists felt that they didn't have enough time to teach chemistry properly. The people who were teaching physics felt the same thing, and, of course, the electrical engineers said they didn't have anywhere near enough time.

Q: Most of these people were officer personnel, were they not?

Adm. S.: When I first went there, all but four or five people in my department were officers, and I found that many of them were officers who didn't have the faintest idea about the subject they were teaching. They were recalled reserves, some of whom had never even had a course in the subject they were sent down to teach. It was outrageous. I started right then a program. I went up to BuPers and I was able to persuade the superintendent and BuPers that we had to have better-qualified instructors. I succeeded in raising the number of civilian instructors considerably during my three years in that job, and I think - I'm not sure - that I was one of those who helped to establish the policy that we should have at least 50 percent civilians.

I felt that in a department as technical as mine, where you taught basic fundamentals in physics and chemistry and electrical engineering, the civilians should be in the great majority, with enough naval officers to teach the applications of the fundamentals that were being taught in the department.

Q: With a teaching faculty like that, how was the academy able to maintain accreditation with the Association of

American Universities?

Adm. S.: I don't honestly think at that time that we were very highly thought of by the accreditors. That's about all I can say about that.

Q: Who was superintendent at that time?

Adm. S.: Admiral Holloway was superintendent the first part of that tour and Admiral Harry Hill was superintendent the second part of my tour. Holloway was the one who brought me there and he stayed about a year or a year and a half, and then the second year and a half it was Harry Hill.

Q: Harry Hill began to put an emphasis on sports and that sort of thing?

Adm. S.: That's right.

Q: I might ask you what innovative things you did because you are an innovative person?

Adm. S.: Actually, as I think back on that tour, I have a little difficulty because I think also about some of the things that happened when I was superintendent later, and I have a little difficulty in my mind separating the two. It's been a long time since those days.

Q: Did you suffer because of an inadequacy in knowledge of electrical engineering?

Adm. S.: Did I personnally?

Q: Yes.

Adm. S.: Yes, I did. As a matter of fact, I was always on the side of the midshipmen against the instructors. One of the first things that I did when I got there was to sit in the classrooms and monitor the instruction. I did it for two reasons. I wanted to learn a little something about the subject and I wanted to see how well the subjects were being taught.

Well, I immediately ran into great indignation on the part of the civilians, who objected to the head of the department sitting in and listening to their presentations.

Q: It curbed their style somewhat!

Adm. S.: Yes. I found that they thought it was unethical. In the case of the officers, of course they couldn't say anything about it. But I could tell, after listening to an instructor, whether or not he was getting his subject across and how well he was getting it across. And, since I had to mark the fitness reports of all officers who were teaching and had a hand in the reports that were being made on the civilians, although my senior professor was actually making up the civilian reports, I felt that I should know a little something about them.

Q: That seems very logical.

Adm. S.: Yes, and it took me a long time to understand that I was not welcome in the classrooms.

Q: I can see where it would provide difficulties for the instructor, but also it seems like a necessary thing.

Adm. S.: It seemed necessary to me, but I gradually got out of the habit of going into the classrooms because I felt distinctly uncomfortable in there. The one classroom that I always went into was a special one - we had a special section for the football team in every subject - I had the best instructors that I had in physics, chemistry, electrical engineering, and electronics for the football team section. In those days, the football team went into their own sections.

Q: This was while you were head?

Adm. S.: This was while I was head of the department. I

told the instructors who were teaching the football squad that I expected them to really be tutors to the football team. They spent a lot of time on the practice field, they had to leave on trips, often on Fridays, they were denied opportunities to study that the other youngsters in the academy got, and I had a tremendous empathy for the burden we were putting on the members of the football team.

Q: Does it imply in any way an inadequacy in scholastic matters?

Adm. S.: That's right. And not only that, you know, but when you've been out there for two hours in a scrimmage on a football field you don't feel too much like coming back and studying that night. You're tired. So I had great sympathy for them, and every Monday morning I went into every class of every football section and we talked about the game the time before, the Saturday before. In those days, we lost practically all our games. I think we had seasons like two wins and six losses, one win and seven losses. We had some terrible seasons.

I remember one time particularly, we'd been beaten by Notre Dame 40 to 0, and I went into the classroom, the first class, Jim Baldinger was our captain, I remember, and I looked at the bruised faces, the closed eyes, and the battered people with bandages on their hands, and I said:

"How would you fellows feel about our giving up Notre Dame as an opponent? They're beating us so badly every year. Do you fellows think we ought to give them up, take them off our schedule?"

And Baldinger said: "Yes, Sir, after we've licked them. I think we ought to keep them there until we can beat them."

I thought that was the greatest thing I ever heard. Our kids had just had the hell beaten out of them by a very fine Notre Dame team.

Q: What did this do, however, to the training of the naval officer, the limited time you had him at the academy for training, when so much energy was going into the athletic program?

Adm. S.: I really don't think any more energy was poured into the program then than is poured in today. I really am not familiar with what they're doing today in the way of athletics, and I know that shortly after I left they did away with the special sections for football. I felt they were necessary and even had the instructors go with them on the planes to the games, which, of course, they enjoyed. They went along as guests of the Athletic Association and they were able to do some work with the boys that were having the hardest time on the planes.

Smedberg #4 - 401

If we flew out to California, say, for a game out there, they'd be a long, long time on the plane, coming and going, when the boys could have a little help from a very good instructor.

Q: What comment do you have to make on Harry Hill's thesis that the athletic program was a great boon in that it developed a community spirit, a community effort, the sort of thing that is necessary on board ship?

Adm. S.: I was with Harry Hill on that pretty much. I think that if you can get people together behind any endeavor, whether it's athletic or some other endeavor, you're increasing the spirit of the group. My feeling at the Naval Academy was that the varsity athletes were not, as they are in some colleges, the goons who were set aside from the student body, but they were part of the student body and regarded as such.

One of the criticisms that I later heard about our policy of having the special football sections was that that set those boys too much apart from the rest of the midshipmen. And I think that may have been one of the reasons those sections were done away with.

Q: Who suffered from that, the team itself or the rest of them?

Adm. S.: It sort of put a separation, a separator, between the midshipmen group as a whole and the teams, when they had their own sections, and I think some of the midshipmen suspected that maybe we were tipping off the boys on the football squad what was going to be in the exams. We weren't, but I was insisting that these boys be properly prepared for the examinations. They took the same exam everybody else did.

One other thing I did there that met with very little favor from the civilian members of my faculty. When I first got there I said:

"Now, I want to have on every examination one of the problems that has been assigned as homework during the term, and I want to have in every examination one of the problems that was assigned in a quiz."

Oh, they protested, but I insisted on it.

Q: Why did they protest?

Adm. S.: They said that would make the exam too easy. "Well," I said, "That's all right. I think it will encourage them to do their homework and to find out how to do the quiz problem that they busted on during the quiz. That's my idea. I know that when I was here, if I missed something on a quiz, I wasn't interested in finding out how I should have done it. If I'd known that that question might be on the examination, I would have asked and found out how

I should have worked that problem."

Well, the very first examination, the senior professor "Slipstick" Willy Thomson, who was a great fellow and who had taught me when I was a midshipman, or attempted to, came in with the examinations for each of the four classes. He laid the first one down in front of me and I said:

"Show me the problem that was in the book assigned as a homework problem." So he said:

"It's this one here, Sir."

I said: "Now let me see the book."

"Well, Sir," he said, "I want you to understand it's the same problem but we've changed the figures."

"That's no good," I said. "I want the identical figures of the problem."

"Sir, they'll all recognize it and a lot of them will know the answers."

"Fine," I said, "if they've done that problem in their homework and recognize it, that's a little bonus for them. Let me see the quiz."

He got the quiz and said:

"Well, Sir, we've changed the figures in that problem. It's the same identical problem, but we just changed the figures."

I made them put the figures back and they didn't like that. And I understand that right after I left, they were thrown out. Whether that was good or not, I don't have any idea, but I think and I hope that it did encourage the boys to do their homework and to try to find out where they made their mistakes in the quiz problems.

Q: I believe it was during Harry Hill's regime, and perhaps while you were there, that there was a cheating scandal at West Point and it had repercussions down here at the academy. Do you recall anything in connection with that?

Adm. S.: Yes. As a matter of fact, we heads of department were very incensed when Admiral Hill announced that he was going to talk to the first class and he did not want any heads of department present, and I think he excluded the commandant of midshipmen. He, Admiral Hill, got the first class and talked to them about the honor system, and we were furious that we were not allowed to hear what he was telling them. We had to find out about it from the midshipmen themselves.

Q: Why did he make it so classified?

Adm. S.: I don't have any idea, but I've always felt in connection with the honor system at the Naval Academy that ours was not really a system, as such. Ours was sort of a feeling about integrity. West Point had a black and white rule, which we didn't approve of at the Naval Academy. If at West Point one cadet sees another cadet cheating, he has to report him. If he doesn't report him, he is in violation of the honor code himself. We don't believe in that. We feel that every midshipman should police his own actions. He shouldn't lie and he shouldn't steal and he shouldn't cheat, but he's not set up to tell on his classmates.

So we felt that we didn't have a system. We had a concept, and I think that maybe that's what Harry Hill was trying to tell the first class. And I think that our concept has served the Naval Academy far better than the West Point system served West Point. I wouldn't be surprised if, today, the West Point system isn't more like the Naval Academy concept that it used to be.

Q: Was there an academic board at that time, when you were head of a department?

Adm. S.: Oh, yes. The academic board met on every student who failed, and each one of us voted as to whether or not he would be discharged or given a reexamination. Every midshipman who failed appeared before that board and was entitled to have his say, and say whether or not he would like to take a reexamination and why he thought he'd failed, why he wanted to stay in the Navy. Very often a boy who had done very poorly in academics but who convinced us that he was gung-ho Navy and really wanted a naval career, we'd give him all kinds of chances, rather than the brilliant boy who failed one subject and didn't give a damn, you know, about the Navy.

Q: Yes. Well, in that time there weren't so many youngsters seeking an education without regard to future service in the Navy, were there?

Adm. S.: Yes, I think so. We've always said that we would take only boys who were motivated toward a naval career, but there isn't anyone, I know today, who can tell whether a boy is motivated toward a naval career when he's seventeen or eighteen or nineteen years of age. He doesn't know what a naval career is.

Q: Including the boy himself.

Adm. S.: That's right. He doesn't know.

Q: That's a part of what you must accomplish during the time he's at the Naval Academy.

Adm. S.: It's our business at the Naval Academy to motivate

the boy toward a naval career, make him feel that it's worthwhile, that he's serving his country, and that the rewards that will come from that service are worthwhile to him.

Q: What could you, as head of department, do to advance this effort, to promote it?

Adm. S.: It's pretty hard to say right now what any one individual could do. We tried to sell the rewards of a naval career to the youngsters. We tried to make it seem attractive to them without hiding the fact that there are a lot of difficult periods that they had to go through. I can't think of any specific thing that I did to sell any particular individuals on the Navy.

Q: Well, you yourself, even then, I suppose, were a kind of a lightning rod in the sense that you inspired people to be naval officers. Did you then utilize this, perhaps unconsciously, in your home - you had quarters on the grounds, did you not?

Adm. S.: Yes.

Q: Did you entertain many of them?

Adm. S.: Oh, yes, we had mids at our house constantly, all the time. Yes, indeed. And I'll never forget my indignation when we came from the Army-Navy baseball game one day back to my house, the game had been played on the field here at the Naval Academy. I remember that in the fifteenth inning - we had come from behind in the ninth and tied it up in the last of the ninth, we had come from behind in the last of the thirteenth to tie it up, and in the fifteenth Army had men on - we were leading by one run - second and third, two out, Arnold Califfa at bat. He hit a pop fly right over the pitcher's box, Zastro, our third baseman, called for it. The pitcher got out of the way. Zastro stood there, and the captain of our team, the second baseman, who didn't think Zastro would get it, came over calling that he had it. They bumped together. The ball fell between them, two runs scored and we lost the Army-Navy game.

When I got back to my house, I found two plebes playing bridge with my daughter and a friend of hers in my quarters. I don't think any two plebes ever got a bawling out such as I gave them for not having been out there supporting their team that day. I don't think they'll ever forget that!

Q: Did the instructors do very much of that sort of thing, having the midshipmen in all the time?

Adm. S.: Yes.

Q: It seems to me this is a way of instilling -

Adm. S.: That's right. I think most of the instructors did, the military more than the civilians, perhaps, as was natural because when you're teaching a midshipman you realize that someday he's liable to be a shipmate of yours. And if you're teaching him navigation, you want to be sure he's a pretty good navigator because he may be navigating the destroyer that you're the captain of or squadron commander in, so I think naval officers have a tremendous interest in the people with whom they're going to serve later.

I'll say another thing about the civilian faculty at the academy. I think they're a magnificent bunch of men because they are just as proud of the naval officers who do well later on as we are who are naval officers. I know I think with tremendous affection of people like Professors Thompson, Potter, Jeffries, I bowled on the bowling team, for instance, with my civilians for three years in the Department of Electrical Engineering.

Was it Ed Crowe who was acting dean here a year or two years ago? Yes, he was one of my top civilian instructors, as were John Daly, "Pinky" Pinkston, Sid Goodwin, Bill Smedley - these are only a few of the civilians for whom I have the greatest, I had and still have, the greatest admiration and affection because they were just as interested in turning out good naval officers as I was.

Q: I suppose a naval officer had this advantage in terms of his relationship with the midshipmen, he had quarters on the grounds and most of the civilians didn't?

Adm. S.: In those days the senior officers had quarters on the grounds, but most of the instructors didn't.

Q: I see.

Adm. S.: They had to find themselves places to live outside. As they built those apartments over where the old golf course used to be, beyond the PG school, more and more of the younger officers who were teachers had quarters. Particularly the company officers had quarters and they had midshipmen from their companies in all the time. But in the day when I was a head of department, there were not that many quarters. Mostly just the heads of departments and the executive officers had the quarters on Upshur and Porter rows.

Q: As head of the department, did you have anything to do with the summer cruises?

Adm. S.: Yes. One summer I was in command of the midshipman detachment in the Missouri. We took the midshipmen over to England. I remember getting together with Lady Astor on one occasion to arrange a party. This was in 1948, the summer of 1948, I think.

Q: That was your first summer there?

Adm. S.: Yes. Perhaps it was the summer of '49. Anyway, England still didn't have very much food, and I remember that Lady Astor was very excited because I told her that I would bring a lot of turkeys and hams for a buffet. She furnished all the girls, and I spent a good deal of my time -

Q: Was this at her country place?

Adm. S.: No, this was in a local hall that they hired for the purpose, but the girls were the daughters of dukes and duchesses, earls, and so forth. I spent my time getting a stag line going, introducing the idea of cutting in. I would go round and I would ask a girl her name who wasn't dancing, and get a midshipman, introduce them and get them dancing, and then get somebody else to break on them. I spent quite a little time doing that!

Anyway, the Astors' gratitude for the wonderful

turkeys and hams - but the minute they were put on the table, all the girls left their partners and gathered around the turkeys and hams and ate as though they hadn't seen meat like that in years.

Q: A cruise in an opportunity for some implementation of learning acquired in the classroom. Were you able to assist in that?

Adm. S.: Oh, we had regular classes on the cruise, not academic classes but classes in seamanship and navigation. In those days every midshipman had to have about a third of the cruise in the engine room, a third of the cruise on the bridge, and a third of the cruise on deck. Each midshipman was rotated through three different environments in the ship.

Q: Was he rated on that summer activity?

Adm. S.: Yes, he was rated on his summer activities in all areas. The first class took the part of junior officers. I thought the cruises were wonderful things, frankly, because, although the midshipmen didn't participate to the extent that we did on our cruises, which we did in battleships in '23, '24, and '25, about half of the enlisted complement of the ship would be taken off the ship and sent on leave, and we midshipmen took their places and actually did every thing they would do as seamen. And I thought that was very valuable experience.

Q: But this wasn't so later on?

Adm. S.: No. Later on they weren't required to do that kind of work as much.

Q: When you had them all on a battleship like that, it was like having a floating academy, wasn't it?

Adm. S.: Yes, it was. In a ship as large as the Missouri, we had adequate space for classrooms and compartments, and the ship, of course, was always comfortable. In a smaller ship, very often in rough weather, you can't keep many people interested in lectures or demonstrations or anything. It's too uncomfortable.

Q: What sort of leave did they have on that particular cruise, continental leave? I mean what kind of leave did they have and what kind of supervision did they have on leave, and what moneys did they have to spend?

Adm. S.: We didn't try to supervise them ashore. They had liberty by sections. I think they had two days ashore for each day of duty, or maybe it was three days ashore for one day of duty, in a port. When in port, they'd go ashore around ten or eleven in the morning and were back at midnight most nights. We made trips that we thought were valuable for educational purposes available to them, which they paid for. We gave them extra money for the cruise from their amounts available, in addition to their monthly stipend which, in those days, was not very much.

Q: A cruise like that is complicated in terms of planning. Who accomplished the planning for it?

Adm. S.: The planning was all done by the Naval Academy staff in conjunction with people in Washington and the naval attaches abroad in the ports we visited.

Q: Months in advance?

Adm. S.: Oh, yes. That's still true, when you're going to have ships visit a port, you have to have a lot of advance planning.

Q: Are there any specific recollections of those three years on campus when you were head of the department, not necessarily related to what you've been saying so far?

Adm. S.: That was a long time ago. I can just say that we thoroughly enjoyed our association with the midshipmen. I felt very strongly then and I feel just as strongly today that the required attendance at Sunday service was as much a part of the education of a naval officer as anything else he got there. It was with a tremendous amount of disgust that I viewed the Congress' action in making attendance at divine service no longer a requirement at the service academies.

Q: Actually, it was the action of the courts, wasn't it?

Adm. S.: Yes, I believe it was. I feel that it is the responsibility of the Naval Academy to take a boy -- many of those youngsters who came there had never had any church-going in their lives, didn't know much about the Bible, and I think that when a man gets to be commanding officer of a ship he should run his ship on Christian principles and he learns many of those in church.

I know that when I was skipper of the *Iowa*, for instance, I always had a morning prayer over the loudspeaker every morning. Of course, today they're not allowed to do that. And when my chaplain was on leave or sick, I personnally gave the prayer every morning at eight o'clock. Every man in the ship stood bare-headed with his head bowed. You'd be surprised. You could go any place in that ship and you'd find during the very short morning prayer that every man throughout the ship would be standing bare-headed.

And in my little destroyers during the war I always had a prayer, particularly before we were going into action. On one occasion, when I picked up some 500 survivors from the Wasp - I may have mentioned this before, in which case you can delete it - the next morning my exec came to me and said:

"Sir, four of the badly wounded died during the night. I have them ready for burial on the fantail, if you would come back and read the burial service."

I said, "Fine, have you got the prayer book?" And he said no, he couldn't find one on the ship.

"Gee," I said, "I don't have one either. Just get a Bible and I'll pick a passage out of the Bible."

We didn't have a Bible on that ship. Now, that's a terrible thing.

Q: Weren't the Gideons active in getting Bibles on the ships?

Adm. S.: I don't know; it could be. I do know that, in the South Pacific Command, an order was issued directing us to throw all books over the side before going into action; throw everything that would burn over the side.

That was an order at one time, in one of the task forces I was in.

Q: Chip all the paint and throw the books over.

Adm. S.: I think I told you before that on my way back to the fantail, when I was thinking of a prayer that I would make up as we tipped the bodies over the side, a man in oil-soaked skivvies came up to me - that's all he had on - and said:

"Captain, I understand you're going to have a burial service?" I said yes, so he said:

"I wonder if I could be of assistance? I was the assistant chaplain of the Wasp and I was Dean Williams at the National Cathedral in Washington."

"You're sent by the good Lord," I said, "you certainly can."

He conducted the service from memory and it was magnificent. I'm sure I told you that several weeks later he was back in Washington preaching at the National Cathedral and my mother happened to be in the audience. He mentioned this incident, which was the first she had heard about me in many, many months.

That was some digression.

Q: As head of a department, were you ever involved with the

Smedberg #4 - 418

Board of Visitors that came periodically to the academy? Were the heads invited in to talk with them and that sort of thing?

Adm. S.: Yes. I personally always enjoyed the Board of Visitors because the more serious members, and by that I mean the ones who were academicians and who were genuinely interested in what we did here, were awfully interesting to talk to, and were interested in what we had to say about what we did. I always enjoyed the Board of Visitors' meetings when I was a head of department, and even more when I was superintendent.

Q: Were the heads of departments in any way related to the heads of departments, corresponding departments, in West Point?

Adm. S.: Yes, except that at West Point they had more permanent tenure in those days. I think they had some professional heads of department at West Point, who were officers who had been kept on for long periods of time and made professor, in uniform. We didn't do that. Our tenure was three years.

I should say that in this group that Admiral Holloway got together as heads of departments, most of us were later selected for rear admiral. There was Cooper, who later became a vice admiral, William G. Cooper. There was Kenny Craig, who later became a rear admiral. Bob Pirie, and myself who later became vice admirals. Admiral McCorkle - Tiny McCorkle - Bob Rice who later became rear admirals. Right there is a very impressive list. We were all there together.

I know that my golf foursome when we were heads of department was later Vice Admiral Pirie, later Vice Admiral Cooper, myself, and Rear Admiral Kenny Craig. We played golf together for almost three years, every chance we got. This was after very few people who'd had head of department duty at the Naval Academy had ever been selected for flag rank.

Q: I guess Holloway was an awfully good influence on the academy, wasn't he?

Adm. S.: He was.

Q: He had the intellectual emphasis -

Adm. S.: Well, he had tremendous enthusiasm and vigor, and he wasn't afraid to say what he thought and throw his weight around up in Washington to require that the Naval Academy get more attention.

One of the things that impressed me while I was a

head of department was the often lack of proper qualification to teach of the officers who were sent here. As a result, when I got to be chief of Naval Personnel I set up a program that required that instructors going to the Naval Academy would have to take a course to get a master's degree in the subject he was going to teach. In other words, I was always impressed by the fact that at West Point they had a program that envisioned taking the man, sending him to college, and then sending him to teach. He would have studied the subject he was going to teach and that's what I tried to set up when I was chief of the Bureau of Personnel and, to quite a large extent, I was able to do that.

But in 1949 and 1950 we still had a thoroughly chaotic condition in personnel, due to the rapid demobilization after the war, and we called reserves just to teach at the Naval Academy who had no qualifications to teach the subject for which they were ordered at all, and no particular interest in it. That was a thing that was very distressing.

Of course, when I was a midshipman we had officers who taught who really were lousey teachers, didn't know their subjects very well in some cases.

Q: There seemed to be a feeling that just a body there -

Adm. S.: Yes, that's right.

Q: - leading a class was sufficient.

Adm. S.: There are too many instances in the history of the Naval Academy where the Bureau of Personnel and the old Bureau of Navigation just ordered somebody that nobody else had any particular requirement for to the Naval Academy to teach whatever was necessary. In other words, a man would be ordered to the Naval Academy and the Naval Academy would say:

"What subject would you like to teach?"

The fellow would say: "I really don't care about teaching any subject," and they'd say:

"Well, you're going to teach English," or whatever subject it was.

That's not true today.

Q: So much of the classroom work was learning by rote, wasn't it?

Adm. S.: Actually, the philosophy for years was that it was all in the book and it was up to the student to dig it out of the book, and the instructor would mark. He was not really a teacher. He was a referee between the book and what the midshipman was able to produce.

Yes, a lot of it was learning by rote rather than instruction.

Q: You spent three profitable years as head of a department and I expect they were more profitable in terms of what you came back to eventually, as superintendent. I mean it must have been very useful to have had three years here as head of a department?

Adm. S.: It was extremely useful because I understood the problems of the department heads probably better than most superintendents ever have, having been one myself.

I remember on one occasion going to Harry Hill and saying that about one-third of a class was unsatisfactory in chemistry at the end of the term and we felt that the boys had not been studying and we wanted that to stand up. Admiral Hill told me to go back and reduce the number of unsats, he wouldn't accept it. That was an order. We had to go back and reduce the number of unsatisfactory midshipmen.

Q: It was too demoralizing to the -

Adm. S.: No, he didn't want to have to report it up to Washington, the fact that we'd failed that many of the same class. It was the first semester, the first term, and we just wanted to make them work harder the second term, but Admiral Hill felt that it might cause us to lose too many youngsters.

He had the same problem with math. Math also had a tremendous number of unsats because the kids weren't working.

Q: Something must have been failing at that point. Where was their motivation?

Adm. S.: Something was failing. Right after the war, you know, you don't have as much motivation as you do at some other period, and this was in 1949, 1950. I can't put my finger on the reason for this, whether it was because we didn't have as good instructors - I know we didn't have very good instructors in my department.

But my experience as head of department was very valuable to me later when I was superintendent.

Q: Well, we'll hear more about that later in the story. Now you were about to leave the academy after three years and you were promised -

Adm. S.: I was told that I was to go in command of the Sixth Fleet flagship, the USS Columbus, in the Mediterranean. Had my orders - I was very pleased and excited about that because that was a top sea job. I expressed my uniforms over to the Med, to the Columbus, and about a week before I was to leave, I got a telephone call from a detailer in Washington, later Vice Admiral Frank Watkins, saying that he hated to tell me but he had to cancel my orders to the Columbus.

I was shocked and I asked him why. He said:

"Well, because you are going to take the battleship Iowa out of "mothballs", put her back in commission, and take her out to the Korean War."

Q: That really was an accolade, was it not?

Adm. S.: To me, it was a shock. I mean I wanted this active cruiser. I didn't want to take an old battleship out of mothballs and train the crew. It was a terrible shock to me. I said:

"Where in the world is the Iowa?" and he said: "Frankly, I don't know where she is."

Q: She wasn't such an old battleship, really, was she?

Adm. S.: No, she was still one of the four most powerful ones in the world, but she had been put into "mothballs" several years before. We found that she was out in Seattle, out in Bremerton. I was called up by Admiral Sherman and he said:

"I want you to get that ship in commission as fast as you can. I'm going to give you the officers who have been trained for the cruiser Bremerton and the crew who have been trained for another cruiser," and I think it was the Pittsburgh.

Q: Sherman was CNO at that time?

Adm. S.: Sherman was then CNO, and he said:

"I want to tell you that the one thing you cannot do is run that ship aground." This was after the Missouri had gone aground at Norfolk. He said: "No matter what orders you get, if you don't think it's safe for that ship, don't carry them out. If you have any problems, refer them to me."

And later on I had a couple of occasions when I remembered that advice with the Iowa.

Anyway, I went out to San Francisco from that nice house on Porter Road and went into half a quonset with my wife at Hunter's Point, where the shower was in the living room. If you dropped the soap and leaned over to pick it up, you propelled yourself out into the living room, the little thin shower was so narrow. The bed we slept in was under the eaves of this rounded quonset, so that you had about a six-inch breathing space, and if you turned over you hit your head on the top of the quonset.

We lived in that thing for thirty days while I was

getting the Iowa back in commission. And, incidentally, I incurred the almost lifelong enmity of two good friends of mine. One was later Admiral Jim Ward, who was to have commanded the Bremerton, and the other one, I think, Preston Mercer, who was to have command of the Pittsburgh.

Q: Why, because you took their officers?

Adm. S.: I got all their officers and their men and both ships were held up about three months going into commission while they trained other crews.

You see, in those days they used to take these crews, officers and enlisted men, and send them to all the schools in San Diego and train them in the job they would have on board ship. Unfortunately, these people were trained for those specific cruisers, so when they came on board the Iowa I didn't have a single soul who had ever been in a 16-inch turret before. And the first problem we had was to find somebody who knew something about a 16-inch gun turret, so I requested permission from the shipyard commander, who was also my boss there, while getting the ship ready for commissioning, to send one officer and I think it was thirteen enlisted men across the continent to the New Jersey, which was in commission on the East Coast, to find out how to operate a 16-inch gun turret. We didn't even know how to load the ammunition. He turned me down, so I sent a dispatch to the CNO and said it was imperative that I do this. He answered "affirmative," so I sent three officers and thirteen men per turret - I had three turrets - to the East Coast where they got trained, came back, and we loaded the ammunition; powder and shells and went ahead with our drills.

Q: A comment. How quickly the glory of the battleship had vanished?

Adm. S.: Yes, that's right. Well, you see, they could have dug up people with experience in 16-inch turrets, had those crews been readied for the Iowa, but nobody was trained for the Iowa. These crews were trained for the light cruisers, or heavy cruisers - they were heavy cruisers with 8-inch guns.

We took that ship out of mothballs and within twenty-five days we had her at sea making 25 knots off the Farcellon Islands.

Q: So she must have had a good period in mothballs. There wasn't much that was wrong with her.

Adm. S.: There wasn't anything wrong with her. We just had to learn how to put her back together again. I remember they had sealed up the voids and every void that we unsealed - they had welded them shut - had something in it. One small void we opened up had a wonderful ship's log in it and the last sentence in that was, "A great ship never dies." So that was our motto when we put her back in commission.

Q: Did you seek or were you asked to take a brief course in shiphandling when you took charge of her?

Adm. S.: No, there was no time. I was ordered right out there, to find her, put her in shape, train the crew and get into the Korean War, in the shortest possible time.

Q: I remember that Charlie Melson was a little bit annoyed when he took the New Jersey, I guess it was, and he had to have a course in shiphandling. He didn't like this idea, the inference being that perhaps he didn't know how!

Adm. S.: I had commanded and put in commission two destroyers and trained the crews for World War II, and I'd handled plenty of ships in my time, including cruisers. Frankly, I handled the Iowa just like a destroyer, and we traveled fast. We traveled around 30 knots most of the time. We could do 32 and ofttimes did out in Korea. I had no fuel restrictions, and I was often ordered to go from one spot to another where I had to make 28 to 30 knots to do it. The only problem was we had stern tubes that fit in the bearings so loosely that when I got up to 30 knots, the chief petty officers had to abandon their quarters aft because they were shaken up like mexican jumping beans. And I always tried to slow during the meal hour so that the petty officers could sit down and have their meals, if I had to make a high-speed run.

Q: Was the Iowa relieving another battleship on station?

Adm. S.: We were relieving the Wisconsin, which was out in Korea.

Q: Was the Iowa the flagship of the - ?

Adm. S.: Of the Seventh Fleet.

Q: So you had Jocko?

Adm. S.: I had, first, Admiral Briscoe and then Jocko Clark. I'd never known Jocko before, and he and I had quite a few disagreements. He was not a good man to disagree with. I'm getting a little ahead of my story.

Q: Yes.

Adm. S.: We took the Iowa and in twenty-five days we had her making 25 knots. The very first time we got her underway I was ordered to steam around San Francisco Bay to test out the engines and so forth. So my navigator and I laid out what we called a fairly safe course, from the head of the bay we'd go under the Bay bridge, down around close to Alcatraz, and then close to the Golden Gate Bridge, and then back, and we had to do that three or four times.

Well, the first day we did that, we damned near went aground on Alcatraz, because the tide was flooding and, coming in from the Golden Gate, my ship was being set right over on Alcatraz. To this day, I don't think we missed a grounding by more than six feet. I was holding my breath.

Q: Why such a hazardous operation? Why not go out in the open water?

Adm. S.: I was ordered to do this by the shipyard commander, who was my boss. He was afraid she'd break down in the open sea. If she broke down in the bay, he could handle it with tugs.

That night, Claudia and I went over and had dinner with Admiral and Mrs. Nimitz at their house in Berkeley, and the first thing Admiral Nimitz said to me was:

"Smedberg, that was the most foolhardy thing I've

ever seen a naval officer do. Do you know how many battleships have gone aground in San Francisco Bay in the past?"

"Well," I said, "Admiral, I was ordered to do that."

He said: "I wouldn't give a damn. I don't care who ordered me to do that, I wouldn't do it. I would have said 'I won't do it.'"

I said, "Admiral, you're a fleet admiral, a five-star admiral. It's very easy for you to say you wouldn't do it. I'm a junior captain and when I'm ordered to do something, I do it." He said:

"Smedberg, remember, if anybody tells you to do something as risky as that, refuse to do it."

Well, to jump ahead a little bit, when I took <u>Iowa</u> down to San Diego for the refresher training with my new crew, I had orders from the senior officer present there to take a berth inside San Diego Harbor. I'd operated in and out of there in destroyers for years and I knew there was a shallow spot off Ballast Point, in the channel going in and out. So I got my chart out and I found there were 34 feet of water at high water there at Ballast Point. I was drawing 38 feet. So I sent a message back:

"Cannot enter the harbor. Request anchor in Coronado Roads," which is outside. The answer came back:

"Carry out your original orders."

The admiral who was the senior officer present

afloat was a vice admiral, Tommy Sprague, who, when I was a young captain in the office of the secretary of the Navy and he was chief of Naval Personnel, had shaken his fist under my nose and said:

"Young man, if it's the last thing I ever do, I'm going to get you." The reason being that, when he had recommended that the Navy not go for a pay increase in 1946, I had persuaded the secretary of the Navy that the reason he had done that was because he was afraid the naval aviators were going to lose their flight pay. And I said the Navy desperately needed a pay increase and we had to support it. Forrestal overturned the chief of naval personnel and the chief of naval operations, by the way. We got the pay increase through the Congress with no difficulty whatsoever, and Sprague came to me and shook his fist under my nose and said:

"By God, I'm going to get you if it's the last thing I ever do."

Q: Did you think he was actually trying to implement that threat at that point?

Adm. S.: Well, I knew he didn't like me and I knew he felt that, again, I was trying to thwart his orders. He'd given me an order to come in. So, when I got down there, I anchored out in Coronado Roads, and I immediately got a signal:

"Commanding officer report to the SOPA immediately." So I got my boat, went through the channel, and he was livid when I got in there. He said:

"You had your orders to come in and take a certain berth in this harbor, didn't you?" And I said:

"Yes, Sir."

"Why didn't you do it?"

"Sir, I told you I can't enter the harbor." And he said:

"Of course, you can. My carriers go in and out of there every day."

I said: "Your carriers don't draw anything like the water I draw, Sir."

"Oh," he said, "the hell they don't. They draw a lot more water than you do."

"Well," I said, "how much do you think your carriers draw, Sir?"

He said: "They draw about 32 feet."

I said: "I'm drawing 38 and there's a 36-foot spot coming into the entrance. Furthermore, Admiral Sherman has told me that if anybody gives me an order to do something that might hazard the ship, I'm to refuse it. If you wish, I'll report this to Admiral Sherman."

He let the matter drop, but he had it investigated and found that I did, in fact, draw 38 feet, and I don't think he ever forgave me, but I never once entered the harbor. I wouldn't enter the harbor, naturally. I would have liked to be in the harbor because it was very inconvenient sending my crews ashore on liberty.

Q: Of course, it was.

Adm. S.: We actually didn't get much liberty because we were working like the devil to get ready to go to the war and relieve the Wisconsin, which we did.

Q: What was the real mission of the ship in Korea?

Adm. S.: The real mission was to provide fire support to the Marines who were inland in Korea and the first ROK (Republic of Korea) division, which was along the shore. We provided support with our 5-inch guns to the ROK division and with our 16-inch guns to the Marines, who were fifteen or sixteen miles inland and over the mountains. We also almost daily knocked out the railroads all along the coast, closed up the tunnels. It was the most fascinating shooting I've ever done in all my years in the Navy. We bombarded Wonsan, we bombarded the big port just south of the Russian border whose name has escaped me for the moment. I'll never forget it.

Q: Chongjin?

Adm. S.: Yes, Chongjin.

Q: We were talking about the mission.

Adm. S.: Yes. The mission of the ship actually was to furnish fire-support to the Marine division inland and the First ROK division on the coast with our 16-inch battery and our 5-inch battery, which we did on call, always with either spotting planes or Marine gunfire liaison officers in the territory.

One day, Easter Sunday 1952, we bombarded Chongjin, which was close to Russia, all day long from about seven in the morning until five or six in the afternoon with 16-inch shells, with air spot, and all the time we were bombarding we had on our radars large groups of Russian planes orbiting about 40 miles north of us. We never knew when they might come down. I had a combat air patrol over me of two Navy fighters furnished by the carriers, and we could count as many as forty or fifty Russian planes in the air all day long, circling around. We never knew whether they would come down or not.

Q: What was the intelligence interpretation of their action?

Adm. S.: We had no intelligence interpretation. We didn't know. All we knew was that the planes were there, circling out there at sea, and I guess they were trying to scare us off. But they were a little afraid to come down. I know that we heard a broadcast that evening that we had been sunk and that one of the destroyers with me had been sunk. We destroyed all of the big gantry cranes along the seafront. We blew up a train of oil tankers in the big marshalling yards. We were very careful not to fire into any of the housing settlements on the hills around the industrial part of the city. We never fired a shot without air spot, and the pilot would tell us that we were ten yards to the left or 100 yards to the right. He'd get us right on and then sometimes we'd fire a three-gun salvo at a worthwhile target, like a group of trains, for instance.

When we hit the train of oil cars, it went up like an atomic explosion, with a great mushroom. The whole train blew up. It was the most spectacular thing you ever saw in your life.

Q: What sort of instructions were you operating under that caused you to have such concern for the civilian population?

Adm. S.: We always tried to concern ourselves with the

civilians. Even in World War II, when I was chief of staff of the bombardment force in Saipan, Guam, and Tinian, we tried to keep out of the civilian population sections of whatever we were shooting at. I know that on Saipan we were supporting - this is a throwback - but on Saipan my cruisers, of which I was chief of staff, were supporting the Marines. We were about a mile and a half off the beach, in line with the Marines who were advacing. They would call for us to destroy a certain resistance point ahead of them. We would put shells in there and destroy it, then they would give us another one.

In one case, there was a perfectly beautiful little village that was holding up the Marines. We could see people in the village, women and children. I had a spotting plane up, and the Marines said that there was heavy resistance there. They had stone basements and there were a lot of snipers in the stone basements, and they wanted us to wipe out the village. So, with reluctance, we gave the order to fire into the village. The first salvo appeared to me to land right in it, and my spotter spotted us 500 yards over. I got on the earphones and I said to the plane spotter:

"Wasn't that last salvo right in the village?" and he said:

"Yes, Sir, but there are a lot of women and children in there."

We burned that village down, though. We fired phosphorescent shells in there, set fire to the village, and burned it down because it was offering resistance to the marines. We didn't want to do it, and this young aviator was terribly upset. He was the son of a minister, it turned out later, and he just couldn't see killing innocent women and children. Neither could we, but if we didn't, then our Marines were going to be killed.

The same way in the Korean War. We tried very hard not to let shells burst in the area of just civilian housing.

Q: Tell me more about the daily or nightly destruction of the railroads.

Adm. S.: The Koreans had crews right near every tunnel and, as you know, the railroad runs right along the coast and goes through tunnel after tunnel after tunnel. Every morning the tunnels would be opened, or almost every morning, and we'd put a 16-inch shell right into the entrance or above it and put an avalanche down and close the tunnel. Then they'd work all night and open it up.

On one or two occasions I was able to sort of cap the T on the mouth of a tunnel, and on one occasion I got a 16-inch shell right smack into a tunnel and hit a train that was hiding in there. It blew up in the tunnel.

That was one of the most successful things we ever did while we were there.

We used to cut the rail beds, and I've got many pictures today taken by our helicopter, which used to spot for us. I had a young Marine captain in the helicopter and he was my spotter. He'd say "Tunnel closed," then we'd cut the railroad. We'd put a 16-inch shell right onto the track and we'd blow the track apart, so that would take care of that. Then we'd move on up the coast and destroy another piece of the track. Once or twice we caught a train, but we never were able to hit a train before it got into a tunnel. We never really got a direct hit on a fast-moving train, which was always a source of great sorrow to me.

Q: How far off did you stand?

Adm. S.: Only about a mile or a mile and a half off the beach. It was a direct line-of-sight shot, really, for a 16-inch gun. Then we were firing our 5-inch, too, at the livestock and, of course, whenever any kind of a car, a freight car, was abandoned, we always set them on fire and turned them up or knocked them off the track. That was like shooting ducks in a shooting gallery.

We had two significant things happen. We had gotten on line and we had an urgent call for firing on a battery of 3-inch that was firing on the Marines and they were nineteen miles from where my ship was. I took my ship right in, almost with her bow on the beach, because I could shoot about twenty miles. We set up our problem, we fired one 16-inch shot. The spotter came back. We waited I think it was 70 or 75 seconds for the shell, the time of the flight of the shell, and when we said splash, in almost the same voice he said: "My God, you landed right between the things and destroyed three of the four guns." That was the greatest single shot we ever made.

Q: That's really being accurate!

Adm. S.: Oh, yes. Then, on another occasion, we were assigned a very secret mission. Our coast watchers had come out and said that there was to be a meeting, the whole area had been sealed off, and the dope was that all the leaders from North Korea were coming down to confer in this little town, which was just about eighteen miles from the coastline. We knew that they were going to meet at eight o'clock in the morning. They had a big conference arranged. They'd all come in the day before, so obviously they were all encamped there that night.

The decision was made by the higher-ups not to send planes over because their radars would pick them up and they would all take shelter. So it was decided to order the _Iowa_ to creep in during the night at low speed, fix our position, get an accurate fix, and fire a nine-gun salvo of 16-inch shells at this meeting. So we crept in very quietly at two o'clock in the morning, got in position, I lowered the anchor very quietly so my ship would not be affected by current, we got an absolutely accurate gunfire solution. We had the spot on our chart where this meeting was to be held, and just before dawn we let go with nine 16-inch shells. But we never could find out what happened because the entire area was sealed off. We couldn't get a coast watcher in or out. We never heard what happened but for weeks they wouldn't let anybody in or out of that area. And to this day I've wanted to know what result we got from that salvo.

You know, there's no warning on a 16-inch shell. When it goes over you, it sounds like a freight train going by, but until it arrives you don't hear it. So they had no warning and these things just must have landed in amongst them or close to them without any warning whatsoever, and I just can't imagine the chaotic conditions that existed in that camp, because they didn't know what had happened, whether it was an air attack or what it was.

That is the one thing that I wish I could have found out about.

Q: Did you ever ask the commission at Panmunjon to try to find out?

Adm. S.: No. I've meant to for years but I've just never done it.

Q: You mentioned coast watchers. No one has ever mentioned coast watchers in connection with Korea. Tell me about them.

Adm. S.: Actually, I used the term "coast watchers" because that's what we used down in the Solomons in World War II. These were agents who actually were landed at night and they would infiltrate the area. Then they'd come out and would be picked up and we would get the intelligence from them about activities in the area behind the North Korean lines.

There was one other thing that we did regularly. We interdicted the enemy all night long. In other words, we would be assigned a fire support mission for the night by the Marine commanders or the First ROK Corps commanders. They would give us their front line, and the enemy, of course, was to the north of their lines, and all night long I would fire occasional 5-inch into their lines so they wouldn't get any sleep. And, every now and then, just for the hell of it, I would fire a 16-inch shell in.

They never knew when it was going to come. I'd wait till the movies were over on the ship, then I'd tell all hands to stand by for a 16-inch shell over the loudspeaker. Then we'd let go a 16-inch, and you can imagine the little 5-inchers popping in there and suddenly one 16-inch going off. We did this all night long, at intermittent times. In other words, we'd fire one, two, three, then we wouldn't fire any for an hour, or maybe twenty minutes, then we'd fire two or three. Then we'd wait half an hour and fire some more. So they never knew when they were coming.

Q: Like somebody upstairs dropping a shoe -

Adm. S.: And you're waiting for the other one, that's right. It must have been extremely difficult for those enemy troops in there, with shells coming all night long. Occasionally, we'd fire star shells at night to illuminate the enemy when our people were going to advance at night. It was a fascinating experience.

Q: How often did you have to refuel - I mean, not refuel, but ammunition?

Adm. S.: Well, we were three weeks on the line. We had to re-ammunition a great deal. After three weeks on the line, we'd get back to Japan, load up with ammunition in Sasebo, and we'd generally get two weeks' relaxation, either in Sasebo if we had to load the ammunition there - that's where our 16-inch ammunition was, or in Yokosuka, and that was recreation for all hands.

For six months we had this regular routine of three weeks on the line shooting every day, occasionally out with the carriers. When Admiral Briscoe was my fleet commander on board, he loved the shooting, and he was relieved by Jocko Clark. I have to tell you about Jocko Clark's reporting on board.

He came on board in Pusan, relieved Admiral Briscoe, and immediately summoned me to his cabin. He said:

"Captain, I've been quite shocked by this ship. I find there are a tremendous number of beards and mustaches among your men."

I said, yes, Sir, and he said: "I don't approve of it."

"Well," I said, "Sir, when we left the States, as a morale factor, I announced that we would have a beard-growing contest. I appointed a group of chief petty officers as a committee. If a man, after two weeks, was unable to grow a successful beard, he was told to shave and he was out of the contest. We have a $500 prize for the best beard. We had many, many other prizes that go down to $300, $200, and $150 for the most unique beard, the fullest beard, the oddest beard, and so forth and so on."

He said: "Well, I don't like it."

So I said: "I'm terribly sorry, Admiral, but this contest runs until we start back for the States."

I went back to my cabin. I thought, he told me he didn't like it. He never ordered me to have the men shave -

Q: That was within his rights, wasn't it?

Adm. S.: Oh, he could have ordered me to. So I did nothing about it, and every now and then he'd say:

"I still don't like those beards and mustaches."
And I'd say: "I know it, Admiral." That's all I'd say.

He used to give me hell all the time because he was a carrier admiral. He wanted to be out with the carriers. The carriers were flying every day also and dropping bombs, and on occasion I would go out to the carriers and fuel from the carriers, from the tanker that was with the carriers. That was his happiest time. He'd get in my helicopter, go off to the carrier, and if I was there twenty-four hours, he would come back to the ship.

I was under the orders of the bombardment commander, who gave me my assigned targets every night for the next day, and I would have 5-inch targets and 16-inch targets. Then I also was subject to what we called "call fire."

In other words, the Marines could say they needed fire urgently on such and such a target. My radioman would tell me this. We'd give them the fire. But Clark used to take a terrible pounding when the 16-inch guns were going off. He would never come up on the open bridge with me and watch the magnificent results of our shooting. I'd say:

"Admiral, come up, we're going to do four or five tunnels tomorrow." He wouldn't come up on that bridge. He'd just sit in his cabin and get the hell shaken out of him. He finally ordered me to quit firing turret 1 and turret 2, so we had to fire turret 3.

Q: Because he was near them?

Adm. S.: Yes, his cabin was up there. So we fired turret 3 most of the time. The liners kept creeping out and finally we had to cut off six inches of the liner of turret 3, because, you know, the liner creeps out as it gets hot and expands. And we had to carry the ammunition and the powder all the way from turret 1 and turret 2 back to turret 3. It was a terrible job, but we had to do it for Admiral Clark.

Q: Didn't he appreciate the effectiveness of all this?

Adm. S.: Oh, I think he did, but he really was so little interested in this bombardment that on one occasion he came up on the open bridge when I was shooting and said:

"Captain, let's knock this all off. Let's go down to Pusan. I've got some fellows who can take us to the best duck-hunting there is in the whole peninsula of Korea."

I said: "Admiral, do you mean to say that you'd rather go duck-hunting than knock out these railroads and these tunnels?"

He said: "You're damned right I would," and stalked below to his cabin, and wouldn't talk to me for two or three days.

On another occasion - one of the things we used to do was send our helicopter in to rescue downed pilots. Quite often we'd be the closest people to a downed pilot. We'd steam up the coast, send my helicopter over, pick him up, and bring him back. On one occasion we got a call to go up and rescue a downed pilot. My helicopter went over and found that he was way up near the top of a mountain and the pilot wasn't able to get up there. So he came back to the ship. Admiral Clark told me to send him back again and make him pick the aviator up.

Well, when we sent him the first time, we knew it was quite an elevation, so we stripped that helicopter down, took out the "mech," and sent only the pilot, with his revolver. That's the only thing that was heavy in that cockpit, and he still said: "I can get to the altitude but I can't pick up a man and get my helicopter out."

So I said to Admiral Clark:

"Admiral, I'm sorry but this helicopter cannot lift the man out of there."

"Oh," he said, "I want you to send him in, anyway." So I said: "Do you mind if I check with Admiral Souchek," who was out with the carriers. He said no, so I sent a dispatch to the admiral saying my helicopter was such and such a model helicopter and we believed it could not lift a man out at this altitude, even with all the weights out of it. He came back and said:

"Under no circumstances send that helicopter. It is impossible for that helicopter to take another man aboard at that altitude."

Admiral Clark was mad about that. Another helicopter was sent, an Army helicopter, and tried to lift him out. It crashed and it had three more men in there, so they had four men in there. Later on, the Army sent one of these great big troop-carrying helicopters, which got them all out. But my helicopter would have crashed in there if I'd sent it back with the admiral's orders.

All this time, I thought I was building up an awful reputation with Admiral Clark, and about a year later when I was in Washington I had occasion to look up my fitness report and found he'd given me one of the best fitness reports I ever had in my life, when all the time I thought he was going to crucify me. He always acted as though he were mad as the devil at me.

Q: I knew that attitude of his also.

When you were in Korean waters, were you ever actually threatened by the enemy in any way? They lacked planes, did they not? They were reported to have used mines extensively. Was the *Iowa* ever threatened by them?

Adm. S.: It was the potential of the threat that bothered us. The fact that on many occasions we could see large flights of hostile aircraft on our radars. We never knew when they were coming down. They had the potential to do us great damage. There was the potential for them to float mines down against us. We kept expecting them. As I recall it, we sighted perhaps two mines during the time I was out there in the *Iowa*. In both cases, we had the destroyer with me go over and sink them.

I wasn't too concerned about mines because the *Iowa* herself was practically unsinkable. She had so many compartments, such good watertight compartmentation, that even if we had hit a mine and it had blown a hole in us, it wouldn't really have taken us off station, unless it hit our props, perhaps, or rudder.

We were under fire on a number of occasions by shore batteries, and we rather welcomed that because then we could locate shore batteries and dig them out with our 16-inch guns.

Q: How accurate was the enemy?

Adm. S.: When we relieved the Wisconsin, she told us of a shore battery and gave us its location, which was in a cave. They would wheel the gun out, shoot it, then put it back in the cave. That battery had hit the Wisconsin and put a shell actually in the junior officers' bunkroom, where they had seven officers. It just happened that it didn't hurt anybody, but it made a mess in the bunkroom. So the first chance we got when we were on the line, after we relieved her, we went up and we blew that gun right out of that tunnel. We put a 16-inch shell right at the base of the cave and we saw the whole gun go right up in the air about 30 or 40 feet. It was a beautiful sight.

We had other occasions when we were bombarding in Wonsan Harbor, and there's no such prickly feeling as being in a completely landlocked harbor, which Wonsan Harbor is, knowing that there were guns in all the hills and caves all around you, and just wondering why the hell they didn't open up on us. All the time, we're trying to find these caves and guns, and we're shooting around, trying to pick the guns out of the holes. Well, they finally got so they wouldn't open up on a big ship because they were afraid of giving away their position, and once they gave it away they lost their guns. We'd blow them out.

Q: And their lives, presumably.

Adm. S.: That's right. One of the worst things that happened. I was in the harbor at Wonsan and a fog shut down and closed us in. It was one of these fogs that came and hung over the water. You could get up on level 8 of the *Iowa* and you were just above the fog. You could just see the tips of our masts sticking up through the fog. That would have been the most marvelous time for them to open up with all their guns because we couldn't see anything to shoot back at. I never could understand why they didn't do it.

But your question about whether we were ever damaged by a gun. Rarely did they come very close to us. They almost always withdrew into their caves and hid themselves when we came along. As you know, they would fire at the minesweeps when they were sweeping Wonsan Harbor, but when one of the big ships would go in they'd keep quiet. They didn't want to take a chance on getting blown up themselves by return fire.

I would say that, aside from the apprehension over the potential of the air threat and the mine threat and possibly motor torpedo boats at night, which we thought about from time to time -

Q: They did have MTBs?

Adm. S.: We never knew whether they did or not. We had reports that they did, but I never saw any. There was always the possibility that they would utilize one of those methods against us. And, of course, the thing that bothered me more than anything else was that some day they might have a submarine torpedo us. We didn't know what - they had submarines up in Vladivostok, and the Russians had submarines. We never knew but what some submarine would come down under the guise of being a North Korean submarine, because they didn't have any, to our knowledge. At least, we didn't think they did. I was very concerned over the fact that we might get torpedoed by a submarine. We could never prove whose it was.

Q: From what you say about their withdrawing and hiding in the caves and so forth, is it right to assume, perhaps, that as protagonists they weren't as sophisticated as our people were, in terms of modern warfare?

Adm. S.: No, I'm sure they weren't. They were primitive compared to us, really.

Q: And yet they had the advantage of help from Russia? and the Chinese?

Adm. S.: Yes, yes, they did. They had the advantage, too, of having that fanatical purpose of the communists, whereas the South Korean, really, didn't care much about fighting. He's a peace-loving man and he didn't like to fight.

Q: Earlier, you mentioned the bombardment command. Would you talk more about your relationship on the battleship with the bombardment command and the interplay?

Adm. S.: The bombardment commander was a rear admiral, the cruiser division commander, who was charged with all of the sea-to-shore bombardments and the support from the sea of the First ROK Corps, which was in the first five miles of the advance to the north, and the Marine Division, which was ten to fifteen miles inland, over two mountain ranges.

From his intelligence sources, and I can't tell you what all of them were, he would assign targets to the cruisers and the battleship each evening for the next day's firing, and he would assign our interdiction firing for the night, every night. He was the commander of the bombardment group. In one case it was Admiral Earl Stone. In another case, it was Admiral Hopwood.

The thing that used to bother the fleet commander most of all was being tied to the *Iowa* - you see, the fleet commander had to live in his flagship, which was the *Iowa*. His heart was in the carriers, and we'd have one or two carriers on station, protected by destroyers and cruisers, steaming around all the time off the coast of Korea, off the east coast of Korea. He wanted to be out there with them, but since I was under the operational orders of the bombardment commander, he kept me on the coast all the time, bombarding, which used to irritate the devil out of the Seventh Fleet commander, whose real interest was in the carriers. Whenever I didn't have a bombardment assignment, we'd whip out at 30 knots, join the carriers, and steam with them maybe twenty-four hours, and I'd go back in for my next assignment. The carriers would rarely be more than 60 or 80 miles out from us.

I remember one occasion when I was coming back to join the carrier group - I always operated the *Iowa* as a destroyer - and I picked up the carrier group dead ahead, just before dawn. I was ordered to join at dawn. I came in at 30 knots. I came in through the two lead destroyers, came in between the two carriers, whipped around, and was in absolutely perfect position at the center of the formation. I was assigned the guide station at the center of the circular formation, and ran up my "affirm posit," which means that I am in position. It was as beautifully done a job as you've ever seen, thanks to my young officers who were working the mooring board and so forth. I expected a well done, but instead of that I got a blast:

"You have seriously endangered this whole formation by entering at high speed. In the future you will always enter this formation from the rear."

Q: This was Clark?

Adm. S.: No, this was Admiral Perry - Smiling Jack Perry, they called him. After he was relieved by Admiral Souchek, I made the same maneuver with the new admiral, came smartly into position, and, bang, a big well done came out from the flagship.

Q: Was that Apollo Souchek?

Adm. S.: It was Apollo, the carrier division commander at the time.

Q: Another question about Jocko, the Seventh Fleet Commander. In World War II he had the reputation of being the charging warrior type. Was this somewhat dissipated when he was there in the Korean waters?

Adm. S.: I saw very little evidence that he was a very charging warrior type in the Korean War. He was frankly very much bored with it. He was certainly bored with our role of bombardment. As I said, he wanted to go duck-shooting instead of knocking out tunnels and railroad trains.

We had one experience in the *Iowa* that was horrifying to me. We had been way up bombarding the northern part of Korea, when I was ordered to bring Admiral Clark down for a meeting with General Van Fleet in Pusan Harbor.

Q: It was safer down in Pusan!

Adm. S.: Oh, yes, we had complete control in Pusan.

I looked at the chart, measured off the distance, and found that I had to make about 28 knots all night long in order to get to Pusan in time. I had never been in Pusan Harbor at that time, nor had anybody on board the *Iowa*. I made the run down the coast in a thick fog, in an absolute fog, and I'm doing 28 knots down the coast in solid fog, navigating by radar. We got down to where my navigator said it was time to turn in for the entrance to Pusan and we had on our radar the jagged coastline of Korea, but we can't see anything, solid fog. I turned in and slowed to 25 knots. I'd been making 28 or 29 all night. I was on the bridge with my navigator, who had his chart right there. I said:

"Are you absolutely certain where we are?"

He said, "Frankly, no, Sir."

I grabbed the enunciators and called "Back, emergency, full." The ship shuddered to a stop in about a mile, because you couldn't stop that ship in under a mile from 28 knots. The fog lifted a little bit and I caught sight of three little islands down to the south of us. I jumped out and personally took three bearings on those little islands, pushed the navigator aside, plotted those bearings myself on his chart, and I couldn't get anything that looked like a fix. So we lay-to there for about half an hour. The fog lifted a little more. We could get some good cross bearings and I found we were ten miles south of the entrance to Pusan Harbor. We were within 600 yards of about 12 feet of water. We would have run high and dry on that rocky coast and been there forever as a monument. You never could have gotten her off.

Just something made me stop that ship. So then we turned north and got in to Pusan Harbor. Well, the little destroyer that had been coming down the coast with me and that had a hard time keeping up with me, frankly, I had told to fall in astern. She was supposed to be screening me, but at 28 or 29 knots I didn't need a screen, so she followed me down. He sent me over a message:

"We felt when you ordered the turn in toward the coast that we were ten miles south of the entrance to Pusan." He told me this later. I said:

"Why didn't you tell me?"

"Oh, Sir," he said, "I thought with all that talent you had on the battleship, my navigator must have been wrong."

And I said: "Well, if you ever have that feeling again, suggest to the commander that, although you may be wrong, this is what you think. With all the talent we had on our ship, we were wrong."

Our investigation showed that at four o'clock in the morning when the radar watch had turned over, they were navigating on peaks and jagged points on the coast of Korea. They had turned over the wrong set of landmarks to three farther south than the ones the watch before them had been taking their bearings on, so that we just were set ten miles to the south from four o'clock on.

Q: So this exonerated your navigator at that time?

Adm. S.: No, it didn't exonerate anybody. It was just a mistake. I wasn't trying to pin the blame on anybody.

Q: How do you react to a navigator who does this?

Adm. S.: This particular navigator of mine was somewhat careless, so I always had - I had three ensigns who were assistant navigators - one of them with him twenty-four hours a day when he was navigating, three brilliant young ensigns. In this case, they weren't brilliant enough to discover this error, and it wasn't really his fault because he was taking the radar bearings that were being sent up from CIC. This is one of those things that can happen. We were alert against that possibility in the future, but since this had never happened to me before I hadn't even considered it as a possibility. Since we were taking our bearings on points of land that jutted out into the sea, we had no way of really verifying those points because we were in solid fog and never once could see them visually.

That was one time when we almost came a cropper. It was just the good Lord stepping in to keep us off the beach.

Q: It would almost appear, from what you tell me about the battleship, that she must have had a guardian angel!

Adm. S.: I think she did have a guardian angel with her.

Q: Another and more important question about the battleship.

Has the development of missiles, for instance, really taken the place of the 16-inch shell, when used as you used it from the <u>Iowa</u> against coastal targets?

Adm. S.: I don't think that the missile has taken the place of a battleship in bombardment, but the missile is far better than the battleship against other ships at sea. In other words, it can shoot farther and more accurately than can a battleship today. A battleship would have no chance against a ship equipped with missiles, because the ship equipped with missiles could stay over the horizon out of reach of the battleship's guns and could sink the battleship with missiles, if she could get enough in her to breach her watertight integrity. She could wreck her topsides.

So the battleship is properly relegated to the past, I think.

Q: But, as a floating gun platform - ?

Adm. S.: The fact that that type battleship was recalled in Vietnam indicates that she had a very valuable purpose and she was valuable again in Vietnam. If we got into that kind of war again, I think we would probably pull the battleships out again, but I can't conceive of our ever getting into that kind of war again. We've made that mistake twice now and I don't think we should make it a third time.

Q: Is the Iowa in mothballs now?

Adm. S.: Yes, the Iowa is in mothballs. Her sister ships, the Missouri, the New Jersey, and the Wisconsin, are also in mothballs. Fortunately, you can't get the Iowa up any river in Iowa, so she hasn't been made a state memorial.

Q: Have the others?

Adm. S.: Well, the North Carolina is a state memorial in North Carolina.

Q: The Massachusetts is?

Adm. S.: Yes, and the Texas is.

Q: But the most recent battleships are not?

Adm. S.: No, the four big battleships are still available, and I hope they will be for a long time because I can conceive of their being useful sometime in a limited war situation. I don't believe that the limited war has gone forever.

Q: In 1952, Sir, you ended your tour of duty in Korean waters and came back to the States and then to the Atlantic. In September of 1952 you became chief of staff and aide to Commander, Destroyer Force, Atlantic.

Adm. S.: That's right, who was then Admiral Wellborn.

Q: Were you reluctant to leave the battleship?

Adm. S.: Oh, yes. That was, of course, the greatest command that a man could have at sea. I hated to leave. I can't imagine anything more wonderful than having your own ship. I'm fortunate in having had that experience several times.

Q: A ship of that magnitude?

Adm. S.: Yes. There were four of these big ships and four of my classmates got command of them during the Korean War. John Sylvester and Tiny McCorkle, later both admirals, were the two perhaps tallest men in our class, and Admiral Chester Bruton, later, and I were perhaps two of the shortest men in our class. We had the four battleships, the four Iowa-class battleships, in the

Korean War. It was a tremendous experience for all of us.

I went to the destroyer force. Being an old destroyer sailor, I was delighted with that job, delighted to work with Admiral Wellborn, one of my close friends, and later with Admiral Chick Hartman, who relieved him. Our major problem during that period was the age and the rapidly deteriorating condition of our destroyers. We had a constant fight to keep them steaming, repaired, operable. We had a campaign to convince the Congress that we needed to start building destroyers. These destroyers that we were operating had all been in World War II, many of them we had before World War II.

Q: Actually, a destroyer that was commissioned during World War II was not that old at that point?

Adm. S.: No, but they had had tremendous wear and tear during the war with almost no upkeep. Some of those destroyers steamed almost continuously for four years, three and four years, during the war, and you probably got in eight or ten years' peacetime steaming in those three or four wartime years.

We had the same problems then, too, of shortage of money, shortage of personnel, skilled personnel, and we had a hard time to keep our ships operating.

Q: But that personnel problem had been dissipated somewhat, had it not, from the immediate postwar years?

Adm. S.: That's right. It was not as bad as it was right after the demobilization after World War II.

Q: By 1952 it had been pretty well determined what the size of the fleet was going to be, hadn't it?

Adm. S.: That's right.

Q: You weren't busy decommissioning ships?

Adm. S.: That's correct. We had a very stable navy by that time, but we were very much concerned with the material condition of our ships, which was not good.

Q: Had not the Korean conflict assisted the Navy in maintaining its ships and adding to them? There was an upsurge in military endeavor, as a result of the Korean War?

Adm. S.: Yes, there was a big upsurge, but I think most of the money was expended in or near or around Korea, rather than on the destroyers of the Atlantic Fleet, where I was on this particular tour.

As I remember that tour, the biggest headaches were the material condition of our ships and the numbers of courts-martial we had to contend with. As chief of staff, I had to review all the courts-martial and that was one tremendous headache for me.

Q: Do you imply that there was an exceptional number of them?

Adm. S.: I thought there was an awful lot of them.

Q: What was the general reason?

Adm. S.: I can't tell you what the general reason was, unless it was general resentment against military discipline on the part of the young people who entered the Navy from the country in those days.

Q: Was that beginning to be reflected in the service in those days?

Adm. S.: Yes. Not to the point that it got to be later when they had mutinies, but they were careless. They'd go AWOL-over staying liberty. We had a lot of discipline to take care of, and that's one of the chief of staff's primary duties, to handle those problems that you don't bother the admiral with.

That was the thing I enjoyed least about that job as chief of staff on the destroyer force.

Q: That was a personnel problem that you got into in a big way later on?

Adm. S.: That's right. It was the beginning of my personnel problems.

Q: Was the concern on the part of the Navy large enough to attempt to do something about it in the Navy training schools, to indoctrinate them, perhaps, a little more severely in terms of discipline?

Adm. S.: I can't remember anything significant along those lines to comment on now.

Q: Did the Navy think in those terms, trying to go back to the roots of the problem and do something about it in time?

Adm. S.: I just don't feel that my memory is adequate to comment on that. Nothing sticks out as being particularly significant in that line.

Q: What was the overall mission of the destroyers in the Atlantic at that time?

Adm. S.: The usual destroyer mission, the primary mission of locating and being able to destroy submarines. We had ASW exercises. We were constantly operating with submarines, trying to locate them and destroy them, trying to improve our underwater equipment, being constantly frustrated by the various layers and barriers that prevented our reaching out longer distances to locate submarines, problems they're still having today. We still are a long way from licking that underwater location.

We kept our gunnery up. We had the wonderful training available to the Atlantic Fleet of Guantanamo, where all our ships went for refresher training. Our new ships went down there for shakedown training. We sent our ships down there after shipyard overhauls for refresher training, to bring them up to operational efficiency, after a shipyard overhaul.

As chief of staff, I went to Guantanamo once or twice to see how the training effort was working out there. We did our shore bombardments down there at Culebra. It's almost impossible to operate in the Atlantic Ocean during the winter. Conditions are so miserable.

Q: Especially the North Atlantic.

Adm. S.: That's right. I trained two of my earlier destroyers during the war in Casco Bay, in February, March, and April. Those are stinking months. The weather was poor, lots of fog, lots of rough weather, very hard to get your crews adequately trained.

Today, the uninformed are talking about our giving up Guantanamo. Guantanamo is one of the most valuable things we can have for our fleet in peacetime, a place where you can go during the severity of the winter and have optimum conditions for your gunnery practices and every other kind of practice, shore bombardments, antisubmarine practice, and so forth. You have your crews not distracted in any way by the fleshpots. They don't get any liberty down there, except to go ashore and have a beer and play baseball.

Q: There used to be a spot across the bay, did there not - ?

Adm. S.: Over at Gonaives or up at Caimanera?

Q: Caimanera, yes.

Adm. S.: Yes, we used to be able to go up to Caimanera and get a beer.

Q: There were a few fleshpots there, weren't there?

Adm. S.: Well, I don't know. I never investigated them myself, nor did very many of my officer friends. Yes, we had some problems.

Q: Talk to the chaplains, they'll tell you about it!

Adm. S.: The chaplains were more aware of the problems, yes.

They didn't get much liberty in Guantanamo. They went down there to work and they worked hard in the winter.

And, of course, we had the fleet problems, the fleet cruises.

Q: Say something about the value of Vieques and Culebra.

Adm. S.: You mean the place we just lost?

Q: Yes, to the fleet, the value, as you saw it.

Adm. S.: It was tremendously valuable. It was to the Atlantic Fleet what the little island of San Clemente is to the Pacific destroyers, off San Diego. For instance, we'd go out to San Clemente and we'd do all our shore bombardment there. We learned how to destroy targets on land. You've got to be able to practice it in order to be able to do it. In both cases, we have tanks ashore and houses ashore, we have every kind of thing that you'd be asked to destroy in a war.

There are very few places, you know, in the Atlantic where you can fire against the shore.

Q: Roosevelt Roads is still an answer to that?

Adm. S.: Roosevelt Roads is a good base from which you can operate, but it isn't a place like Guantanamo Bay, where you can steam out just three, four, or five miles and start shooting, there's so little traffic around that area that your operating area is only, instead of hours, just a few minutes from the entrance to the harbor. That's important when you have a lot of practices to do. In San Diego, for instance, our operating areas were some distance from the port. With restricted use of our fuel, we take hours to get to the operating areas, and then when we get through, we have to come back at the prescribed speed of, say, 12 knots, and it takes you from six o'clock in the morning until eight, nine, or ten o'clock at night to go out and come back each day. And that's pretty wearing.

In the old days, in San Diego, the worst thing we ever did was to require the ships to return to port every night to save fuel. We saved a little fuel, perhaps, because when we'd get to port three or four destroyers would nest. One destroyer would keep her boilers going to furnish the water, light, and power to the other three destroyers. So we'd burn very little fuel oil. But the crew would get in around nine or ten o'clock at night and those who were married would go ashore and be back on the ship at four or five in the morning to go out again. You can see how wearing that is, when you do that Monday, Tuesday, Wednesday, Thursday, and Friday nights for a three-week operating period.

Q: Was this prior to World War II?

Adm. S.: Prior to World War II, that's right, when we were restricted in our speeds. I don't know what the restrictions are in the fleet today. It must be cutting down on the operating speeds to save fuel, because the amount of money for fuel is not, I hear, sufficient for operating purposes of a really efficient fleet.

I think that's about all that I can say about the time I was with the destroyers of the Atlantic Fleet.

Q: Did you use the Azores in any way with the destroyers?

Adm. S.: No.

Q: You didn't go that far afield?

Adm. S.: No. We deployed our destroyers to the Med, you know, for regular cruises.

Q: For six months?

Adm. S.: Yes. At one time it was four months and another time it was six months. That was a regular rotation. We had sort of a cycle. A destroyer would go to the shipyard, and she had her refresher training out of the shipyard in Guantanamo, where you brought the ship right up to efficiency. You'd get her ready and the crew trained to go to the Mediterranean for six months. Then she'd come back from the Med and you'd give her as much time in the home port as you could give her before she starts another cycle over again.

That's about all of the Newport destroyer experience that I think is significant.

Q: What about the use of Narragansett Bay? This had its value, did it not, as a base for destroyers?

Adm. S.: You mean Newport Harbor?

Q: Yes, operating out of that harbor in the Atlantic.

Adm. S.: It did, but it never, in my opinion, was as

good a base as San Diego, for instance. The weather in the winter is miserable, and when I was chief of staff all of our destroyers anchored out. Of course, until we were recently kicked out of Newport, the destroyers were all berthed alongside piers, which made it extremely pleasant for the crews. Many is the time when we were in our home port of Newport, the weather was so rough that we couldn't get our crews ashore.

Q: What I was thinking about was the fact that from Newport you did have to operate in very bad weather, with fog, rough seas, and so forth?

Adm. S.: That's right. It was very tough to get to an operating area.

Q: Now they operate out of Norfolk, where it's much calmer most of the time, and yet in case there is a conflict, say, with Russia, crews will have to operate in northern waters around Norway. So isn't there an advantage in imposing this kind of training upon them in bad weather out of Newport? In terms of readiness?

Adm. S.: I think a certain amount of that is advantageous, but you get a certain amount of rough weather in the Navy, no matter where you're operating. There are always storms, every place.

Q: Off Hatteras.

Adm. S.: That's right. I've had plenty of rough weather out of Norfolk. In fact, once, when I had the Second Fleet, we had to ttake the whole fleet to sea and try to escape a hurricane that kept changing course, and kept me changing the fleet course for two days. We couldn't figure where it was going.

Q: How adequate was the weather reporting when you were with Destroyers, Atlantic?

Adm. S.: I would say it was adequate. Even today, though, nobody can adequately predict the course of a hurricane. It keeps changing course and even though we follow it, you never quite know where it's going next. You don't know whether it's going to head out to sea or come into land.

Q: As Destroyers, Atlantic, did you engage in any amphibious operations in your time?

Adm. S.: We had ships assigned to amphibious commanders for their exercises, yes, as a routine matter. Various destroyers would be rotated to assist in amphibious landings.

Q: What was the nature of amphibious operations in the early fifties? Had they benefited by experiences in Korea?

Adm. S.: Not having been an amphibious commander, I don't think I ought to comment on that stage of warfare because I was not an expert in it. I had supported many amphibious landings in my own destroyers in World War II, but I'm not really competent to comment now on the state of the amphibious art later. I don't feel that I'm competent to comment when you've got a lot of people who are experts in that.

Q: Exactly, but I was trying to get your recollections on it and wondering whether the amphibious operation was solely a Navy-Marine operation, or whether the Army cooperated?

Adm. S.: It was solely Navy-Marine, as far as we were concerned. The Navy always put the Marines ashore and always put the Army ashore. Once they got ashore, they could take care of themselves. We were responsible for getting both of them ashore, and I would hope that that is still the way it is.

Index to

Series of Interviews with

Vice Admiral William R. Smedberg, III
U. S. Navy (Retired)


VOLUME I

ANDERSON, VADM Walter Stratton:  p. 128; p. 132; p. 151;

ATHLETICS:  Smedberg on importance of athletics in the fleet, p. 67-68;

AVIATION:  and the fleet in the 1930s, p. 75 ff; Smedberg's interest in aviation, the deterrents, p. 81-4;

BADGER, Admiral Oscar C.:  in command at Caso Bay, p. 195-6;

BERTIL - Prince of Sweden:  p. 342-4;

BLANDY, Adm. Wm. H.P.:  gunnery officer on the BB NEW MEXICO, p. 45;

BOUGAINVILLE:  The DD HUDSON has a dangerous mission - to escort marine transports into Empress Augusta Bay with inadequate charts, p. 255 ff;

BRAINARD, VADM Roland M.:  p. 147;

BRITISH INTELLIGENCE:  an arrangement with U. S. representatives for the post war period, p. 317-8; wartime cooperation, p. 318-9;

BROWN, Capt. Wm.:  Smedberg relieves him as Chief of Staff to Adm. Merrill, p. 264; p. 269-70;

CAPE ESPERANCE:  Battle of, p. 220-2;

CASCO BAY:  p. 234-5;

CHARLESTON NAVY YARD:  Forrestal's attempt to close it, p. 354-5;

USS CHAUMONT:  p. 57;

SS CITY OF BIRMINGHAM:  torpedoed and sunk off Cape Hatteras, p. 207-8;

CLARK, Admiral John J. (Jocko):  relieves Adm. Briscoe as Commander of the 7th fleet - his objection to beards, p. 444; uninterested in shore bombardment with 16" guns, p. 445-7; p. 448-9; flagship - the IOWA - but preferred to be with carriers, p. 454-6;

USS CLEVELAND:  Skipper of the CLEVELAND apologizes for a bad bit of ship handling, p. 268;

CLIFFORD, The Hon. Clark:  p. 330-2;

CLUVERIUS, Adm. Wat Tyler:  p. 63;

COAST WATCHERS:  p. 257-8; p. 260;

COMBAT INTELLIGENCE:  see entries under FADM KING:  Smedberg relieves Smith-Hutton, p. 281-3; King orders Smedberg to brief the Combined Chiefs on Leyte Gulf, p. 284-5; King interrupts briefing to correct Smedberg, p. 285-7; King asks Smedberg for an estimate when the Japanese might surrender, p. 289-91; the episode involving Forrestal, King and Smedberg on a weekly briefing of the press, p. 293 ff; Smedberg's press conference covering the surrender of Corregidor, p. 295 ff; Smedberg unaware of atomic bomb until it was dropped on Japan, p. 316; Smedberg part of intelligence committee that visits Britain to arrange post WW II exchange, p. 317-8;

COOKE, Admiral Charles M. (Saavy): advises Smedberg to wear the grey uniform designated by King, p. 286-7; p. 311;

CORREGIDOR: p. 295-6;

USS DAUNTLESS: flagship of COMINCH, p. 305-6;

DD DIVISION 31: Smedberg makes operational suggestions to Adm. Forrestal (Comdr. DD's Pac) because of dislocations caused by demobilization, p. 383 ff; Smedberg initiates a very active sports program to build moral, p. 384-7; the excitement of a new sonar, p. 388; the benefit from experience of WWII, p. 390-1;

DD FORCE - ATLANTIC: Smedberg becomes Chief of Staff to Commander DD Force - Admiral Wellborn, p. 462-3; discipline problems, p. 465-6; Atlantic mission, p. 467 ff;

DEMOBILIZATION: the demoralizing effects after WW II, p. 382;

DENNISON, Adm. Robert L.: p. 120;

USS DUNCAN: p. 188; p. 216; lost at the Battle of Cape Esperance, p. 220-2; p. 232;

EDISON, The Hon. Charles: p. 135;

EDWARDS, Admiral R. S.: Chief of Staff to Adm. King, p. 284; p. 286; p. 298-9; p. 311.

USS ENGLAND: p. 260-1; p. 319;

ESPIRITU SANTO: The LANSDOWNE's narrow escape from minefield at Espiritu Santo, p. 197 ff; p. 220;

FAY, Paul B.: his attitude towards the NROTC in several leading universities, p. 374-6;

FOLEY, Comdr. Frank: Executive Officer on the LANSDOWNE, p. 207; his quick action during torpedo attack in South Pacific, p. 212; p. 227-8;

FORRESTAL, The Hon. James: p. 118-9; p. 274; his insistence on Smedberg holding press briefings on naval events - while serving on staff of Admiral King, p. 293 ff; p. 297; p. he "borrows" Smedberg to brief a crowd in Denver, p. 302-3; Smedberg's concern about data in the Forrestal Diaries, p. 303; p. 304; his telephone conversation with Pres. Truman on formation of the Department of Defense, p. 313-5; Smedberg becomes his aide in May, 1946, p. 322 ff; his lack of home life,

p. 324-7; Forrestal's poker game for President Truman, p. 328 ff; the round-the-world trip, p. 334 ff; China; p. 334-5; the Philippines, p. 335-6; Tokyo and Gen. Mac-Arthur, p. 336; Bangkok, p. 337-8; Calcutta, p. 338-9; Stockholm, p. 341-2; objectives of the trip, p. 344-5; p. 347-8; his meeting with navy's ranking officers on future of naval aviation, p. 348-9; Congressional relations, p. 353 ff; his interest in a balanced navy, p. 360; his interest in the Naval Reserve, p. 361; p. 365-7; the misadventure in Japan when the secretary's party got lost in back country, p. 367-8; his faith and trust in naval aviators, p. 377-8; his interest in missiles - and his visit to White Sands to witness small rocket firing, p. 377-8; p. 432;

GANNON, RADM Sinclair: commandant of midshipmen, p. 14; p. 16;

GHORMLEY, VADM Robert L.: p. 135-6; p. 235-6;

GREENSLADE, VADM John Wills: p. 237-8;

GUANTANAMO: value of this base to the fleet for training purposes, p. 647-8; p. 472;

HALSEY, Fleet Admiral Wm. F. Jr.: p. 136; his reaction to Smedberg's account of the would-be mutiny on board the LANSDOWNE in Sydney harbor, p. 229-30; his manner of dealing with his command, p. 236-7; p. 243-4;

HART, Admiral Thos. C.: conducts Pearl Harbor investigation, p. 166; p. 168;

HAYLER, VADM Robert Ward: successor to Adm. Merrill in CTF 39 - Smedberg continues as his Chief of Staff, p. 276; his reaction to Adm. King's orders for detachment of Smedberg just before Battle of Leyte Gulf, p. 277 ff;

HILL, Admiral Harry W.: Superintendent of the Naval Academy, p. 396; p. 401; p. 404-5; p. 422;

HOLLOWAY, Admiral James L. Jr.: as Superintendent of Naval Academy picks his department heads very carefully; Smedberg named as head of Department of Electrical Engineering, p. 394; p. 396; p. 418-9;

HORNE, Adm. Frederick J.: p. 300-1;

USS HUDSON: p. 234; p. 248-9; the influence on additions to a new ship - objections of Buships, p. 250; the crew and advance training, p. 251-2; p. 253; lead ship in escorting the marines into Bougainville, p. 254 ff; p. 292;

HULL, The Hon. Cordell: U. S. Secretary of State - his strong response to Japanese request for easing of sanctions, p. 158-60; his telephone call to Stark on the 2nd or 3rd of December, 1941, p. 161;

INGERSOLL, Admiral Royal E.: p. 135-6;

INGLIS, RADM Thomas: F-2 on COMINCH staff, p. 306; p. 312 provided Combat Intelligence with information from ONI sources p. 312-3;

INITIATIVE: Smedberg's comments on its importance for the advancement of men in the Navy, p. 45-7;

USS IOWA: p. 234-5; Smedberg and the running of trials in San Francisco Bay, p. 270 ff; his orders to enter San Diego Harbor - his refusal to Admiral Sprague, p. 274-5; p. 415; Smedberg given command to take her out of mothballs and into the Korean conflict orders directly from CNO Sherman, p. 424; problems with obtaining trained men for 16" turrets, p. 426-7; p. 428-9; tribulations in San Francisco Bay and in San Diego, p. 430-3; her misssion to bombard Korean coast - fire support to U. S. Marines, p. 434-5; various targets dealt with, p. 438-9-40; use of agents on shore, p. 442; p. 449-50; the hazardous run to Pusan Harbor, p. 456 ff; p. 460-1;

USS KEYES: flagship of Smedberg in DD Div. 31, p. 385;

KIDD, Admiral Isaac Campbell Jr.: aide to Smedberg when he was Superintendent of the Naval Academy, p. 320-1;

KIMMEL, RADM Husband E.: p. 50; his foresight and thoroughness as an officer, p. 51-2; p. 87; p. 105; p. 173; his bitter feeling towards Adm. Stark after Pearl Harbor, p. 181-3;

KING, Fleet Admiral Ernest: p. 76-7; p. 87; p. 100-1; p. 181; p. 238; p. 242; Smedberg delivers message to him about lack of spare parts for Halsey's planes, p. 243-4; p. 257; he calls Smedberg back to Washington just before Leyte Gulf, p. 279 ff; Smedberg's interview with King, p. 280-3; King orders Smedberg to brief Combined Chiefs on Leyte Gulf - with only one hour notice, p. 284; his reaction to Forrestal's insistence that there be weekly briefing of the press on naval events, p. 293 ff; p. 296 ff; p. 304-5; his staff set-up at headquarters, p. 305-6; King and the intelligence shared with the army, p. 306; King and intelligence shared with the British and the Russians, p. 308-9; his ability to trust those in whom he had confidence, p. 309-11; p. 315; Smedberg as Supt. of Naval Academy entertains members of King family after the Admiral's funeral in Annapolis, p. 319-322;

KISSINGER, The Hon. Henry: p. 161-2;

KNOX, The Hon. Frank: Secretary of the Navy, p. 135; p. 174-6; p. 181;

KOREA: BOMBARDMENT COMMAND: the function of the naval command, p. 453-4;

KURUSU, Saburo: Special Japanese emissary to the U. S. (1941), p. 162-3;

USS LANSDOWNE: p. 47; commissioned in Kearny, NJ, p. 188-90; shake down in Hudson River, p. 191-3; ordered to Casco Bay - transit of Cape Cod Canal, p. 193 ff; going through the minefield, p. 195-6; by intuition Smedberg avoids mined area later at Espiritu Santo, p. 197; the ship characteristics, p. 199; a mission to Guadalcanal with ammunition - narrow escape from torpedo attack, p. 200-2; firing of star shells in training off coast of Maine, p. 204-5; Cape Hatteras, p. 206-7; sinking of U.-153, escorts BB WASHINGTON to South Pacific, , p. 209; news of Savo Island battle, p. 209-210; escort work in South Pacific, p. 211 ff; torpedoing of CV WASP, p. 211-12; she escorts PORTLAND to Sydney for repairs, p. 224-7; lack of food and supplies in South Pacific, p. 237-8; p. 239;

LAYTON, RADM Edwin T.: p. 166-7;

LEAHY, Fleet Admiral Wm.: Wellborn and Smedberg serve with him for some months in advance of Adm. Stark taking office as CNO, p. 123;

LEE, VADM Willis A. Jr.: Smedberg's estimate of him, p. 178-80; p. 210;

LEYTE GULF: Smedberg briefs the Combined Chiefs, p. 284-5;

LOCKWOOD, Admiral Charles: Naval Attache to London, p. 137;

LOWE, VADM Frank Loper (Frog): Commander Tenth Fleet - asks for intelligence data on subs in the Pacific - King refuses, p. 304-5;

MacARTHUR, General Douglas: p. 295-6; MacArthur and Forrestal, p. 336;

McCAIN, Admiral John Sydney: executive on the BB MEXICO, p. 38;

USS MAJARA: ammo ship - sunk by Japanese torpedo off Guadalcanal, p. 202;

MARSHALL, General George C.: he and Stark at the White House to urge moderation in our message to the Japanese on sanctions, p. 58-9; p. 164-5; p. 174;

USS McCALL: in same division with DD LANSDOWNE - rescues survivors from the DUNCAN, p. 220-1;

McNAMARA, Robert S.: Secretary of Defense - on the pay bill (1962), p. 356; his reaction to report of the special study commission on the pay bill, p. 357-8; Smedberg's testimony before the Congressional Committee, p. 357-9;

MERRILL, VADM Aaron S. (Tip): Requests Smedberg to serve as his Chief of Staff in the MONTPELLIER (1944), p. 263-4; p. 266-8; p. 276;

USS MINNEAPOLIS: torpedoed in the SLOT (Nov. 30) - escorted to Tulagi, p. 224; p. 230;

USS MISSOURI: p. 269-70; Smedberg takes a summer cruise with midshipmen; p. 411 ff;

USS MONTPELIER: flagship of Adm. Merrill, p. 263;

MORISON, RADM Samuel E.: p. 261;

MORREEL, RADM Ben: his reaction immediately after attack on Pearl Harbor, p. 172;

USS MOUNT VERNON: LANSDOWNE escorts her from New Jersey to Noumea, p. 229;

USS MULLANY: Smedberg transferred to her for cruise to Nicaragua, p. 40-1; extra fuel oil to aid in winning the competition, p. 42; p. 48; Nicaragua, p. 48; fleet problems, p. 48-50;

U. S. NAVAL ACADEMY: Smedberg's general attitude towards the Academy, p. 9; his difficulties with upper classmen, p. 10-11; demerits, p. 12 ff; comments on the classes at the Academy, p. 19; Trident scholars, p. 21-22; summer cruises, p. 23 ff; aviation summer, p. 32; Smedberg invited to teach French at the Academy, p. 56; ordered to Academy (in Superintendency of Admiral Holloway) as head of Dept. of Electrical Engineering, p. 393 ff; Smedberg makes great effort to have better qualified instructors, p. 395; Smedberg sits on various classes, p. 397-9; Smedberg on the football squad and tutoring, p. 399-420; Smedberg changes content of examinations, p. 402-3; Smedberg comments on the honor system, p. 404-5; in praise of the civilian faculty, p. 409-410; a summer cruise (1949), p. 411-412; Smedberg's emphasis on chapel, p. 415;

NAVAL COMMUNICATIONS: Smedberg studies applied communications at P.G. school, p. 94; discussion of state of communications prior to WWII, p. 92-5; Smedberg finds the field very limited and hard to get out of, p. 94; need for radio-telephone between ships, p. 96-100; post WW II agreement with the R.N. on exchange of information, p. 103-4; Smedberg's various tasks in field of communications on staff of Adm. Vernou, p. 104-6; in CruBatFor, p. 109-11; p. 116; Smedberg on communications on staff of Adm. Stark, p. 131-2; closely held secret of code breaking activities, p. 132-3;

NAVAL RESERVE: Forrestal's great interest, p. 361; Smedberg's example of a reserve captain who was dropped from the continued list and then put back by a Secretary of the Navy - the repercussions, p. 370 ff;

USS NEW MEXICO: first duty of Smedberg after graduation, p. 37 ff; story of Rickover and the fuel oil, p. 43; ensigns required to keep journals, p. 52-3;

NEWPORT, R.I.: Smedberg comments on Newport as a base for Destroyers, p. 472-3;

NEWS MEDIA AND THE NAVY: see entries under:
FADM KING; FORRESTAL, James.

NICARAGUA: p. 40; p. 48;

NIMITZ, Flt. Adm. Chester W.: his comments on Smedberg's handling of the IOWA in San Francisco Bay, p. 273; p. 315; p. 430-1;

NOMURA, Admiral Kiskisaburo: his secret meeting with Admiral Stark in November, 1941, p. 156-8; p. 162;

USS NORTHAMPTON: fitting out the new ship (1930), p. 58-60; p. 65; p. 74; availability of ammunition in the 1930s, p. 88-9; p. 224;

NOYES, VADM Leigh: p. 213; p. 216;

NROTC: p. 374-7;

NULTON, Adm. Louis M.: Superintendent, Naval Academy, p. 16

PEARL HARBOR: p. 66-7; the night before the attack in Washington, p. 163 ff;

PERSONNEL PROBLEMS IN THE NAVY: p. 117-20; spark plugs among the personnel, p. 129-30;

USS PORTLAND: LANSDOWNE escorts her with wooden bow to Australia for repairs, p. 224-5;

POST GRADUATE SCHOOL: BuPers insists that Smedberg attend PG school even though he had accepted to teach at the Naval Academy, p. 56; p. 91; Smedberg specializes in Applied Communications, p. 92;

PRATT, RADM Richard R.: Smedberg selects him for duty on the DD LANSDOWNE, p. 189-90; p. 232-3; becomes Executive Officer on the DD HUDSON, p. 252-3; p. 265;

RADAR: p. 99-100; p. 102-3;

REEVES, Adm. Joseph Mason: his order to the fleet to go to sea at once, p. 63-65; p. 107-8;

RICHARDSON, Admiral J.O.: p. 146;

RICKOVER, Admiral Hyman G.: assistant engineer in BB NEW MEXICO, p. 43;

ROOSEVELT, The Hon. Franklin D.: President of the United States; p. 120-1; his practice of passing on every addition to navy personnel, p. 124-5; his method of giving orders to Stark, p. 128-9; p. 142; p. 144; p. 146-8; his reversal on the proposed message to the Japanese (Nov. 1941) on lifting sanctions, p. 159; p. 164;

RYAN, Comdr. Thos. J.: Destroyer Squadron Commander in Solomons, p. 219; p. 223-4;

SEBALD, The Hon. Wm.J.: p. 283-4; p. 287; p. 289-31; p. 296;

SELECTION BOARDS: p. 112-5;

SETTLE, VADM Thos. G. W.: (Tex): navy member of the McNamara pay bill committee (1962), p. 357;

SHERMAN, Admiral Forrest: p. 348; p. 350;

SMEDBERG, Vice Admiral Wm. R. III: personal background, p. 1-3; attends Middlesex School, p. 4-5; destined for West Point he shifts at the last moment to the Naval Academy, p. 6-7; early years in various army posts, p. 8; attacks of asthma, p. 35-6; marriage, p. 53-5; Flag Lieutenant to Admiral Stark, p. 123 ff; his five Legions of Merit, p. 301; the 'high naval spokesman', p. 295 and p. 301;

SMITH, Senator Margaret Chase: her interference in a reserve selection board matter, p. 372-4;

SMITH-HUTTON, Captain Henri: relieved as head of Combat Intelligence on staff of Adm. King by Smedberg, p. 281-3;

SOUCHEK, RADM Apollo: Carrier Division Commander, p. 448; p. 455;

USS SOUTH DAKOTA: p. 233-4;

SPENAVO - in London: his purpose, p. 136-7;

SPRAGUE, Adm. Thomas: orders Smedberg to berth the IOWA in San Diego Harbor - Smedberg demurs, p; 274-5; p. 432;

STANDLEY, Adm. Wm. H.: p. 15-16;

STARK, Adm. Harold R.: succeeds Adm. Vernou in Cruisers - retains Smedberg on his staff - p. 94; as CNO asks Smedberg to become flag lieutenant - Smedberg demurs but finally stays, p. 95; p. 99; p. 107-8; p. 115; Smedberg's opinion of how Stark came to be selected as CNO, p. 120-3; Stark's need to get FDR approval for every personnel increase, p. 124; Flag lieutenant, p. 123; p. 126; p. 127-8; telephonic communications from FDR to Stark, p. 128-9; Stark's efforts to build up the navy, 1939-40, p. 141 ff; p. 144-5; impression made on him by the British raid on Italian fleet at Taranto, p. 149; his correspondence with senior admirals in long hand, p. 152; p. 153-5; Stark and his talk with Japanese Admiral Nomura, p. 156-7; p. 164-5; attempt to pin Pearl Harbor disaster on Stark, p. 165-6; p. 172; Kimmel entertains bitterness towards Stark, p. 181-2; p. 243; p. 247;

SWANSON, The Honorable Claude: Secretary of the Navy, p. 121-2; p. 134;

TAUSSIG, VADM Joseph K.: his speech on the immanence of war, p. 107-8; p. 143;

TAYLOR, VADM E. B. (Whitney): commissioning the USS DUNCAN, p. 188-9; rescued from DD sunk in Battle of Cape Esperance, p. 220; p. 232-3; p. 248-9;

THEBAUD, RADM Leo: Chief of Naval Intelligence, p. 305;

TRUMAN, The Hon. Harry S.: his telephone call to Forrestal in San Francisco on formation of Department of Defense, p. 313-4; his poker game at Forrestal residence, p. 328-9 ff;

TULAGI: LANSDOWNE ordered to patrol entrance to Tulagi the night of Battle of Cape Esperance, p. 223;

TURNER, Admiral Richmond Kelly: p. 127-8; p. 147; p. 150; sends Smedberg in DD LANSDOWNE with ammunition for marines on Guadalcanal, p. 199 ff;

VERNOU, VADM Walter N. (Wally): Smedberg on his staff in USS CONCORD, p. 42 ff; p. 59-60; p. 75-7; p. 85; illustrations of his training tactics p. 86-7; requests Smedberg on his staff as Commander, CruDiv 3, p. 92; promises Smedberg job as Executive of DD but his successor, Adm. Stark, would not let him go, p. 94; p. 104-5;

VINSON, The Hon. Carl: p. 143; p. 371;

WAR CORRESPONDENTS: p. 255-7;

USS WASHINGTON: p. 233;

USS WASP: torpedoed in South Pacific, p. 211-13; DD LANSDOWNE ordered to sink the WASP, p. 216-7; she sinks shortly before Japanese task force arrives on the scene, p. 219;

WAVES: Smedberg comments on the WAVES in COMINCH office, p. 287-8;

WELLBORN, VADM Charles: p. 99-100; p. 123-4; p. 128; p. 132; p. 145; p. 151; p. 153; p. 164; p. 392; Smedberg becomes Chief of Staff to Wellborn as Commander, DD Force, Atlantic, p. 462-3;

USS WISCONSIN: p. 450;

WONSAN HARBOR: p. 450-1;

ZUMWALT, Adm. Elmo R. Jr.: Smedberg expresses himself to Zumwalt on standards in dress and conduct, p. 73;

www.ingramcontent.com/pod-product-compliance
Lightning Source LLC
Chambersburg PA
CBHW080626170426
43209CB00007B/1525